A

DEFENCE

OF THE

TRUE AND CATHOLIC DOCTRINE OF THE SACRAMENT
OF THE BODY AND BLOOD

OF

OUR SAVIOUR CHRIST,

WITH

A CONFUTATION OF SUNDRY ERRORS CONCERNING THE SAME GROUNDED
AND STABLISHED UPON GOD'S HOLY WORD, AND APPROVED BY
THE CONSENT OF THE MOST ANCIENT DOCTORS
OF THE CHURCH.

MADE BY THE MOST REVEREND FATHER IN GOD,

THOMAS,

Archbishop of Canterbury,

PRIMATE OF ALL ENGLAND AND METROPOLITAN.

It is the spirit that giveth life, the flesh profiteth nothing.—John vi.

Wipf and Stock Publishers
199 W 8th Ave, Suite 3
Eugene, OR 97401

A Defence of the True and Catholic Doctrine of the Sacrament
of the Body and Blood of Our Savior Christ
With a confutation of sundry errors concerning the same grounded
and stablished upon God's holy word, and approved by the consent of
the most ancient doctors of the church
By Cranmer, Thomas
ISBN: 1-59244-777-5
Publication date 8/9/2004
Previously published by Chas. J. Thynne, 1907

PREFACE.

A VALUABLE and opportune service is rendered by the republication in a convenient form of this important treatise by Archbishop Cranmer. It affords at once a comprehensive and a popular statement of the views respecting "the Sacrament of the Body and Blood of our "Saviour Christ" which animated Cranmer at the critical period at which the two Prayer Books of King Edward the Sixth's reign were formed, and it must thus be regarded as expounding the principles on that subject embodied in our present Communion Service, which has not been modified in any material points from the Second Book. The First Book, moreover, must be regarded as embodying in substance the same principles. The cardinal controversy of the Reformation centred around the Mass, and Cranmer went to the heart of the issue in publishing this "Defence of the true and Catholic Doctrine of the Sacra-"ment." It has the advantage, moreover, of being written with a popular and practical purpose. "God I take to "witness," he says, (*Preface to the Reader,*) "... that I "take this labour for none other consideration but for "the glory of his name, and the discharge of my duty, "and the zeal that I bear toward the flock of Christ. I "know in what office God hath placed me, and to what "purpose; that is to say, to set forth His word truly "unto his people, to the uttermost of my power, without "respect of person, or regard of thing in the world, but "of Him alone.... I know how Antichrist hath "obscured the glory of God and the true knowledge of "his word, overcasting the same with mists and clouds of "error and ignorance, through false glosses and interpre-"tations. It pitieth me to see the simple and hungry "flock of Christ led into corrupt pastures, to be carried

vi.   PREFACE.

"blindfold they know not whither, and to be fed with "poison in the stead of wholesome meats." The treatise, accordingly, though dealing effectively with the questions of formal theology which are involved, is addressed to lay as well as clerical readers, and is suited to the general intelligence. Having a distinctly practical object in view, and intended for "the simple and hungry "flock of Christ," it will be found to have a singularly personal and living interest. It is written for the most part in that large English style which is characteristic of Cranmer, and which, no doubt through his influence, has moulded so much of the language of our Prayer Book. It is more flowing and natural than the stately language of Hooker, and, apart from some antique expressions, is in harmony with the best English of a later date. We are told (Todd's Life of Cranmer, ii., 237) that "so eager "was the demand for the work that in the same year "(1550) three impressions of it appeared;" and it may be hoped that in its present more accessible form it may receive at least similar attention.

Its main object is clearly indicated in the Preface to the Reader. "What availeth it," he says, "to take away "beads, pardons, pilgrimages, and such other like popery, "so long as two chief roots remain unpulled up? whereof, "so long as they remain, will spring again all former im-"pediments of the Lord's harvest, and corruption of his "flock. . . . The very body of the tree, or rather the "roots of the weeds, is the popish doctrine of transub-"stantiation, of the real presence of Christ's flesh and "blood in the sacrament of the altar, (as they call it,) and "of the sacrifice and oblation of Christ made by the "priest for the salvation of the quick and the dead. "Which roots, if they be suffered to grow in the Lord's "vineyard, they will overspread all the ground again "with the old errors and superstitions." Transubstantiation, however, as Cranmer shows, is but a particular form of the error which is at the root of the mischief. The ultimate question is as to the alleged fact of the sacred presence in the bread and wine, not as to the manner of the presence. The cardinal issue on this point is stated clearly in the second chapter of the Third Book. "Though we do affirm," he says, "according to "God's word, that Christ is in all persons that truly "believe in him, in such sort, that with his flesh and "blood he doth spiritually nourish them and feed them, "and giveth them everlasting life, and doth assure them "thereof, as well by the promise of his word, as by the "sacramental bread and wine in his holy Supper, which "he did institute for the same purpose, yet we do not a "little vary from the heinous errors of the papists.

"For they teach, that Christ is in the bread and wine, "but we say, according to the truth, that he is in them "that worthily eat and drink the bread and wine.

"They say, that Christ is received in the mouth, and "entereth in with the bread and wine. We say that he "is received in the heart, and entereth in by faith."

This is the position asserted by Hooker fifty years later, that "the real presence of Christ's most blessed "body and blood is not to be sought for in the sacra-"ment, but in the worthy receiver of the sacrament." It is striking thus to find the same principle, in very similar words, thus asserted by one of the chief composers of the Prayer Book, and fifty years later by the chief defender and expounder of the Prayer Book. Thus the main "root of error" which Cranmer denounces is not the mere technical doctrine of transubstantiation, but the assertion of a presence of Christ's body and blood "in "the bread and wine." As Mr. Dimock has said, in his statement to the late Fulham conference, the presence of Christ in the Holy Communion is both real and objective, "for faith believes only what is really and objectively "true, and takes and receives only what is really and "objectively offered. But it is not a presence *in* or *under* "the elements considered in themselves." Persons may deny, therefore, as many do in the present day, that they hold the Roman doctrine of transubstantiation, and may yet hold an essential part of the Roman doctrine by maintaining a presence in the elements themselves; and what Cranmer said of the abuses of that time may be said in our own, that the root of all the superstitious practices against which Evangelical Churchmen are contending is to be found in this doctrine—not of a real and objective presence of Christ in the Holy Communion, but—of the real and objective presence of his body and blood in the elements.

The case is similar with the second "root of error" which Cranmer denounces. No one denies that in the Eucharist sacrifice is offered to God—a commemorative memorial of the sacrifice of Christ's death, and in that sense a commemorative sacrifice, a sacrifice of praise and thanksgiving, and the sacrifice of ourselves, our bodies and souls. The question is whether a sacrifice more or less propitiatory is made or applied by the priest. "They "say," according to Cranmer, in the same place, "that the "mass is a sacrifice satisfactory for sin, by the devotion of "the priest that offereth, and not by the thing that is "offered; but we say, that their saying is . . . a detest- "able error against the glory of Christ. For the satis- "faction for our sins is not the devotion nor offering of the "priest; but the only host and satisfaction for all the "sins of the world is the death of Christ, and the oblation "of his body upon the cross, that is to say, the oblation "that Christ himself offered once upon the cross, and "never but once, nor none other but he. And therefore "that oblation, which the priests make daily in their

PREFACE. ix.

"papistical masses, cannot be a satisfaction for other "men's sins by the priest's devotion"—still less can "the "mass" be, as Lord Halifax urged the other day, an application of the Passion of our Lord, not only to "those "members of Christ's body who happen at the moment "to be living upon earth," but "to the far greater number "within the veil." It is the question of the sacrificial and applicatory power of the priest in this matter which is of vital consequence. As Cranmer says again in Book V., chap. x., "Briefly to conclude, he that thinketh to come "to the kingdom of Christ himself must also come to His "sacraments himself, and keep His commandments him-"self, and do all things that pertain to a Christian man "and his vocation himself; lest if he refer these things to "another man to do them for him, the other may with as "good right claim the kingdom of heaven for him. "Therefore Christ made no such difference between the "priest and the layman, that the priest should make "oblation and sacrifice of Christ for the layman, and eat "the Lord's Supper for him all alone, and distribute and "apply it as him liketh. Christ made no such difference; "but the difference that is between the priest and the "layman in this matter is only in the ministration; that "the priest, as a common minister of the Church, doth "minister and distribute the Lord's Supper unto other, "and other receive it at his hands. But the very Supper "itself was by Christ instituted and given unto the whole "Church, not to be offered and eaten of the priest for "other men, but by him to be delivered to all that would "duly ask it."

These references will illustrate the main contentions of Cranmer's work, and will show that he is dealing directly, and in a trenchant manner, with the vital questions at issue in our controversies in the Church of England at the present day. He approaches them however, in no merely controversial spirit, but starts from a large view of the purpose and method of our redemption by Christ, and of the sacred and vital nature of our participation in Christ's body and blood. It is a treatise which takes us deep into the heart of the Gospel, and assists us to a living apprehension of the great truths which were reasserted at the Reformation. As he grounds his position in the first instance on the Scriptures, he reviews their language on the subject in detail, and throws great light, as it seems to me, on the symbolical and figurative method of expression which is characteristic of them. He is not less illuminative in his discussion of the language of the Fathers; and it is important to notice, as the present Bishop of Edinburgh has observed, that he earnestly maintains that the doctrine he upholds is not merely the Scriptural, but the "Catholic" doctrine. On the whole, the treatise may be regarded as the most authoritative, the ablest, and the most impressive statement of the doctrine respecting the Holy Communion which is embodied in our Prayer Book and Articles, and which was held by the chief English Divines at the Reformation; and at the present crisis in our Church it deserves wide attention and the most thoughtful consideration.

H. WACE.

The Deanery, Canterbury,
June, 1907.

PREFATORY REMARKS BY THE EDITOR.

This edition of Cranmer's work on the Lord's Supper is reprinted from *The Remains of Thos. Cranmer*, D.D., Archbishop of Canterbury, collected and arranged by Rev. Henry Jenkyns, M.A., Fellow of Oriel College. That work was published in four volumes at Oxford, University Press, 1833. Cranmer's work on the Lord's Supper was first published in 1550, under the title of "*Defence of the True and Catholic Doctrine of the Sacrament of the Body and Blood of our Saviour Christ.*" Cranmer's main arguments in defence of "the true and catholic doctrine" were taken from Holy Scripture, and from it he refuted the four chief errors of the Romanists, namely, Transubstantiation, the Real Presence of Christ in the consecrated elements, the eating and drinking of Christ by the wicked and the Propitiatory Sacrifice of the Mass. Two replies to that work were speedily published, first by Richard Smythe (or Smith), who had been Regius Professor of Divinity at Oxford, and then by Stephen Gardiner, some time Bishop of Winchester. In the edition of his work published in reply to those assailants, Archbishop Cranmer introduced answers to their arguments. Gardiner had, when in prison, composed a second reply which he wrote in London, and published in Paris under the fictitious name of Marcus Antonius Constantius, a divine of Louvain. That work was publicly acknowledged later in the reign of Queen Mary to have been the composition of Bishop Gardiner. Archbishop Cranmer replied to that work, but two parts of that reply perished, as John Foxe informs us, at Oxford. The third part, too, though once in Foxe's custody, has also been lost.

The fact that in the edition published in the collection of the Parker Society by Rev. J. E. Cox, M.A., Cranmer's original work is in that edition, combined with the answers to his Roman opponents, has made the work less easy to read, and therefore it has been for popular purposes considered advisable here to reprint it in its original form.

There are, however, notes of importance in the Parker Society's edition which do not appear in this, and *vice versa*. The notes in this edition at the foot of the page, unless when specially otherwise indicated, are those of Rev. Henry Jenkyns. It would have involved a large amount of extra labour and expense to have revised those notes, and to have brought the quotations from the Fathers up to the present standpoint of information. The means, however, were not forthcoming for accomplishing such a revision; but, even in its present form, this reprint of Archbishop Cranmer's work ought to prove of considerable importance at the present time.

A few supplementary notes have been added at the conclusion of the volume which it may be hoped may be useful to many who would not be inclined to read the work in the shape presented in the Parker Society's edition.

CHARLES H. H. WRIGHT, D.D.
90, Bolingbroke Grove, London, S.W.
June, 1907.

A PREFACE TO THE READER.

[Prefixed to the edition of 1551, which contained a reply to Gardiner's Criticisms.]

IT has been thought well to add the following Preface from the edition of 1551 because it deals with the mistakes as to his real meaning which on the first appearance of this work Cranmer had found most prevalent. The double sense in which the word "sacrament" is popularly used, Cranmer found, had caused some readers to "stumble." It does so still.

The presence of Christ to the worthy receiver, he explains, is not peculiar to the Lord's Supper, or to sacraments, but belongs to every occasion when "two or three are gathered together in Christ's name." The argument that two substances cannot coexist in the same space, which was supposed to prove transubstantiation, he parries by shewing that "the natural cause wherefore two bodies cannot be together in one place is their accidents and not their substance." This last hardly appeals to modern readers because the scholastic philosophy has now been so completely exploded; but as transubstantiation is based on that same metaphysical theory, this discrimination is still useful in refutation of the mistaken inference from an unproved hypothesis. Each of these fallacies is as prevalent to-day as in the 16th century and still calls for Cranmer's lucid exposure.

THE FOLLOWING IS FROM CRANMER :—

I think it good, gentle reader, here in the beginning, to admonish thee of certain words and kinds of speeches,

PREFACE.

which I do use sometimes in this mine answer to the late Bishop of Winchester's book, lest in mistaking thou do as it were stumble at them.

Sacrament First, this word "sacrament" I do sometimes use (as it is many times taken among writers and holy doctors) for the sacramental bread, water, or wine; as when they say, that *sacramentum est sacræ rei signum,* "a sacrament is the sign of an holy thing." But where I use to speak sometimes (as the old authors do) that Christ is in the sacraments, I mean the same as they did understand the matter; that is to say, not of Christ's carnal presence in the outward sacrament, but sometimes of his sacramental presence. And sometime by this word "sacrament" I mean the whole ministration and receiving of the sacraments, either of baptism, or of the Lord's Supper: and so the old writers many times do say, that Christ and the Holy Ghost be present in the sacraments; not meaning by that manner of speech, that Christ and the Holy Ghost be present in the water, bread, or wine, (which be only the outward visible sacraments,) but that in the due ministration of the sacraments according to Christ's ordinance and institution, Christ and his holy Spirit be truly and indeed present by their mighty and sanctifying power, virtue, and grace, in all them that worthily receive the same.

Matt. xxviii.

Christ's presence in the godly receiver. Moreover, when I say and repeat many times in my book, that the body of Christ is present in them that worthily receive the sacrament; lest any man should mistake my words, and think that I mean, that although Christ be not corporally in the outward visible signs, yet he is corporally in the persons that duly receive them, this is to advertise the reader, that I mean no such thing; but my meaning is, that the force, the grace, the virtue and benefit of Christ's body that was crucified for us, and of his blood that was shed for us, be really and effectually present with all them that duly receive the sacraments: but all this I understand of his spiritual presence, of the which he saith, "I will be with you until Matt. vi. the world's end;" and, "wheresoever two or three be Matt.xviii. gathered together in my name, there am I in the midst of them;" and, "he that eateth my flesh and John vi. drinketh my blood, dwelleth in me, and I in him." Nor no more truly is he corporally or really present in the due ministration of the Lord's Supper, than he is in the due ministration of baptism; [that is to say, in both spiritually by grace. And wheresoever in the scripture it is said that Christ, God, or the Holy Ghost is in any man, the same is understood spiritually by grace.][1] . . .

The last admonition to the reader is this, where the said late bishop thinketh that he hath sufficiently proved transubstantiation, (that is to say, that the substance of bread and wine cannot be in the sacrament, if the body and blood of Christ were there, because two bodies cannot be together in one place,) although the truth be, that in the sacrament of Christ's body there is corporally but the substance of bread only, and in the sacrament of the blood the substance of wine only, yet how far he is deceived, and doth vary from the doctrine of other papists, and also from the principles of philosophy (which he taketh for the foundation of his doctrine in this point), the reader hereby may easily perceive. For if we speak of God's power, the papists affirm, that by God's power two bodies may be together in one place, and then why may not Christ's blood be with the wine in the cup, and his flesh in the same place where the substance of the bread is? And if we consider the cause wherefore two bodies cannot be together in one place by the rules of nature, it shall evidently appear, that the body

The real presence of Christ should prove no transubstantiation of the bread and wine.

[1] This passage is only found in the edition of 1580.

of Christ may rather be in one place with the substance of the bread, than with the accidents thereof, and so likewise his blood with the wine. For the natural cause wherefore two bodies cannot be together in one place (as the philosophers say) is their accidents, their bigness, and thickness, and not their substances. And then by the very order of nature it repugneth more, that the body of Christ should be present with the accidents of bread, and his blood with the accidents of wine, than with the substances either of bread or wine. This shall suffice for the admonition to the reader, joining thereto the preface in my first book, which is this:

A TABLE

OF THE

CHIEF AND PRINCIPAL MATTERS

CONTAINED IN THIS BOOK

THE CONTENTS OF THE FIRST BOOK.

	Page
THE abuse of the Lord's Supper	1
The eating of the body of Christ	3
The eating of the sacrament of his body	5
Christ calleth the material bread his body	7
Evil men do eat the sacrament, but not the body of Christ	9
Things sufficient for a Christian man's faith, concerning this sacrament	9
The sacrament which was ordained to make love and concord, is turned into the occasion of variance and discord	10
The purpose of the author	11
The spiritual hunger and thirstiness of the soul	12
The spiritual food of the soul	15
Christ far excelleth all corporal food	17
The sacraments were ordained to confirm our faith	18
Wherefore this sacrament was ordained in bread and wine	21
The unity of Christ's mystical body	22
This sacrament moveth all men to love and friendship	23
The doctrine of transubstantiation doth clean subvert our faith in Christ	24
The spiritual eating is with the heart, not with the teeth	25
Four principal errors of the papists	28
The first is of transubstantiation	28
The second is of the presence of Christ in this sacrament	30
The third is, that evil men eat and drink the very body and blood of Christ	33
The fourth is of the daily sacrifice of Christ	33

THE CONTENTS OF THE SECOND BOOK.

	Page
The confutation of the error of transubstantiation	34
The papistical doctrine is contrary to God's word	34
The papistical doctrine is against reason	40
The papistical doctrine is also against our senses	42
The papistical doctrine is contrary to the faith of the old authors of Christ's church	45
Transubstantiation came from Rome	63
The first reason of the papists to prove their transubstantiation, with the answer thereto	66
The second argument for transubstantiation, with the answer	70
The third reason, John vi.	72
Authors wrested of the papists for their transubstantiation	73
Negatives by comparison	78
Absurdities that follow of transubstantiation	92

THE CONTENTS OF THE THIRD BOOK.

	Page
The presence of Christ in the sacrament	96
Christ corporally is ascended into heaven	97, 102
The difference between the true and the papistical doctrine concerning the presence of Christ's body	97
The proof whereof by our profession in our common creed	102
Another proof by the holy Scripture	103
Also another proof by ancient authors	104
One body cannot be in divers places at one time	112
An answer to the papists, alleging for them these words, "This is my body"	119
The argument of the papists	120
The interpretation of these words, "This is my body"	119 & foll.
Christ called bread his body, and wine his blood	122
"Bread is my body," "Wine is my blood," be figurative speeches	128
"To eat Christ's flesh" and "drink his blood," be figurative speeches	129
"This is my body," "This is my blood," be figurative speeches	136

THE TABLE OF CONTENTS. xvii.

	Page
The bread representeth Christ's body, and the wine his blood	136
Signs and figures have the names of the things which they signify	139 and 221
Five principal things to be noted in Theodoretus	145-152, 153-5
Figurative speeches be not strange	156
Christ himself used figurative speeches	156
The Paschal Lamb	158
The Lord's Supper	158
What figurative speeches were used at Christ's last supper	160
Answers to the authorities and arguments of the papists	161
One brief answer to all	162
The answers to all the doctors	164

THE CONTENTS OF THE FOURTH BOOK.

Whether evil men do eat and drink Christ	199
The godly only eat Christ	199, 204
What is the eating of Christ's flesh, and drinking of his blood	202
Christ is not eaten with teeth, but with faith	202
The good only eat Christ	204
The answer to the papists that do affirm that the evil do eat Christ's body, &c.	217
The answer to the papists' authors, which, at the first show, seem to make for them	219
Figures be called by the names of the things which they signify	221
The adoration in the sacrament	224
The simple people be deceived	224
They be the papists that have deceived the people	229
An exhortation to the true honouring of Christ in the sacrament	230

THE CONTENTS OF THE FIFTH BOOK.

The sacrifice of the mass	232
The difference between the sacrifice of Christ, and of the priests of the old law	232

DEFENCE, &c

	Page
Two kinds of sacrifices	234
The sacrifice of Christ	235
A more plain declaration of the sacrifice of Christ	236
The sacrifices of the old law	237
The mass is not a sacrifice propitiatory	239, 241
A confutation of the papists' cavillation	241
The true sacrifice of all Christian people	242
The popish mass is detestable idolatry, utterly to be banished from all Christian congregations	244
Every man ought to receive the sacrament himself, and not one for another	244
The difference between the priest and the layman	246
The answer to the papists, concerning the sacrifice propitiatory	247
An answer to the authors	249
The lay persons make a sacrifice as well as the priest	251
The papistical mass is neither a sacrifice propitiatory, nor of thanksgiving	252
There were no papistical masses in the primitive Church	253
The causes and means how papistical masses entered into the Church	255
The abuses of the papistical masses	255
Which Church is to be followed	256
A short instruction to the holy communion	257
Supplementary Notes by the Editor	259

(xix.)

To His Most Illustrious and Most Noble Prince Edward the Sixth, King of England, France and Ireland, Defender of the Faith, and on earth after Christ Supreme Head of the Church of England and Ireland, Thomas Canterbury, Archbishop.

In accordance with the care committed to me of the Lord's Flock in instructing which in the wholesome pasture of the Divine Word I ought to place all my care and thought, Most Illustrious Prince, I have considered that the Supper of the Lord (which has been violated by many and great superstitions, and turned into gain) should be renovated and restored according to the institutions of our Saviour Christ; and I have considered that all should be performed concerning its true use according to the authority of the Divine Word and of the Ancient and Holy Church, the care and instruction of which belong in some part to the authority of my office.

Accordingly about three years ago I confuted in a certain English book the principal abuses of the Popish Mass, (by which not only the English Church, but almost even the whole world had been defiled and infected,) and I showed that the true and Christian practice should be restored. By which book so many persons were drawn to a correct opinion concerning that very thing that I perceived how great was the power of truth, and understood the benefits of the grace

[a] This Letter was first prefixed to the Latin translation of the *Defence* published in 1553. It was reprinted in the Embden edition of 1557.

of our Saviour Christ, so that men who had been darkened to the light of truth received the splendour of the light, and like Paul at the preaching of Ananias, received the sight of their eyes. Stephen Gardiner, then Bishop of Winchester, took this so badly, that he thought that nothing ought first to be done by himself, before he had confuted a book so useful and plausible; having thought that unless by his own work some hindrances could be placed in the way, there would be no favourers of the opinion already deplored and almost abandoned. He wrote accordingly in the same language a book concerning those same things, and endeavoured to overthrow the opinion which had been proved concerning the true use of the Supper, and endeavoured to bring back again the Popish opinion with its superstitions which was fading away on every side. After him, Marcus Constantius, so akin and closely connected with Stephen Gardiner, that he appeared to be his very self; so great was the subtlety of disposition, the similarity of his sophistic interpretation of Scripture. But both handled the same point, but in a different manner.

For Constantius in the book he wrote in Latin so handled my arguments as it appeared best to himself; and that he might benefit his cause he thus brought them in often clipped, often inverted, often dislocated, so that they could not be recognised by me any more than the children of Medea when divided into many members, and defaced. For we cannot correctly judge of the form of the human body, nor indeed about any matter when the whole appearance has not been placed before our eyes, on which we ought to gaze as on the Minerva of Phidias, and not to find fault with some small point, as Momas did with the slipper of Venas. So in order that my views may be better understood upon this controversy, I took care that my book should be translated from English into Latin, that all might understand, that we neither wished our opinion to be obscure or hidden, which we hold in common with many good and learned men, and to be in accordance with the Word of God, and the true Church which is a defender of the Word.

But there is no one of all who is more worthy, that this book should appear in his name, than in yours. For you are not only in the opinion of the Papists the Defender of the Faith, (who not only brought this out by themselves, but God warning by them to their destruction,) but even by the authority of all good men, you are worthy person upon whom so great a gift of the Church should be conferred. You are the supreme ruler on earth of this English and Irish Church, under whom, as under Moses, a place may be left in which I have some part of the Spirit and a great care and administration of many committed to me: for which reason I think it may not only be satisfactory to one, but even to Gardiner and Constantius; and what the latter said about the comedies may also be said of those personated: "When you know "one, you know both." Because if any things have been treated in the one book, which have been omitted in the other, I will join my reply to them, so that the adversaries, if any should be left, shall either have nothing to object to, or if they do object to it, they may see what answer could be made to those objections. These are the causes, O Most Noble King, which induce me to publish this book and to spread it abroad under the authority of your Majesty. I hope that you will accept this my study, as both the equity of the cause demands, and ask for my offices as your clemency is wont to do in all honorable causes. The Lord Jesus preserve your Majesty. Ides of March, 1553.

A

PREFACE TO THE READER.

The great mercy and benefits of God towards us. [1580] OUR Saviour Christ Jesus according to the will of his eternal Father, when the time thereto was fully complished, taking our nature upon him, came into this world from the high throne of his Father, to declare unto miserable sinners good news; to heal them that were sick; to make the blind to see, the deaf to hear, and the dumb to speak; to set prisoners at liberty; to show that the time of grace and mercy was come; to give light to them that were in darkness and in the shadow of death; and to preach and give pardon and full remission of sin to all his elected. And to perform the same, he made a sacrifice and oblation of his own body upon the cross, which was a full redemption, satisfaction, and propitiation, for the sins of the whole world. And to commend this his sacrifice unto all his faithful people, and to confirm their faith and hope of eternal salvation in the same, he hath ordained a perpetual memory of his said sacrifice, daily to be used in the Church to his perpetual laud and praise, and to our singular comfort and consolation; that is to say, the celebration of his holy supper, wherein he doth not cease to give himself with all his benefits, to all those that duly receive the same supper according to his blessed ordinance.

The erroneous doctrine of the papists obscuring the same. [1580.] But the Romish Antichrist, to deface this great benefit of Christ, hath taught that his sacrifice upon the cross is not sufficient hereunto, without another sacrifice devised by him, and made by the priest, or else without indulgences, beads, pardons, pilgrimages, and such other pelfry, to supply Christ's imperfection: and that Christian people cannot apply to themselves the benefits of Christ's passion, but that the same is in the distribution of the Bishop of Rome, or else that by Christ we have no full remission, but be delivered only from sin, and yet remaineth temporal pain in Purgatory due for the same, to be remitted after this life by the Romish Antichrist and his ministers, who take upon them to do for us that thing, which Christ either would not or could not do. O heinous blasphemy and most detestable injury against Christ! O wicked abomination in the temple of God! O pride intolerable of Antichrist, and most manifest token of the son of perdition, extolling himself above God, and with Lucifer exalting his seat and power above the throne of God! For he that taketh upon him to supply that thing, which he pretendeth to be unperfect in Christ, must needs make himself above Christ, and so very Antichrist. For what is this else, but to be against Christ, and to bring him into contempt, as one that either for lack of charity would not, or for lack of power he could not, with all his blood-shedding and death, clearly deliver his faithful, and give them full remission of their sins, but that the full perfection thereof must be had at the hands of Antichrist of Rome and his ministers? *2 Thess ii.*

What man of knowledge and zeal to God's honour can with dry eyes see this injury to Christ, and look upon the state of religion brought in by the papists, perceiving the true sense of God's word subverted by false glosses of man's devising, the true Christian religion turned into certain hypocritical and superstitious sects, the people praying with their mouths and hearing with their ears they wist not what, and so ignorant in God's word, that they could not discern hypocrisy and superstition from true and sincere religion? This was of late years the face of religion within this realm of England, and yet *The state of religion brought in by the papists. [1580.]*

remaineth in divers realms. But, (thanks be to Almighty God and to the King's Majesty, with his father, a prince of most famous memory,) the superstitious sects of monks and friars, that were in this realm, be clean taken away; the Scripture is restored unto the proper and true understanding; the people may daily read and hear God's heavenly word, and pray in their own language which they understand, so that their hearts and mouths may go together, and be none of those people of whom Christ complained, saying, *These people honour me with their lips, but their hearts be far from me.* Thanks be to God, many corrupt weeds be plucked up, which were wont to rot the flock of Christ, and to let the growing of the Lord's harvest.

Matt. xv.

But what availeth it to take away beads, pardons, pilgrimages, and such other like popery, so long as two chief roots remain unpulled up? whereof, so long as they remain, will spring again all former impediments of the Lord's harvest, and corruption of his flock. The rest is but branches and leaves, the cutting away whereof is but like topping and lopping of a tree, or cutting down of weeds, leaving the body standing, and the roots in the ground; but the very body of the tree, or rather the roots of the weeds, is the popish doctrine of transubstantiation, of the real presence of Christ's flesh and blood in the sacrament of the altar, (as they call it,) and of the sacrifice and oblation of Christ made by the priest for the salvation of the quick and the dead. Which roots, if they be suffered to grow in the Lord's vineyard, they will overspread all the ground again with the old errors and superstitions.

The chief roots of all errors. [1580.]

These injuries to Christ be so intolerable, that no Christian heart can willingly bear them. Wherefore seeing that many have set to their hands and whetted their tools, to pluck up the weeds, and to cut down the tree of

What moved the author to write [1580]

error, I, not knowing otherwise how to excuse myself at the last day, have in this book set to my hand and axe with the rest to cut down this tree, and to pluck up the weeds and plants by the roots, which our heavenly Father never planted, but were grafted and sown in his vineyard by his adversary the Devil, and Antichrist his minister. The Lord grant that this my travail and labour in his vineyard be not in vain, but that it may prosper and bring forth good fruits to his honour and glory. For when I see his vineyard overgrown with thorns, brambles, and weeds, I know that everlasting woe appertaineth unto me, if I hold my peace, and put not to my hands and tongue to labour in purging his vineyard. God I take to witness, (who seeth the hearts of all men throughly unto the bottom,) that I take this labour for none other consideration, but for the glory of his name, and the discharge of my duty, and the zeal that I bear toward the flock of Christ. I know in what office God hath placed me, and to what purpose; that is to say, to set forth his word truly unto his people, to the uttermost of my power, without respect of person, or regard of thing in the world, but of Him alone. I know what account I shall make to Him hereof at the last day, when every man shall answer for his vocation, and receive for the same, good or ill, according as he hath done. I know how Antichrist hath obscured the glory of God and the true knowledge of his word, overcasting the same with mists and clouds of error and ignorance, through false glosses and interpretations. It pitieth me to see the simple and hungry flock of Christ led into corrupt pastures, to be carried blindfold they know not whither, and to be fed with poison in the stead of wholesome meats.

And moved by the duty, office, and place, whereunto it hath pleased God to call me, I give warning in his *A warning given by the author.*

name unto all that profess Christ, that they flee far from Babylon, if they will save their souls, and to beware of that great harlot, that is to say, the pestiferous see of Rome, that she make you not drunk with her pleasant wine. Trust not her sweet promises, nor banquet with her; for instead of wine she will give you sour dregs, and for meat she will feed you with rank poison. But come to our Redeemer and Saviour Christ, who refresheth all that truly come unto him, be their anguish and heaviness never so great. Give credit unto him, in whose mouth was never found guile nor untruth. By him you shall be clearly delivered from all your diseases, of him you shall have full remission, *a pœna et a culpa*. He it is that feedeth continually all that belong unto him with his own flesh that hanged upon the cross; and giveth them drink of the blood flowing out of his own side, and maketh to spring within them water that floweth unto everlasting life. Listen not to the false incantations, sweet whisperings, and crafty jugglings of the subtle papists, wherewith they have this many years deluded and bewitched the world; but harken to Christ, give ear unto his words, which shall lead you the right way unto everlasting life, there with him to live ever as heirs of his kingdom. Amen.

[a] *The First Book is of the True and Catholic Doctrine and Use of the Sacrament of the Body and Blood of our Saviour Christ.*

The Supper of the Lord, otherwise called the

CHAP. 1.

The abuse of the Lord's Supper.

a [The library of Corpus Christi College Cambridge possesses a Collection of authorities *De Re Sacramentaria*, which was probably used by Cranmer in the composition of his *Defence*, &c. The extracts made from thence by Strype, with his accurate account of the manuscript, are subjoined, because they state briefly many of the principal points discussed in the following work. This Note-book, as Strype calls it, " consists of nothing but "quotations out of ancient ecclesiastical authors about the "Lord's Supper; interlined in many places by the Archbishop's "pen. On the top of some of the pages are these sentences "writ by himself, being doctrines provable out of the sentences "there produced and transcribed.

" Panis vocatur corpus Christi, et vinum sanguis.

" *Panis est corpus meum*, et *Vinum est sanguis meus*, figura"tivæ sunt locutiones.

" Quid significet hæc figura, *Edere carnem*, *et bibere* " *sanguinem*.

" Mali non edunt et bibunt corpus et sanguinem Domini.

" Patres Vet. Testamenti edebant et bibebant Christum, sicut " et nos.

" Sicut in Eucharistia, ita in Baptismo, præsens est Christus.

" Contra Transubstantiationem.

" After this follow these writings of the Archbishop's own " hand.

" Multa affirmant crassi papistæ, seu Capernaitæ, quæ neque " Scriptura neque ullus veterum unquam dixerat; viz.

" Quod accidentia maneant sine subjecto.

" Quod accidentia panis et vini sunt sacramenta: non panis " et vinum.

" Quod panis non est figura, sed accidentia panis.

" Quod Christus non appellavit panem corpus suum.

" Quod cum Christus dixit, *Hoc est corpus meum*, pronomen " *hoc* non refertur ad panem, sed ad corpus Christi.

" Quod tot corpora Christi accipimus, aut toties corpus ejus

Holy Communion or Sacrament of the Body and Blood of our Saviour Christ, hath been of many men, and by sundry ways, very much abused ; but specially within these four or five hundred years. Of some it hath been used as a sacrifice propitiatory for sin, and otherwise superstitiously, far from the intent that Christ did first ordain the same at the beginning ; doing therein great wrong and injury to his death and passion. And of other some it hath been very lightly esteemed, or rather contemned and despised, as a thing of small or of none effect. And thus between both the parties hath been much variance and contention in divers places of Christendom. Therefore to the intent that this holy sacrament, or Lord's Supper,

" accipimus, quoties, aut in quot partes, dentibus secamus
" panem.

" Thus having set down divers assertions of papists, or Caper-
" naites, as he styled them, which neither Scripture nor ancient
" fathers knew any thing of ; his Notes proceed to state where-
" in papists and protestants disagree.

"Præcipua capita in quibus a papistis dissentimus.

" Christum papistæ statuunt in pane, nos in homine come-
" dente :

" Illi in comedentis ore, nos in toto homine.

" Illi corpus Christi aiunt evolare, masticato vel consumpto
" pane : nos manere in homine dicimus, quamdiu membrum
" est Christi.

" Illi in pane statuunt per annum integrum, et diutius, si
" duret panis : nos in homine statuimus inhabitare, quamdiu
" templum Dei fuerit.

"Illorum sententia, quod ad realem præsentiam attinet,
" non amplius edit homo quam bellua, neque magis ei prodest,
" quam cuivis animanti." Strype, *Cranm.* p. 262. The manuscript contains also some other scattered remarks by the Archbishop, besides those which are here extracted. C.C.C.C. CII. p. 151.]

may hereafter neither of the one party be con- CHAP. temned or lightly esteemed, nor of the other party be abused to any other purpose than Christ himself did first appoint and ordain the same, and that so the contention on both parties may be quieted and ended; the most sure and plain way is, to cleave unto holy Scripture. Wherein whatsoever is found, must be taken for a most sure ground and an infallible truth; and whatsoever cannot be grounded upon the same (touching our faith) is man's device, changeable and uncertain. And therefore here are set forth the very words that Christ himself and his apostle St. Paul spake, both of the eating and drinking of Christ's body and blood, and also of the eating and drinking of the sacrament of the same.

First, as concerning the eating of the body and drinking of the blood of our Saviour Christ, he speaketh himself, in the sixth chapter of St. John, in this wise:

CHAP. II.
The eating of the body of Christ.
John vi.

Verily, verily, I say unto you, Except you eat the flesh of the Son of man, and drink his blood, you have no life in you. Whoso eateth my flesh, and drinketh my blood, hath eternal life; and I will raise him up at the last day. For my flesh is very meat, and my blood is very drink. He that eateth my flesh, and drinketh my blood, dwelleth in me, and I in him. *As the living Father hath sent me, and I live by the Father: even so he that eateth me, shall live by me. This is the bread which came down from heaven: not as your fathers did eat manna, and are dead:* he that eateth this bread shall live for ever. Of these words of Christ[b] it is plain and manifest, that the eating of Christ's flesh, and drinking of his blood, is not like to the eating and drinking of other meats and drinks. For although without meat and drink man cannot live, yet it followeth not, that he that eateth and drinketh shall live for ever.

But as touching this meat and drink of the body and blood of Christ, it is true, both he that eateth and drinketh them, hath everlasting life; and also he that eateth and drinketh them not, hath not everlasting life. For to eat that meat and drink that drink, is to dwell in Christ and to have Christ dwelling in him[c].

And therefore no man can say or think[d], that he eateth the body of Christ or drinketh his blood, except he dwelleth in Christ and hath Christ dwelling in him. Thus have ye heard of the eating and drinking of the very flesh and blood of our Saviour Christ.

---

[b] Augustin. *In Joan. Tractat.* 26. [d] Aug. *De Civitate*, lib. 21. cap. 25.
[c] Eodem Tract.

THE USE OF THE LORD'S SUPPER.

Now as touching the sacraments of the same, our Saviour Christ did institute them in bread and wine, at his last supper, which he had with his Apostles the night before his death: at which time, as St. Matthew saith, *(CHAP. III. The eating of the sacrament of his body. Matt. xxvi.)*

When they were eating, Jesus took bread, and when he had given thanks, he brake it, gave it to his disciples, and said, Take, eat; this is my body. And he took the cup, and when he had given thanks, he gave it to them, saying, Drink ye all of this; for this is my blood of the new testament, that is shed for many for the remission of sins. But I say unto you, I will not drink henceforth of this fruit of the vine, until that day when I shall drink it new with you in my Father's kingdom.

This thing is rehearsed also of St. Mark, in these words:

As they did eat, Jesus took bread, and when he had blessed, he brake it, and gave it to them, and said, Take, eat; this is my body. And taking the cup, when he had given thanks, he gave it to them: and they all drank of it. And he said to them, This is my blood of the new testament, which is shed for many. Verily I say unto you, I will drink no more of the fruit of the vine, until that day that I drink it new in the kingdom of God. *(Mark xiv.)*

The Evangelist St. Luke uttereth this matter on this wise:

When the hour was come, he sat down, and the twelve Apostles with him. And he said unto them: I have greatly desired to eat this Pascha with you *(Luke xxii.)*

before I suffer: for I say unto you, henceforth I will not eat of it any more, until it be fulfilled in the kingdom of God. And he took the cup, and gave thanks, and said, Take this, and divide it among you: for I say unto you, I will not drink of the fruit of the vine, until the kingdom of God come. And he took bread, and when he had given thanks, he brake it, and gave it unto them, saying, This is my body which is given for you: this do in remembrance of me. Likewise also when he had supped, he took the cup, saying, This cup is the new testament in my blood, which is shed for you.

Hitherto you have heard all that the Evangelists declare that Christ spake or did at his last supper, concerning the institution of the communion and sacrament of his body and blood. Now you shall hear what St. Paul saith concerning the same, in the tenth chapter of the First to the Corinthians, where he writeth thus:

Is not the cup of blessing which we bless, a communion *of the blood of Christ? Is not the bread which we break, a communion of the body of Christ? We being many are one bread and one body: for we all are partakers of one bread and of one cup.*

And in the eleventh he speaketh on this manner:

That which I delivered unto you I received of the Lord. For the Lord Jesus the same night in the which he was betrayed, took bread, *and when*

THE USE OF THE LORD'S SUPPER. 7

he had given thanks, he brake it, *and said,* Take, *eat; this is my body, which is broken for you: do this in remembrance of me. Likewise also he took* the cup, *when supper was done, saying, This cup is the new testament in my blood: do this, as often as you drink it, in remembrance of me. For as often as you shall eat this* bread, *and drink* this cup, *show forth the Lord's death* till he come. *Wherefore whosoever shall eat of this* bread *or drink of this* cup *unworthily, shall be guilty of the body and blood of the Lord. But let a man examine himself, and so eat of the* bread, *and drink of the* cup. *For he that* eateth and drinketh *unworthily, eateth and drinketh his own damnation, because* he maketh no difference of the Lord's body. *For this cause many are weak and sick among you, and many do sleep.*

By these words of Christ rehearsed of the Evangelists, and by the doctrine also of St. Paul, (which he confesseth that he received of Christ,) two things specially are to be noted.

CHAP. III.

First, that our Saviour Christ called the material bread which he brake, his body, and the wine which was the fruit of the vine, his blood.

And yet he spake not this to the intent that men should think, that material bread is his very

CHAP. IV.

Christ called the material bread his body.

body, or that his very body is material bread; neither that wine made of grapes is his very blood, or that his very blood is wine made of grapes; but to signify unto us (as St. Paul saith) that the cup is a communion of Christ's blood that was shed for us, and the bread is a communion of his flesh that was crucified for us. So that although, in the truth of his human nature, Christ be in heaven, and sitteth on the right hand of God the Father, yet whosoever eateth of that bread in the supper of the Lord, according to Christ's institution and ordinance, is assured of Christ's own promise and testament, that he is a member of his body, and receiveth the benefits of his passion which he suffered for us upon the cross. And likewise he that drinketh of that holy cup in that supper of the Lord, according to Christ's institution, is certified by Christ's legacy and testament, that he is made partaker of the blood of Christ which was shed for us. And this meant St. Paul, when he saith, *Is not the cup of blessing which we bless, a communion of the blood of Christ? Is not the bread which we break, a communion of the body of Christ?* So that no man can contemn or lightly esteem this holy communion, except he contemn also Christ's body and blood, and pass not, whether he have any fellowship with him or no. And of those men St. Paul saith, that they eat and drink their own damnation, because they esteem not the body of Christ.

THE USE OF THE LORD'S SUPPER.

The second thing which may be learned of the foresaid words of Christ and St. Paul is this, that although none eateth the body of Christ and drinketh his blood, but they have eternal life (as appeareth by the words before recited of St. John), yet both the good and the bad do eat and drink the bread and wine, which be the sacraments of the same: but, beside the sacraments, the good eateth everlasting life; the evil, everlasting death. Therefore St. Paul saith: *Whosoever shall eat of the bread or drink of the cup of the Lord unworthily, he shall be guilty of the body and blood of the Lord.* Here St. Paul saith not, that he that eateth the bread or drinketh the cup of the Lord unworthily, eateth or drinketh the body and blood of the Lord, but is guilty of the body and blood of the Lord. But what he eateth and drinketh St. Paul declareth, saying, *He that eateth and drinketh unworthily, eateth and drinketh his own damnation.*

CHAP. V.
Evil men do eat the sacrament, but not the body of Christ.
John vi.

1 Cor. xi.

1 Cor. xi.

Thus is declared the sum of all that Scripture speaketh of the eating and drinking, both of the body and blood of Christ, and also of the sacrament of the same.

And as these things be most certainly true, because they be spoken by Christ himself, the author of all truth, and by his holy apostle St.

CHAP. VI.
These things

BOOK I.

Suffice for a Christian man's faith, concerning this sacrament.

Paul, as he received them of Christ, so all doctrines contrary to the same be most certainly false and untrue, and of all Christian men to be eschewed, because they be contrary to God's word. And all doctrine concerning this matter, that is more than this, which is not grounded upon God's word, is of no necessity, neither ought the people's heads to be busied, or their consciences troubled with the same. So that things spoken and done by Christ, and written by the holy Evangelists and St. Paul, ought to suffice the faith of Christian people, as touching the doctrine of the Lord's Supper, and holy communion or sacrament of his body and blood.

Which thing being well considered and weighed, shall be a just occasion to pacify and agree both parties, as well them that hitherto have contemned or lightly esteemed it, as also them which have hitherto, for lack of knowledge or otherwise, ungodly abused it.

CHAP. VII.

The sacrament which was ordained to make love and concord, is turned into the occasion of variance and discord.

Christ ordained the sacrament to move and stir all men to friendship, love, and concord, and to put away all hatred, variance and discord, and to testify a brotherly and unfeigned love between all them that be the members of Christ; but the Devil, the enemy of Christ and of all his members, hath so craftily juggled herein, that of nothing riseth so much contention as of this holy sacrament.

THE USE OF THE LORD'S SUPPER.

CHAP. VII.

God grant, that all contention set aside, both the parties may come to this holy communion with such a lively faith in Christ, and such an unfeigned love to all Christ's members, that as they carnally eat with their mouth this sacramental bread and drink the wine, so spiritually they may eat and drink the very flesh and blood of Christ, which is in heaven, and sitteth on the right hand of his Father; and that finally by his means they may enjoy with him the glory and kingdom of heaven. Amen.

CHAP. VIII.
The purpose of the author.

Although in this treaty of the sacrament of the body and blood of our Saviour Christ, I have already sufficiently declared the institution and meaning of the same, according to the very words of the Gospel and of St. Paul, yet it shall not be in vain somewhat more at large to declare the same, according to the mind as well of holy Scripture as of old ancient authors; and that so sincerely and plainly, without doubts, ambiguities, or vain questions, that the very simple and unlearned people may easily understand the same, and be edified thereby.

And this by God's grace is mine only intent and desire, that the flock of Christ dispersed in this realm (among whom I am appointed a special pastor) may no longer lack the commodity and fruit which springeth of this heavenly knowledge. For the more clearly it is understood, the more sweetness, fruit, comfort, and edification it bringeth to the godly receivers thereof. And to the clear understanding of this sacrament, divers things must be considered.

CHAP. IX.

The spiritual hunger and thirstiness of the soul.
Ephes. ii.
Rom. iii.

First, that as all men of themselves be sinners, and through sin be in God's wrath, banished far away from him, condemned to hell and everlasting damnation, and none is clearly innocent but Christ alone: so every soul inspired by God is desirous to be delivered from sin and hell, and to obtain at God's hands mercy, favour, righteousness, and everlasting salvation.

And this earnest and great desire is called in Scripture the hunger and thirst of the soul; with which kind of hunger David was taken, when he said: *As an hart longeth for springs of water, so doth my soul long for thee, O God.* My soul hath thirsteth *after God, who is the well of life. My soul thirsteth for thee, my flesh wisheth for thee.*

Psalm xlii.
Psalm lxiii.

And this hunger the silly, poor, sinful soul is driven unto by means of the law, which showeth unto her the horribleness of sin, the terror of God's indignation, and the horror of death and everlasting damnation.

Rom. iv. vii. viii.

And when she seeth nothing but damnation for her offences by justice and accusation of the law,

THE USE OF THE LORD'S SUPPER.

and this damnation is ever before her eyes; then, in this great distress, the soul being pressed with heaviness and sorrow seeketh for some comfort, and desireth some remedy for her miserable and sorrowful estate. And this feeling of her damnable condition, and greedy desire of refreshing, is the spiritual hunger of the soul.

And whosoever hath this godly hunger is blessed of God, and shall have meat and drink enough, as Christ himself said: *Blessed be they that hunger and thirst for righteousness, for they shall be filled full.* And on the other side, they that see not their own sinful and damnable estate, but think themselves holy enough, and in good case and condition enough, as they have no spiritual hunger, so shall they not be fed of God with any spiritual food. For as Almighty God feedeth them that be hungry, so doth he send away empty all that be not hungry.

But this hunger and thirst is not easily perceived of the carnal man: for when he heareth the Holy Ghost speak of meat and drink, his mind is by and by in the kitchen and buttery, and he thinketh upon his dishes and pots, his mouth and his belly.

But the Scripture in sundry places useth special words, whereby to draw our gross minds from the phantasying of our teeth and belly, and from this carnal and fleshly imagination. For the Apostles and disciples of Christ, when they were yet carnal, knew not what was meant by this kind of hunger and meat, and therefore, when they desired him to eat, to withdraw their minds from carnal meat, he said unto them: *I have other meat to eat, which you know not.* And why knew they it not? Forsooth because their minds were gross as yet, and had not received the fulness of the Spirit. And therefore our Saviour Christ, minding to draw them from this grossness, told them of another kind of meat than they phantasied; as it were, rebuking them, for that they perceived not that there was any other kind of eating and drinking, besides that eating and drinking which is with the mouth and the throat.

Likewise when he said to the woman of Samaria: *Whosoever shall drink of that water that I shall give him shall never be thirsty again:* they that heard him speak those words might well perceive, that he went about to make them well acquainted with another kind of drinking, than is the drinking with the mouth and throat. For there is no such kind of drink, that with once drinking can quench the thirst of a man's body for ever. Wherefore in saying, He shall never be thirsty again, he did draw their minds from drinking with the mouth unto another kind of drinking whereof they knew not, and unto another kind of thirsting wherewith as yet they were not acquainted. Also when our Saviour Christ said, *He that cometh to me shall not hunger; and he that believeth on me shall never be thirsty;* he gave them a plain watchword, that there was another kind of meat and drink than that wherewith he fed them at the other side of the water, and another kind of hungering and thirsting than was the hungering and thirsting of the body. By these words therefore, he drove the people to understand another kind of eating and drinking, of hungering and thirsting, than that which belongeth only for the preservation of temporal life.

CHAP. IX.

Now then as the thing that comforteth the body is called meat and drink, of a like sort the Scripture calleth the same thing that comforteth the soul, meat and drink.

Wherefore as here before in the first note is declared the hunger and drought of the soul, so is it now secondly to be noted, what is the meat, drink, and food of the soul.

CHAP. X.

The spiritual food of the soul.

The meat, drink, food, and refreshing of the soul, is our Saviour Christ; as he said himself: *Come unto me all you that travail and be laden, and I will refresh you.—And if any man be dry*, saith he, *let him come to me and drink. He that believeth in me, floods of water of life shall flow out of his belly.—And I am the bread of life*, saith Christ; *he that cometh to me shall not be hungry; and he that believeth in me shall never be dry.* For as meat and drink do comfort the hungry body, so doth the death of Christ's body, and the

Matt. xi.

I John vii.

John vi.

Not the actual body, but the

BOOK I.

death of the body, because from death all spiritual benefits flow.

shedding of his blood, comfort the soul, when she is after her sort hungry. What thing is it that comforteth and nourisheth the body? Forsooth, meat and drink. By what names then shall we call the body and blood of our Saviour Christ (which do comfort and nourish the hungry soul) but by the names of meat and drink? And this similitude caused our Saviour to say, *My flesh is very meat, and my blood is very drink.* For there is no kind of meat that is comfortable to the soul, but only the death of Christ's blessed body; nor no kind of drink that can quench her thirst, but only the blood-shedding of our Saviour Christ, which was shed for her offences.

For as there is a carnal generation, and a carnal feeding and nourishment, so is there also a spiritual generation, and a spiritual feeding.

And as every man, by carnal generation of father and mother, is carnally begotten and born unto this mortal life, so is every good Christian spiritually born by Christ unto eternal life.

And as every man is carnally fed and nourished in his body by meat and drink, even so is every good Christian man spiritually fed and nourished in his soul by the flesh and blood of our Saviour Christ.

And as the body liveth by meat and drink, and thereby increaseth and groweth from a young babe unto a perfect man, (which thing experience teacheth us,) so the soul liveth by Christ himself, by pure faith eating his flesh and drinking his

THE USE OF THE LORD'S SUPPER. 17

blood. And this Christ himself teacheth us in the sixth of John, saying, *Verily, verily, I say unto you, Except ye eat the flesh of the Son of man, and drink his blood, you have no life in you.* Whoso eateth my flesh, and drinketh my blood, hath eternal life; and I will raise him up at the last day. *For* my flesh is very meat, and my blood is very drink. *He that eateth my flesh, and drinketh my blood, dwelleth in me, and I in him. As the living Father hath sent me, and I live by the Father: even so* he that eateth me, shall live by me. And this St. Paul confessed of himself, saying, *That I have life, I have it by faith in the Son of God. And now it is not I that live, but Christ liveth in me.*

CHAP. X.

John vi.

Gal. ii.

The third thing to be noted is this, that although our Saviour Christ resembleth his flesh and blood to meat and drink, yet he far passeth and excelleth all corporal meats and drinks. For although corporal meats and drinks do nourish and continue our life here in this world, yet they begin not our life. For the beginning of our life we have of our fathers and mothers; and the meat, after we be begotten, doth feed and nourish us, and so preserveth us for a time. But our Saviour Christ is both the first beginner of our spiritual life, (who first begetteth us unto God his Father,) and also afterward he is our lively food and nourishment.

CHAP. XI.

Christ far excelleth all corporal food.

Moreover, meat and drink doth feed and nourish only our bodies; but Christ is the true and perfect nourishment both of body and soul. And besides that, bodily food preserveth the life but for a time, but Christ is such a spiritual and perfect food, that he preserveth both body and soul for ever; as he said unto Martha: *I am resurrection and life. He that believeth in me, although he die, yet shall he live. And he that liveth and believeth in me shall not die for ever.*

CHAP. XII.

The sacraments were ordained to confirm our faith.

Fourthly, it is to be noted, that the true knowledge of these things is the true knowledge of Christ; and to teach these things is to teach Christ; and the believing and feeling of these things is the believing and feeling of Christ in our hearts. And the more clearly we see, understand, and believe these things, the more clearly we see and understand Christ, and have more fully our faith and comfort in him.

And although our carnal generation and our carnal nourishment be known to all men by daily experience and by our common senses; yet this our spiritual generation and our spiritual nutrition be so obscure and hid unto us, that we cannot attain to the true and perfect knowledge and feeling of them, but only by faith, which must be grounded upon God's most holy word and sacraments.

THE USE OF THE LORD'S SUPPER.

And for this consideration our Saviour Christ hath not only set forth these things most plainly in his holy word, that we may hear them with our ears; but he hath also ordained one visible sacrament of spiritual regeneration in water, and another visible sacrament of spiritual nourishment in bread and wine, to the intent that, as much as is possible for man, we may see Christ with our eyes, smell him at our nose, taste him with our mouths, grope him with our hands, and perceive him with all our senses. For as the word of God preached putteth Christ into our ears; so likewise these elements of water, bread, and wine, joined to God's word, do after a sacramental manner put Christ into our eyes, mouths, hands, and all our senses.

And for this cause Christ ordained baptism in water, that as surely as we see, feel, and touch water with our bodies, and be washed with water; so assuredly ought we to believe, when we be baptized, that Christ is verily present with us, and that by him we be newly born again spiritually, and washed from our sins, and grafted in the stock of Christ's own body, and be apparelled, clothed, and harnessed with him in such wise, that as the Devil hath no power against Christ, so hath he none against us, so long as we remain grafted in that stock, and be clothed with that apparel, and harnessed with that armour. So that the washing in water of baptism is, as it were, a showing of Christ before our eyes, and a sensible touching,

CHAP. XII.

feeling, and groping of him, to the confirmation of the inward faith which we have in him.

And in like manner Christ ordained the sacrament of his body and blood in bread and wine, to preach unto us, that as our bodies be fed, nourished, and preserved with meat and drink, so (as touching our spiritual life towards God) we be fed, nourished, and preserved by the body and blood of our Saviour Christ; and also that he is such a preservation unto us, that neither the devils of hell, nor eternal death, nor sin, can be able to prevail against us, so long as by true and constant faith we be fed and nourished with that meat and drink. And for this cause Christ ordained this sacrament in bread and wine[e], (which we eat and drink, and be chief nutriments of our body,) to the intent that as surely as we see the bread and wine with our eyes, smell them with our noses, touch them with our hands, and taste them with our mouths; so assuredly ought we to believe, that Christ is our spiritual life and sustenance of our souls, like as the said bread and wine is the food and sustenance of our bodies. And no less ought we to doubt, that our souls be fed and live by Christ, than that our bodies be fed and live by meat and drink. Thus our Saviour Christ knowing us to be in this world, as it were, but babes and weaklings in faith, hath ordained sensible signs and tokens, whereby to allure and draw us

[e] Hugo de S. Victore, *De Sacramentis*, tract. vi. cap. 3. [1580.]

to more strength and more constant faith in him. So that the eating and drinking of this sacramental bread and wine is, as it were, a showing of Christ before our eyes, a smelling of him with our noses, a feeling and groping of him with our hands, and an eating, chewing, digesting, and feeding upon him to our spiritual strength and perfection.

CHAP. XII.

Fifthly, it is to be noted, that although there be many kinds of meats and drinks which feed the body, yet our Saviour Christ (as many ancient authors[f] write) ordained this sacrament of our spiritual feeding in bread and wine, rather than in other meats and drinks, because that bread and wine do most lively represent unto us the spiritual union and knot of all faithful people, as well unto Christ, as also amongst themselves. For like as bread is made of a great number of grains of corn, ground, baken, and so joined together that thereof is made one loaf; and an infinite number of grapes be pressed together in one vessel, and thereof is made wine; likewise is the whole multitude of true Christian people spiritually joined, first to Christ, and then among themselves together, in one faith, one baptism, one holy spirit, one knot and bond of love. [See Suppl. Note.]

CHAP. XIII.

Wherefore this sacrament was ordained in bread and wine.

[f] Hugo de S. Victore, *De Sacramentis*, tract. vi. cap. 3. [1551.]
Rabanus, *De Inst. Clericorum*, lib. i. cap. 31. Bernardus, *De Cœna Dom*

Sixthly, it is to be noted, that as the bread and wine which we do eat, be turned into our flesh and blood, and be made our very flesh and very blood, and be so joined and mixed with our flesh and blood that they be made one whole body together, even so be all faithful Christians spiritually turned into the body of Christ, and be so joined unto Christ, and also together among themselves, that they do make but one mystical body of Christ, as St. Paul saith : *We be one bread and one body, as many as be partakers of one bread and one cup.* And as one loaf is given among many men, so that every one is partaker of the same loaf, and likewise one cup of wine is distributed unto many persons, whereof every one is partaker; even so our Saviour Christ (whose flesh and blood be represented by the mystical bread and wine in the Lord's Supper) doth give himself unto all his true members, spiritually to feed them, nourish them, and to give them continual life by him[g]. And as the branches of a tree, or member of a body, if they be dead or cut off, they neither live, nor receive any nourishment or sustenance of the body or tree ; so likewise ungodly and wicked people, which be cut off from Christ's mystical body or be dead members of the same, do not spiritually feed upon Christ's body and blood, nor have any life, strength, or sustentation thereby.

---

[g] Dionysius, *Eccles. Hierar.* cap. 3. [1580.]

THE USE OF THE LORD'S SUPPER.

Seventhly, it is to be noted, that whereas nothing in this life is more acceptable before God, or more pleasant unto man, than Christian people to live together quietly in love and peace, unity and concord: this sacrament doth most aptly and effectuously move us thereunto. For when we be made all partakers of this one table, what ought we to think, but that we be all members of one spiritual body, (whereof Christ is the head,) that we be joined together in one Christ, as a great number of grains of corn be joined together in one loaf. Surely they have very hard and stony hearts, which with these things be not moved. And more cruel and unreasonable be they than brute beasts, that cannot be persuaded to be good to their Christian brethren and neighbours, (for whom Christ suffered death,) when in this Sacrament they be put in remembrance, that the Son of God bestowed his life for his enemies. For we see by daily experience, that eating and drinking together maketh friends, and continueth friendship. Much more then ought the table of Christ to move us so to do. Wild beasts and birds be made gentle by giving them meat and drink; why then should not Christian men wax meek and gentle with this heavenly meat of Christ? Hereunto we be stirred and moved as well by the bread and wine in this holy Supper, as by the words of holy Scripture recited in the same. Wherefore whose heart soever this holy sacrament, com-

CHAP. XV. This sacrament moveth all men to love and friendship.

munion, and supper of Christ, will not kindle with love unto his neighbours, and cause him to put out of his heart all envy, hatred, and malice, and to grave in the same all amity, friendship, and concord, he deceiveth himself if he think that he hath the spirit of Christ dwelling within him.

But all these foresaid godly admonitions, exhortations, and comforts, do the papists (as much as lieth in them) take away from all Christian people by their transubstantiation.

The doctrine of transubstantiation doth clean subvert our faith in Christ.

For if we receive no bread nor wine in the holy communion, then all these lessons and comforts be gone, which we should learn and receive by eating of the bread and drinking of the wine. And that phantastical imagination giveth an occasion utterly to subvert our whole faith in Christ. For if this sacrament be ordained in bread and wine, which be foods for the body, to signify and declare unto us our spiritual food by Christ, then if our corporal feeding upon the bread and wine be but phantastical, (so that there is no bread and wine there indeed to feed upon, although they appear there to be,) then it doth us to understand, that our spiritual feeding in Christ is also phantastical, and that indeed we feed not of him. Which sophistry is so devilish and wicked, and so much injurious to Christ, that it could not come from any other person but only from the Devil himself, and from his special minister Antichrist.

THE USE OF THE LORD'S SUPPER.

The eighth thing that is to be noted is, that this spiritual meat of Christ's body and blood, is not received in the mouth, and digested in the stomach, (as corporal meats and drinks commonly be,) but it is received with a pure heart and a sincere faith. *CHAP. XVI. The spiritual eating is with the heart, not with the teeth.*

And the true eating and drinking of the said body and blood of Christ, is with a constant and lively faith to believe, that Christ gave his body and shed his blood upon the cross for us, and that he doth so join and incorporate himself to us, that he is our head, and we his members, and flesh of his flesh, and bone of his bones, having him dwelling in us, and we in him. And herein standeth the whole effect and strength of this sacrament. And this faith God worketh inwardly in our hearts by his Holy Spirit, and confirmeth the same outwardly to our ears by hearing of his word, and to our other senses by eating and drinking of the sacramental bread and wine in his holy Supper. *True eating.*

What thing then can be more comfortable to us, than to eat this meat and drink this drink? Whereby Christ certifieth us, that we be spiritually and truly fed and nourished by him, and that we dwell in him and he in us. Can this be showed unto us more plainly than when he saith himself, *He that eateth me shall live by me.* John vi.

Wherefore whosoever doth not contemn the everlasting life, how can he but highly esteem this sacrament? How can he but embrace it, as a sure pledge of his salvation? And when he seeth godly people devoutly receive the same, how can he but be desirous oftentimes to receive it with them? Surely no man that well understandeth and diligently weigheth these things, can be without a great desire to come to this holy Supper.

All men desire to have God's favour; and when they know the contrary, that they be in his indignation and cast out of his favour, what thing can comfort them? How be their minds vexed! What trouble is in their consciences! All God's creatures seem to be against them, and do make them afraid, as things being ministers of God's wrath and indignation towards them. And rest and comfort can they find none, neither within them nor without them. And in this case they do hate as well God as the Devil; God as an unmerciful and extreme judge, and the Devil as a most malicious and cruel tormentor.

And in this sorrowful heaviness, holy Scripture teacheth them, that our heavenly Father can by no means be pleased with them again, but by the sacrifice and death of his only-begotten Son, whereby God hath made a perpetual amity and peace with us, doth pardon the sins of them that believe in him, maketh them his children, and giveth them to his first-begotten Son Christ, to be incorporate into him, to be saved by him, and to be made heirs of heaven with him. And in the receiving of the holy Supper of our Lord, we be put in remembrance of this his death, and of the whole mystery of our redemption. In the which Supper is made mention of his testament, and of the aforesaid communion of us with Christ, and of the remission of our sins by his sacrifice upon the cross.

CHAP.
XVI.

Wherefore in this sacrament (if it be rightly received with a true faith) we be assured that our sins be forgiven, and the league of peace, and the testament of God, is confirmed between him and us, so that whosoever by a true faith doth eat Christ's flesh and drink his blood, hath everlasting life by him. Which thing when we feel in our hearts at the receiving of the Lord's Supper, what thing can be more joyful, more pleasant, or more comfortable unto us?

All this to be true, is most certain by the words of Christ himself, when he did first institute his holy Supper the night before his death, as it appeareth as well by the words of the Evangelists as of St. Paul: *Do this*, saith Christ, *as often as you drink it in remembrance of me.* And St. Paul saith: *As often as you eat this bread, and drink this cup, you shall show the Lord's death until he come.* And again, Christ said, *This cup is a new testament in mine own blood, which shall be shed for the remission of sins.* Luke xxii.

1 Cor. xi.

Matt. xxvi.
Mark xiv.
Luke xxii.

This doctrine here recited, may suffice for all that be humble and godly and seek nothing that is superfluous, but that is necessary and profitable. And therefore unto such persons may be made here an end of this book. But unto them that be contentious papists and idolaters, nothing is enough. And yet because they shall not glory in their subtle inventions and deceivable doctrine, (as though no man were able to answer them,) I shall desire the readers of patience, to suffer me a little while to spend some time in vain, to confute their most vain vanities. And yet the time shall not be altogether spent in vain, for thereby shall more clearly appear the light from the darkness, the truth from false sophistical subtleties, and the certain word of God from men's dreams and phantastical inventions.

CHAP. XVII

Four principal errors of the papists. The first is of transubstantiation

But these things cannot manifestly appear to the reader, except the principal points be first set out, wherein the papists vary from the truth of God's word; which be chiefly four.

Transubstantiation

First, the papists say, that in the Supper of the Lord after the words of consecration (as they call it) there is none other substance remaining but the substance of Christ's flesh and blood, so that there remaineth neither bread to be eaten, nor wine to be drunken. And although there be the colour of bread and wine, the savour, the smell, the bigness, the fashion, and all other (as they call them) accidents or qualities and quantities of bread and wine, yet (say they) there is no very bread nor wine, but they be turned into the flesh and blood of Christ. And this conversion they call *transubstantiation*, that is to say, turning of one

THE USE OF THE LORD'S SUPPER.

CHAP.
XVII

substance into another substance. And although all the accidents, both of the bread and wine, remain still, yet (say they) the same accidents be in no manner of thing; but hang alone in the air, without any thing to stay them upon. For in the body and blood of Christ (say they) these accidents cannot be, nor yet in the air, for the body and blood of Christ and the air, be neither of that bigness, fashion, smell, nor colour, that the bread and wine be. Nor in the bread and wine (say they) these accidents cannot be; for the substance of bread and wine (as they affirm) be clean gone. And so there remaineth whiteness, but nothing is white: there remaineth colours, but nothing is coloured therewith: there remaineth roundness, but nothing is round: and there is bigness, and yet nothing is big: there is sweetness, without any sweet thing: softness, without any soft thing: breaking, without any thing broken: division, without any thing divided: and so other qualities and quantities, without any thing to receive them. And this doctrine they teach as a necessary article of our faith.

But it is not the doctrine of Christ, but the subtle invention of Antichrist, first decreed by Innocent the Third[h], and after more at large set forth by school authors, whose study was ever to defend and set abroad to the world all such matters as the Bishop of Rome had once decreed.

[h] *De Summa Trinit. et Fide Catholica*, "Firmiter," "Paragrapho," "Una." [1580.]

And the Devil by his minister Antichrist, had so dazzled the eyes of a great multitude of Christian people in these latter days, that they sought not for their faith at the clear light of God's word, but at the Romish Antichrist, believing whatsoever he prescribed unto them, yea though it were against all reason, all senses, and God's most holy word also. For else he could not have been very Antichrist indeed, except he had been so repugnant unto Christ, whose doctrine is clean contrary to this doctrine of Antichrist. For Christ teacheth that we receive very bread and wine in the most blessed Supper of the Lord, as sacraments to admonish us that as we be fed with bread and wine bodily, so we be fed with the body and blood of our Saviour Christ spiritually. As in our baptism we receive very water to signify unto us, that as water is an element to wash the body outwardly, so be our souls washed by the Holy Ghost inwardly.

The second is of the presence of Christ in this sacrament.

The second principal thing, wherein the papists vary from the truth of God's word, is this. They say that the very natural flesh and blood of Christ, which suffered for us upon the cross, and sitteth at the right hand of the Father in heaven, is also really, substantially, corporally and naturally, in or under the accidents of the sacramental bread and wine, which they call the forms of bread and wine. And yet here they vary not a little among themselves. For some say, that the very natural body of Christ is there, but not naturally nor sensibly.

And other say, that it is there naturally and sensibly, and of the same bigness and fashion that it is in heaven, and as the same was born of the blessed Virgin Mary, and that it is there broken and torn in pieces with our teeth. And this appeareth partly by the school authors, and partly by the confession of Berengarius[i], which Nicholas the Second constrained him to make, which was this[k]: that of the sacraments of the Lord's table, the said Berengarius should promise to hold that faith which the said Pope Nicholas and his council held; which was, that not only the sacraments of bread and wine, but also the very flesh and blood of our Lord Jesu Christ, are sensibly handled of the priest in the altar, broken and torn with the teeth of the faithful people. But the true catholic faith grounded upon God's most infallible word teacheth us, that our Saviour Christ (as concerning his man's nature and bodily presence) is gone up unto heaven, and sitteth at the right hand of his Father, and there shall he tarry until the world's end, at what time he shall come again to judge both the quick and the dead, as he saith himself in many scriptures: *I forsake the world,* said he, *and go to my Father.* And in another place he saith: *You shall ever have poor men among you, but me you shall not ever have.* And again he saith, *Many hereafter shall come and say,*

Christ is not corporally in earth. [1580]

John xvi.

Matt. xxvi

Ibid. xxiv.

---

[i] *De Consecrat.* Distin. 2. "Ego Berengarius." Lege Roffen. *Contra Œcolamp.* in prooemio, lib. iii. corroborat. 5. [1580.]

[k] [See Mosheim, *Eccles. Hist.* Cent. xi. ch. iii. §. 13, &c.]

Look, here is Christ, or Look, there he is, but believe them not. And St. Peter saith in the Acts, That heaven must receive Christ, until the time that all things shall be restored. And St. Paul, writing to the Colossians, agreeth hereto, saying, *Seek for things that be above, where Christ is sitting at the right hand of the Father.* And St. Paul, speaking of the very sacrament, saith: *As often as you shall eat this bread and drink this cup, show forth the Lord's death until he come.* "Till he come," saith St. Paul, signifying that he is not there corporally present. For what speech were this, or who useth of him that is already present to say, "Until he come?" For "Until he come" signifieth that he is not yet present. This is the catholic faith, which we learn from our youth in our common Creed, and which Christ taught, the Apostles followed, and the Martyrs confirmed with their blood.

And although Christ in his human nature substantially, really, corporally, naturally and sensibly, be present with his Father in heaven, yet sacramentally and spiritually he is here present. For in water, bread, and wine, he is present as in signs and sacraments, but he is indeed spiritually in the faithful Christian people, which according to Christ's ordinance be baptized, or receive the holy communion, or unfeignedly believe in him. Thus have you heard the second principal article, wherein the papists vary from the truth of God's word and from the catholic faith.

THE USE OF THE LORD'S SUPPER.

Now the third thing, wherein they vary, is this: The papists say, that evil and ungodly men receive in this Sacrament the very body and blood of Christ, and eat and drink the selfsame thing that the good and godly men do. But the truth of God's word is contrary, that all those that be godly members of Christ, as they corporally eat the bread and drink the wine, so spiritually they eat and drink Christ's very flesh and blood; and as for the wicked members of the Devil, they eat the sacramental bread and drink the sacramental wine, but they do not spiritually eat Christ's flesh nor drink his blood, but they eat and drink their own damnation.

CHAP. XVII.

The third is, that evil men eat and drink the very body and blood of Christ.

The fourth thing, wherein the popish priests dissent from the manifest word of God, is this: they say, that they offer Christ every day for remission of sin, and distribute by their masses the merits of Christ's passion. But the Prophets, Apostles, and Evangelists do say, that Christ himself in his own person made a sacrifice for our sins upon the cross, by whose wounds all our diseases were healed, and our sins pardoned; and so did never no priest, man, nor creature but he, nor he did the same never more than once. And the benefit hereof is in no man's power to give unto any other, but every man must receive it at Christ's hands himself, by his own faith and belief, as the Prophet saith.

The fourth is of the daily sacrifice of Christ.

Habak. ii.

HERE ENDETH THE FIRST BOOK.

The Second Book is against the Error of Transubstantiation.

CHAP. I.
The confutation of the error of transubstantiation.

THUS have you heard declared four things, wherein chiefly the papistical doctrine varieth from the true word of God and from the old catholic Christian faith, in this matter of the Lord's Supper.

Now, lest any man should think that I feign any thing of mine own head without any other ground or authority, you shall hear by God's grace as well the errors of the papists confuted, as the catholic truth defended, both by God's most certain word, and also by the most old approved authors and martyrs of Christ's Church.

CHAP. II.
The papistical doctrine is contrary to God's word.

And first, that bread and wine remain after the words of consecration, and be eaten and drunken in the Lord's Supper, is most manifest by the plain words of Christ himself, when he ministered the same Supper unto his disciples.

Matt. xxvi. Mark xiv. For as the Evangelists write, *Christ took bread, and brake it, and gave it to his disciples, and said,* Take, eat, this is my body.

Luke xxii Here the papists triumph of these words, when Christ said, *This is my body,* which they call the words of consecration. For (say they) as soon as these words be fully ended, there is no bread left, nor none other substance, but only Christ's body. When Christ said " this," the bread (say they) remained. And when he said " is," yet the bread remained. Also when he added " my," the bread remained still. And when he said " bo," yet the bread was there still.* But when he had finished the whole sentence, *This is my body*, then (say they) the bread was gone, and there remained no substance but Christ's body! as though the bread could not remain, when it is made a sacrament. But this negative, that there is no bread, they make of their own brains by their Unwritten Verities.

O, good Lord, how would they have bragged if Christ had said, ' This is no bread!' But Christ spake not that negative, ' This is no bread,' but said affirmingly, *This is my body*, not denying the bread, but affirming that his body was eaten (meaning spiritually) as the bread was eaten corporally.

And that this was the meaning of Christ appeareth plainly by St. Paul, in the tenth chapter to the Corinthians, the First Epistle, where he speaking of the same matter saith : *Is not the bread which we break*, the communion of the body of Christ? Who understood the mind of Christ 1 Cor. x.

---

* Gardiner, in his reply to Cranmer, maintains that this was only a " private opinion " of some theologians designed to show the great importance of all the words being pronounced by the celebrant. See Parker's Society Edit., p. 244.—C. H. H. W.

better than St. Paul, to whom Christ showed his most secret counsels? And St. Paul is not afraid, for our better understanding of Christ's words, somewhat to alter the same, lest we might stand stiffly in the letters and syllables, and err in mistaking of Christ's words. For whereas our Saviour Christ brake the bread and said, *This is my body;* St. Paul saith, that the bread which we break is the communion of Christ's body. Christ said, " his body :" and St. Paul said, " the communion " of the body :" meaning, nevertheless, both one thing, that they which eat the bread worthily, do eat spiritually Christ's very body. And so Christ calleth the bread his body, (as the old authors report,) because it representeth his body, and signifieth unto them which eat that bread according to Christ's ordinance, that they do spiritually eat his body, and be spiritually fed and nourished by him, and yet the bread remaineth still there, as a sacrament to signify the same. But of these words of consecration shall be spoken hereafter more at large.

Therefore to return to the purpose, that the bread remaineth and is eaten in this sacrament, appeareth by the words which go before the consecration. For that Christ *took bread, and brake it, and gave it to his disciples, and said, Take eat:* all this was done and spoken before the words of consecration. Wherefore they must needs be understand of the very bread, that Christ took bread, brake bread, gave bread to his disciples, commanding them to take bread, and eat bread. But the same is more plain and evident of the wine, that it remaineth and is drunken at the Lord's Supper, as well by the words that go before as by the words that follow after the consecration. For before the words of consecration, Christ took the cup of wine, and gave it unto his disciples, and said, *Drink you all* of this. And after the words of consecration followeth, *They drank all* of it.

Matt. xxvi.
Mark xiv.

Now I ask all the papists, what thing it was that Christ commanded his disciples to drink, when he said, 'Drink you all of this?' The blood of Christ was not yet there, by their own confession, for it was spoken before the consecration: therefore it could be nothing else but wine that he commanded them to drink.

Then I ask the papists once again, whether the disciples drank wine or not? If they say Yea, then let them recant their error, that there was no wine remaining after the consecration. If they say Nay, then they condemn the Apostles of disobedience to Christ's commandment, which drank not wine as he commanded them. Or rather they reprove Christ as a juggler, which commanded his Apostles to drink wine, and when they came to the drinking thereof, he himself had conveyed it away.

Moreover, before Christ delivered the cup of wine to his disciples, he said unto them, *Divide this among you.*

Luke xxii.

Here I would ask the papists another question; what thing it was that Christ commanded his disciples to divide among them? I am sure they will not say it was the cup, except they be disposed to make men laugh at them. Nor I think they will not say, it was the blood of Christ, as well because the words were spoken before the consecration, as because the blood of Christ is not divided, but spiritually given whole in the sacrament. Then could it be understand of nothing else but of wine, which they should divide among them, and drink all together.

Also when the communion was ended, Christ said unto his Apostles: *Verily I say unto you, that I will drink no more henceforth of this fruit of the vine, until that day that I shall drink it new with you in my Father's kingdom.*

By these words it is clear, that it was very wine that the Apostles drank at that godly supper. For the blood of Christ is not the fruit of the vine, nor the accidents of wine; nor none other thing is the fruit of the vine, but very wine only.

How could Christ have expressed more plainly, that bread and wine remain, than by taking the bread in his hands, and breaking it himself, and giving unto his disciples, commanding them to eat it? And by taking the cup of wine in his hands, and delivering it unto them, commanding them to divide it among them and to drink it, and calling it the fruit of the vine? These words of Christ be so plain, that if an angel of heaven would tell us the contrary, he ought not to be believed: and then much less may we believe the subtle lying of the papists.

If Christ would have had us to believe as a necessary article of our faith, that there remaineth neither bread nor wine, would he have spoken after this sort, using all such terms and circumstances as should make us believe that still there remaineth bread and wine? What manner of teacher make they of Christ that say, he meant one thing, when his words be clean contrary? What Christian heart can patiently suffer this contumely of Christ?

But what crafty teachers be these papists, who devise phantasies of their own heads directly contrary to Christ's teaching, and then set the same abroad to Christian people, to be most assuredly believed as God's own most holy word! St. Paul did not so, but followed herein the manner of Christ's speaking, in calling of bread "bread," and wine "wine," and never altering Christ's words herein: *The bread which we break,* saith he, *is it not the communion of Christ's body?*

1 Cor x.

Now I ask again of the papists, whether he spake this of the bread consecrated or not consecrated? They cannot say that he spake it of the bread unconsecrated, for that is not the communion of Christ's body by their own doctrine. And if St. Paul spake it of bread consecrated, then they must needs confess, that after consecration such bread remaineth, as is broken bread, which can be none other than very true material bread. And straightways after, St. Paul saith in the same place, *that we be partakers of one bread and one cup.* And in the next chapter, speaking more fully of the same matter, four times he nameth the bread and the cup, never making mention of any transubstantiation, or remaining of accidents without any substance; which things he would have made some mention of, if it had been a necessary article of our faith to believe that there remaineth no bread nor wine. Thus it is evident and plain by the words of the Scripture, that after consecration remaineth bread and wine, and that the papistical doctrine of transubstantiation is directly contrary to God's word.

Marginalia: BOOK II. 1 Cor. x.

CHAP. III.

The papistical doctrine is against reason.

Let us now consider also, how the same is against natural reason and natural operation[a]; which although they prevail not against God's word, yet when they be joined with God's word, they be of great moment to confirm any truth. Natural reason abhorreth *vacuum*, that is to say, that there should be any empty place, wherein no substance should be. But if there remain no bread nor wine, the place where they were before, and where their accidents be, is filled with no substance, but remaineth *vacuum*, clean contrary to the order of nature.

[a] See chap. xiv., p. 92 and fol.

TRANSUBSTANTIATION. 41

We see also that the wine, though it be consecrated, yet will it turn to vinegar, and the bread will mould, which then be nothing else but sour wine and moulded bread, which could not wax sour nor mouldy, if there were no bread nor wine there at all.

And if the sacraments were now brent [burned], (as in the old Church they burned all that remained uneaten,) let the papists tell what is brent. They must needs say, that it is either bread, or the body of Christ. But bread (say they) is none there. Then must they needs burn the body of Christ, and be called Christ-burners, (as heretofore they have burned many of his members,) except they will say, that accidents burn alone without any substance, contrary to all the course of nature.

The sacramental bread and wine also will nourish, which nourishment naturally cometh of the substance of the meats and drinks, and not of the accidents.

The wine also will poison, (as divers Bishops of Rome have had experiences, both in poisoning of other, and being poisoned themselves,) which poisoning they cannot ascribe to the most wholesome blood of our Saviour Christ, but only to the poisoned wine.

And most of all, it is against the nature of accidents to be in nothing. For the definition of accidents is to be in some substance, so that if they be, they must needs be in something. And if they be in nothing, then they be not.

And a thousand things more of like foolishness do the papists affirm by their transubstantiation, contrary to all nature and reason; as that two bodies be in one place, and one body in many places at one time, and that substances be gendered of accidents only, and accidents converted into substances, and a body to be in a place and occupy no room, and generation to be without corruption, and corruption without generation, with many such like things, against all order and principles of nature and reason.

CHAP. IV.
The papistical doctrine is also against all our senses.

The papistical doctrine is also against all our outward senses, called our five wits. For our eyes say, they see there bread and wine, our noses smell bread and wine, our mouths taste, and our hands feel bread and wine. And although the articles of our faith be above all our outward senses, so that we believe things which we can neither see, feel, hear, smell, nor taste, yet they be not contrary to our senses; at the least so contrary, that in such things which we from time to time do see, smell, feel, hear, and taste, we shall not trust our senses, but believe clean contrary. Christ never made no such article of our faith.

Our faith teacheth us to believe things that we see not; but it doth not bid us, that we shall not believe that we see daily with our eyes, and hear with our ears, and grope with our hands. For although our senses cannot reach so far as our faith doth, yet so far as the compass of our senses doth usually reach, our faith is not contrary to the same, but rather our senses do confirm our faith. Or else what availed it to St. Thomas for the confirmation of Christ's resurrection, that he did put his hand into Christ's side, and felt his wounds, if he might not trust his senses nor give no credit thereto?

And[b] what a wide door is here opened to Valentinianus, Marcion, and other heretics, which said that Christ was not crucified, but that Simon Cyrenæus was crucified for him, although to the sight of the people it seemed that Christ was crucified! Or to such heretics as said, that Christ was no man, although to men's sights he appeared in the form of man, and seemed to be hungry, dry, weary; to weep, sleep, eat, drink, yea and to die like as other men do. For if we once admit this doctrine, then no credit is to be given to our senses, we open a large field, and give a great occasion unto an innumerable rabblement of most heinous heresies.

And if there be no trust to be given to our senses in this matter of the sacrament, why then do the papists so stoutly affirm, that the accidents remain after the consecration, which cannot be

---

[b] Lege Aug. *In Psal.* xxix. Præfat. Enarrationis 2., et Hilarium *De Trin.* lib. iii. et *Contra Constantium.*

judged but by the senses? For the Scripture speaketh no word of the accidents of bread and wine, but of the bread and wine themselves. And it is against the nature and definition of accidents to be alone without any substance. Wherefore if we may not trust our senses in this matter of the sacrament, then if the substance of the bread and wine be gone, why may we not then say, that the accidents be gone also? And if we must needs believe our senses, as concerning the accidents of bread and wine, why may we not do the like of the substance, and that rather than of the accidents? Forasmuch as after the consecration, the Scripture saith in no place, that there is no substance of bread nor of wine, but calleth them still by such names as signify the substances and not the accidents.

And, finally, if our senses be daily deceived in this matter, then is the sensible sacrament nothing else but an elusion of our senses. And so we make much for their purpose that said, that Christ was a crafty juggler, that made things to appear to men's sights that indeed were no such things, but forms only, figures, and appearances of them.

But to conclude in few words this process of our senses, let all the papists lay their heads together, and they shall never be able to show one article of our faith so directly contrary to our senses, that all our senses by daily experience shall affirm a thing to be, and yet our faith shall teach us the contrary thereunto.

Now forasmuch as it is declared, how this papistical opinion of transubstantiation is against the word of God, against nature, against reason, and against all our senses, we shall show furthermore, that it is against the faith and doctrine of the old authors of Christ's Church, beginning at those authors, which were nearest unto Christ's time, and therefore might best know the truth herein[c].

The papistical doctrine is contrary to the faith of the old authors of Christ's Church.

First, Justinus, a great learned man and holy martyr, the oldest author that this day is known to write any treaty upon the sacraments, and wrote not much above one hundred years after Christ's ascension.

Justinus.

[c] Ignatius, *Ad Philadelphenses:* "Una est caro Domini Jesu, "et unus ejus sanguis qui pro nobis fusus est: unus etiam "panis pro omnibus confractus, et unus calix totius Ecclesiæ." EMBD. [Cranmer quotes from the Epistle as it stood in his time, before the interpolations had been pointed out. Jenkyns gives the *authorities* in his Appendix.]

Clemens in *Pædagogo,* lib. ii. cap. 2. "Ipse quoque vino "usus est, nam ipse quoque homo; et vinum benedixit, cum "dixit; *Accipite bibite, hoc est sanguis meus,* sanguis vitis; "Verbum, quod pro multis effunditur in remissionem peccatorum, sanctum lætitiæ fluentum allegorice significat." Et mox: "Quod autem vinum esset, quod benedictum est, "ostendit rursum dicens discipulis: *Non bibam ex fructu vitis* "*hujus donec bibero ipsum vobiscum in regno Patris mei.*"

"Pontifex opertum panem et indivisum aperit, in frusta con- "cidens, &c." Dionysius, *Eccles. Hier.* cap. iii. EMBD.

He writeth in his second Apology[d], "That the "bread, water, and wine in this sacrament are not "to be taken as other common meats and drinks "be, but they be meats ordained purposely to "give thanks to God, and therefore be called "*Eucharistia* [*thanksgiving*], and be called also "the body and blood of Christ. And that it is "lawful for none to eat or drink of them, but "that profess Christ and live according to the "same. And yet the same meat and drink," "saith he, "*is changed into our flesh and blood,* "*and nourisheth our bodies.*"

By which saying it is evident, that Justinus thought that the bread and wine remained still; for else it could not have been turned into our flesh and blood, to nourish our bodies.

Next him was Irenæus[e], above one hundred and fifty years after Christ, who, as it is supposed, could not be deceived in the necessary points of our faith, for he was a disciple of Polycarpus, which was disciple to St. John the Evangelist. This Irenæus followeth the sense of Justinus wholly in this matter, and almost also his words, saying, "that the bread wherein we "give thanks unto God, although it be *of the* "*earth,* yet when the name of God is called upon "it, it is not then common bread, but the bread "of thanksgiving having two things in it, *one*

[d] [Ed. Bened. *Apol.* i. p. 83. See book iii. ch. 8.]

[e] Irenæus *Contra Valentin.* lib. iv. cap. 34. [ed. Bened. *Contra Hæreses,* lib. iv. cap. 18.]

TRANSUBSTANTIATION. 47

"*earthly*, and the other heavenly." What meant he by the heavenly thing, but the sanctification which cometh by the invocation of the name of God? And what by the earthly thing, but the very bread, which, as he said before, is of the earth, and which also, he saith, doth nourish our bodies, as other bread doth which we do use[f]?

Shortly after Irenæus was Origen, about two hundred years after Christ's ascension; who also affirmeth, that the material bread remaineth, saying, "that *the matter of the bread* availeth nothing, but *goeth down into the belly, and is avoided downward;* but the word of God, spoken upon the bread, is it that availeth[g]."

After Origen came Cyprian the holy martyr, about the year of our Lord 250, who writeth against them that ministered this sacrament with water only, and without wine. "Forasmuch," saith he, "as Christ said, I am a true vine, therefore *the blood of Christ is not water, but wine; nor it cannot be thought that his blood,* whereby

[f] Et idem Irenæus, lib. v: "Quando mixtus calix et fractus "panis percipit verbum Dei, fit Eucharistia corporis et san- "guinis Christi, ex quibus augetur et consistit carnis nostræ "substantia." Et in eodem: "Cum membra ejus sumus, et "per creaturam nutrimur, eum calicem qui est creatura suum "corpus confirmavit, ex quo nostra auget corpora." Idem, lib. iv. cap. 34: "Quomodo constabit eum panem, in quo "gratiæ actæ sunt, corpus esse Domini sui, et calicem san- "guinem ejus, si non ipsum Fabricatoris mundi filium esse "dicant?"

[g] Origenes, *In Matt.* cap. 15.
Idem, *Contra Celsum*, lib. iv: "Ubi pro collatis in nos bene- "ficiis gratias diximus, oblatis panibus vescimur."

"we be redeemed and have life, *is in the cup,* "*when wine is not in the cup, whereby the blood* "*of Christ is showed*[h]."

What words could Cyprian have spoken more plainly, to show that the wine doth remain, than to say thus : " If there be no wine there is no " blood of Christ ? "

And yet he speaketh shortly after, as plainly, in the same Epistle : " Christ," saith he, " taking " the cup, blessed it, and gave it to his disciples, "saying, *Drink you all of this, for this is the* "*blood of the new testament, which shall be shed* "*for many, for the remission of sins.* I say unto " you, that from henceforth I will not drink of this " creature of the vine, *until I shall drink with* "*you new wine in the kingdom of my Father.* By " these words of Christ," saith St. Cyprian, " we " perceive, that the cup which the Lord offered, " was not only water, but also wine ; and that *it* "*was wine, that Christ called his blood ;* whereby " it is clear, that *Christ's blood is not offered, if* " *there be no wine in the chalice.*" And after it followeth : " How shall we drink with Christ new " *wine of the creature of the vine,* if in the sacri- " fice of God the Father and of Christ we do not " *offer wine ?* "

In these words of St. Cyprian appeareth most manifestly, that in this sacrament is not only offered very wine that is made of grapes that come of the vine, but also that we drink the

[h] Cyprian. *Ad Cæcilium,* lib. ii. epistola 3.

same. And yet the same giveth us to understand, that if we drink that wine worthily, we drink also spiritually the very blood of Christ which was shed for our sins[i].

[k]Eusebius Emissenus, a man of singular fame in learning, about three hundred years after Christ's ascension, did in few words set out this matter so plainly, both how the bread and wine be converted into the body and blood of Christ and yet remain still in their nature; and also how besides the outward receiving of bread and wine Christ is inwardly by faith received in our hearts, all this, I say, he doth so plainly set out, that more plainness cannot be reasonably desired in this matter. For he saith, that the conversion of the visible creatures of bread and wine into the body and blood of Christ, is like unto our conversion in baptism, where outwardly nothing is changed but remaineth the same that was before, but all the alteration is inwardly and spiritually.

"If thou wilt know," saith he[l], "how it ought

[i] Idem, in *Sermone de Lapsis:* "Sanctificatus in Domini "sanguinem potus de pollutis visceribus erupit." Et, *De Cœna Domini:* "Sceleratum os panis sanctificatus intravit." Et in eodem: "Ante verba consecrationis panis ille communis," &c. vid. infra cap. xi. [The treatise, *De Cœna Domini*, is now considered spurious, and is attributed by the Benedictine editor to Arnoldus, Abbas Bonæ-Vallis. See Bened. edit. and Cave, *Hist. Liter.*]

[k] [The writings attributed to Eusebius Emissenus are generally held to be spurious. Cave, *Hist. Literaria.* The passage here cited is assigned to him on the authority of the Canon Law, from whence it is extracted.]

[l] *De Consecr.* Dist. 2. "Quia."

"not to seem to thee a new thing and impossible,
" that *earthly and corruptible things be turned into
" the substance of Christ, look upon thyself, which
" art made new in baptism,* when thou wast far
" from life, and banished as a stranger from mercy
" and from the way of salvation, and inwardly
" wast dead, yet suddenly thou beganst another
" life in Christ, *and wast made new* by wholesome
" mysteries, and *wast turned into the body of the
" Church,* not by seeing, but by believing; and of
" the child of damnation, by a secret pureness, thou
" wast made the chosen son of God. *Thou visibly
" didst remain in the same measure that thou
" hadst before, but invisibly thou wast made greater,
" without any increase of thy body. Thou wast
" the selfsame person,* and yet by the increase of
" faith thou wast made another man. *Outwardly
" nothing was added, but all the change was in-
" wardly.* And so was man made the son of
" Christ, and Christ formed in the mind of man.
" Therefore as thou putting away thy former vile-
" ness didst receive a new dignity, not feeling any
" change in thy body; and as the curing of thy
" disease, the putting away of thine infection, the
" wiping away of thy filthiness, be not seen with
" thine eyes, but are believed in thy mind: so
" likewise, when thou dost go up to the reverend
" altar to feed upon spiritual meat, in thy faith
" look upon the body and blood of him that is thy
" God, honour him, touch him with thy mind,
" take him in the hand of thy heart, and chiefly

TRANSUBSTANTIATION. 51

"drink him with the draught of thy inward "man."

Hitherto have I rehearsed the sayings of Eusebius, which be so plain, that no man can wish more plainly to be declared, that this mutation of the bread and wine into the body and blood of Christ, is a spiritual mutation, and that outwardly nothing is changed. But as outwardly we eat the bread and drink the wine with our mouths, so inwardly by faith we spiritually eat the very flesh and drink the very blood of Christ.

Hilarius also in few words saith the same. "There is a figure," saith he, " for *bread and wine* " *be outwardly seen.* And there is also a truth of "that figure; for the body and blood of Christ "be of a truth inwardly believed[m]." And this Hilarius was within less than three hundred and fifty years after Christ.

And Epiphanius, shortly after the same time, saith[n], that *the bread is meat,* but the virtue that is in it, is it that giveth life. But if there were no bread at all, how could it be meat?

About the same time, or shortly after, about the year of our Lord 400, St. John Chrysostome writeth thus against them that used only water in the sacrament[o]: "Christ," saith he, "minding to "pluck up that heresy by the roots, *used wine*, as " well before his resurrection when he gave the

[m] Hilarius, *Dist.* 2. "Corpus." EMBD.
[n] Epiphanius, *Contra Hæreses*, lib. iii. tom. 2. Et in *Anacephaleosi.*
[o] Chrysost. *In Mat.* cap. xxvi. hom. 83.

"mysteries, as after at his table without mysteries. "For he saith, 'of the fruit of the vine;' which "surely bringeth forth no water, but wine."

These words of Chrysostome declare plainly, that Christ in his holy table both drank wine and gave wine to drink, which had not been true, if no wine had remained after the consecration, as the papists feign.

And yet more plainly St. Chrysostome[p] declareth this matter in another place, saying: "The "bread, before it be sanctified, is called bread; "but when it is sanctified by the means of the "priest, it is delivered from the name of bread, "and is exalted to the name of the Lord's body, "although *the nature of bread doth still remain.*"

[p] *Ad Cæsarium Monachum.* [A few passages only of this Epistle are preserved in Greek, by Jo. Damascene, Anastasius, and Nicephorus. A Latin version is the sole authority for the remainder. Its genuineness was disputed by Gardyner, and has been the subject of much controversy since. Its history is curious. Attention was first directed to it by Peter Martyr, who brought a copy to England, which he presented to Cranmer. When the Archbishop's library was dispersed at his death, this copy disappeared, and as Peter Martyr had not stated from whence it was procured, Cardinal Perron ventured to charge him with having forged it. But in 1680, the accusation was proved to be false by the discovery of the original manuscript in the library of the Dominican monastery of St. Mark at Florence. It was immediately printed, together with the extracts extant in Greek and a preface, by the discoverer, Emeric Bigot; but some doctors of the Sorbonne interfered, and prevented its publication. The Latin version, however, was given to the world in 1685, by Stephen Le Moyne, in his *Varia Sacra;* and in the following year, Wake, into whose hands the very leaves cut out at Paris had fallen, reprinted the whole in one of his tracts against Bossuet. The evidence in its

TRANSUBSTANTIATION. 53

"The nature of bread," saith he, "doth still re-main," to the utter and manifest confutation of the papists, which say, that the accidents of bread do remain, but not the nature and substance.

At the same time was St. Ambrose, who declareth the alteration of bread and wine into the body and blood of Christ not to be such, that the nature and substance of bread and wine be gone, but that through grace there is a spiritual mutation by the mighty power of God, so that he that worthily eateth of that bread doth spiritually eat Christ, and dwelleth in Christ and Christ in him.

"For," saith St. Ambrose[q], speaking of this change of bread, into the body of Christ, "if the

---

favour derived from the citations in Damascene, &c. is very conclusive, and has induced even the Roman Catholic writers, Bigot, Hardouin, and Dupin, to place it among the genuine works of Chrysostom. But the Benedictine editor, Montfaucon, condemns it as spurious, though he takes pains to explain away the expressions which it contains against transubstantiation. Walchius, on the other side, says, "Contra pontificios satis pro-"batum est, Epistolæ hujus auctorem omnino esse Chrysosto-"mum." See Gardyner, *Explication*, book v. cap. 5. *Confutatio Cavillationum*, &c. Object. 201. Cranmer, *Disputation with Harpsfield at Oxford*. Wake, *Defence of the Exposition of the Doctrine of the Church of England*. Burnet, *Reformat*. vol. iii. p. 362. Chrysostom. *Opera*, ed. Bened. tom. iii. p. 736. Dupin, *Eccles. Writers*, Cent. v. Walchius, *Biblioth. Patrist.* p. 224. where is a list of other authors who have written on the subject.—*Jenkyns.*]

[q] *De iis qui Mysteriis initiantur*, cap. ult. Et, *De Sacramentis*, lib. iv. cap. 4. [Jenkyns adds the following note:—The genuineness of both of these works was questioned in 1535, by Bullinger, who maintained in a letter to Vadianus, "stupidos hos nequaquam esse "auctoris optimi et judicii emunctissimi fœturam," and asserted that Erasmus also was of the same opinion Both too, as Cranmer

"word of God be of that force that it can make
"things of nought, and those things to be which
"never were before, much more it can make
"*things that were before, still to be, and also to be*
"*changed into other things.*"
And he bringeth for example hereof, the
change of us in baptism, wherein a man is so
changed, (as is before declared in the words of

states in his *Answer*, were suspected by Melancthon; and one of
them, the treatise on the sacraments, was repeatedly denied to
be of any authority by Peter Martyr and Ridley.
The spuriousness indeed of the six books *De Sacramentis*,
seems to admit of little doubt. The Benedictine editors,
though they print them among the genuine works of Ambrose,
do not venture, after giving the arguments on both sides, to
decide in their favour: and the following statement by Cave
can scarcely be shaken. "De Sacramentis libri vi. non tantum
"a theologis reformatæ sed et pontificiæ religionis quam pluri-
"mis Ambrosio abjudicantur; scripsisse quidem Ambrosium
"libros De Sacramentis certissimum est, qui vero hodie ex-
"tant, aut ejus non sunt, aut adeo insigniter interpolati ut no-
"vam plane faciem induerint. Desiderantur in his quæ ex
"illis citant Augustinus et Bertramus; aliam exhibent S. Scrip-
"turæ versionem, quam qua in genuinis operibus usus est
"Ambrosius; repugnat styli diversitas patre mellifluo indigna;
"repugnant haud pauca a sæculo Ambrosiano aliena. Vidit
"hæc omnia ac ingenue agnovit eminentiss. Card. Bona de
"Reb. Liturg. lib. i. cap. 7. § 4. ubi hoc opusculum non nisi
"ab octavi et noni sæculi scriptoribus tanquam legitimum Am-
"brosii fœtum laudari fatetur."
The case is not so strong against the other work, *De
Mysteriis*, and the Benedictine editors stiffly maintain its
genuineness: yet even of this Walchius writes: "Ingenii moni-
"mentum esse adulterinum satis constat." See *Answer*, b. iii.
ch. 15. Peter Martyr, *Tractat. de Eucharist.* Tiguri, 1557.
p. 163. *Disputations at Cambridge, in Foxe*, edit. 1641.
vol. ii. p. 764. Ambros. *Opera*, ed. Bened. tom. ii. p. 321.
Cave, *Historia Literaria*. Walchius, *Biblioth. Patrist.* p. 479.]

Eusebius,) that he is made a new creature, and yet his substance remaineth the same that was before. [See p. 48.]

And St. Augustine[r], about the same time wrote thus: "That which you see in the altar, *is the bread and the cup, which also your eyes do show you.* But faith showeth further, that bread is "the body of Christ, and the cup his blood[s]." Here he declareth four things to be in the sacrament: two that we see, which be bread and wine; and other two, which we see not, but by faith only, which be the body and blood of Christ.

[r] Augustinus in *Sermone ad Infantes.*

[s] Et mox: "Panis non fit ex uno grano, sed ex multis." [ed. Bened. *Serm.* 271. tom. v. p. 1104.] Et mox: "Illas nubes et "ignes quæ fecerint vel assumpserint Angeli, ad significandum "quod annuntiabant, quis novit hominum, sicut infantes non "nôrunt," &c. [*De Trin.* lib. iii. cap. 10. ed. Bened. tom. viii. p. 804.] Et mox: "Infantes non nôrunt quod in altari ponitur "et peracta pietatis celebratione consumitur, unde vel quo- "modo conficiatur, unde in usum religionis assumatur. Et " si nunquam discant experimento vel suo, vel aliorum, et nun- "quam istam speciem rerum videant, nisi inter celebrationes " sacramentorum, cum offertur et datur, dicaturque illis " auctoritate gravissima cujus corpus et sanguis sit, nihil aliud " credent, nisi omnino in illa specie Dominum oculis apparuisse " mortalium, et de latere tali percusso liquorem illum omnino "fluxisse." [*De Trin.* lib. iii. cap. 10. ed. Bened. tom. viii. p. 804.] Et ante cap. 4. "Panis et vinum non sanctificantur, "ut sint tam magnum sacramentum, nisi per invisibilem opera- "tionem Spiritus Sancti." [ed. Bened. tom. viii. p. 798.]

Idem Aug. *De Trin.* lib. iii. cap. 10, loquens de novem modis quibus Deus aliquid nobis annuntiat, nonum modum dicit esse in re, quæ sit quidem eadem specie, sed peracto mysterio transitura: "Aliquando (inquit) ad hoc fit eadem species, vel "aliquantulum mansura, sicut potuit serpens ille æneus ex- "altatus in Eremo, sicut possunt literæ, vel peracto ministerio

And the same thing he declareth also as plainly in another place[t], saying, "The sacrifice of the "Church consisteth of two things, of *the visible* "kind of the *element*, and of the invisible flesh "and blood of our Lord Jesu Christ; both of the "sacrament, and of the thing signified by the "sacrament; even as *the person of Christ con-* "*sisteth of God and man*, forasmuch as he is very "God and very man. For *every thing containeth* "*in it the very nature of those things whereof it* "*consisteth*. Now the sacrifice of the Church "consisteth of two things, of the sacrament, and "of the thing thereby signified, that is to say, "the body of Christ. Therefore there is both "the sacrament, and the thing of the sacrament, "which is Christ's body[u]."

"transitura, sicut panis ad hoc factus in accipiendo sacramento "consumitur. Sed quia hæc hominibus nota sunt, quia per "homines fiunt, honorem tanquam religiosa possunt habere, "stuporem tanquam mira non possunt." [ed. Bened. tom. viii. p. 803.]

Idem, *In Joan. Homil.* 26. "Dominus noster Jesus Chris- "tus corpus et sanguinem suum in iis rebus commendavit, "quæ ad unum aliquid ex multis rediguntur. Aliud enim ex "multis granis conficitur, aliud ex multis racemis confluit." Et mox: "Securus accede, panis est, non venenum." EMBD.

[t] In *Lib. Sententiarum Prosperi.* [This passage is not to be found in the *Lib. Sententiarum Prosperi ex Augustino*, as it is printed in the Appendix to the Benedictine edition of Augustin. Cranmer took it from the *Corpus Juris Canonici, De Consecrat.* Dist. 2. "Hoc est," where *Lib. Sentent. Prosper.* is the authority referred to. See his *Answer to Gardyner*, book ii. ch. 5. where he cites another sentence from the same place.]

[u] Hesychius, *In Levit.* lib. ii. cap. 8. "Simul panis et caro "est."

TRANSUBSTANTIATION. 57

What can be devised to be spoken more plainly against the error of the papists, which say that no bread nor wine remaineth in the sacrament? For as the person of Christ consisteth of two natures, that is to say, of his manhood and of his Godhead, and therefore both those natures remain in Christ; even so, saith St. Augustine, the sacrament consisteth of two natures, of the elements of bread and wine, and of the body and blood of Christ, and therefore both these natures must needs remain in the sacrament.

For the more plain understanding hereof, it is to be noted, that there were certain heretics, as Simon, Menander, Marcion, Valentinus, Basilides, Cerdon, Manes, Eutyches Manichæus, Apollinaris, and divers other of like sorts, which said, that Christ was very God, but not a very man, although in eating, drinking, sleeping, and all other operations of man, to men's judgments he appeared like unto a man.

Other there were, as Artemon, Theodorus, Sabellius, Paulus Samasathenus, Marcellus, Photinus, Nestorius, and many other of the same sects, which said, that he was a very natural man, but not very God, although in giving the blind their sight, the dumb their speech, the deaf their hearing, in healing suddenly with his word all

---

Gregorius, in *Registro*. "Tam azymum quam fermentatum "dum sumimus, unum corpus Domini salvatoris efficimur." Rabanus dicit, "Sacramentum in alimentum corporis redigi." EMBD.

diseases, in raising to life them that were dead, and in all other works of God, he showed himself as he had been God.

Yet other there were, which seeing the Scripture so plain in those two matters, confessed that he was both God and man, but not both at one time. For before his incarnation, said they, he was God only, and not man; and after his incarnation, he ceased from his Godhead, and became a man only, and not God, until his resurrection or ascension, and then, say they, he left his manhood, and was only God again, as he was before his incarnation. So that when he was man, he was not God, and when he was God, he was not man.

But against these vain heresies the catholic faith, by the express word of God, holdeth and believeth, that Christ after his incarnation left not his divine nature, but remained still God, as he was before, being together at one time, as he is still, both perfect God, and perfect man.

And for a plain declaration hereof, the old ancient authors give two examples; one is of man, which is made of two parts, of a soul and of a body, and each of these two parts remain in man at one time; so that when the soul by the almighty power of God is put into the body, neither the body nor soul perisheth thereby, but thereof is made a perfect man, having a perfect soul and a perfect body remaining in him both at one time. The other example which the old authors bring in for this purpose, is of the holy Supper of our

Lord, which consisteth, say they, of two parts; of the sacrament or visible element of bread and wine, and of the body and blood of Christ. And as in them that duly receive the sacrament the very natures of bread and wine cease not to be there, but remain there still, and be eaten corporally, as the body and blood of Christ be eaten spiritually; so likewise doth the divine nature of Christ remain still with his humanity.

Let now the papists avaunt themselves of their transubstantiation, that there remaineth no bread nor wine in the ministration of the sacrament, if they will defend the wicked heresies before rehearsed, that Christ is not God and man both together. But to prove that this was the mind of the old authors, beside the saying of St. Augustine here recited, I shall also rehearse divers other.

St. John Chrysostome writeth against the pestilent error of Apollinaris, which affirmed that the Godhead and manhood in Christ were so mixèd and confounded together, that they both made but one nature. Against whom St. John Chrysostome writeth thus[x] : " When thou speakest of
" God, thou must consider a thing that in nature is
" single, without composition, without conversion;
" that is invisible, immortal, incircumscriptible,
" incomprehensible, with such like. And when
" thou speakest of man, thou meanest a nature
" that is weak, subject to hunger, thirst, weeping,

[x] *Ad Cæsarium Monachum.*

"fear, sweating, and such like passions, which
"cannot be in the divine nature. And when thou
"speakest of Christ, thou joinest two natures
"together in one person, who is both passible and
"impassible; passible, as concerning his flesh, and
"impassible in his Deity."

And after he concludeth, saying, "Wherefore
"Christ is both God and man: God by his im-
"passible nature, and man because he suffered.
"He himself being one person, one son, one Lord,
"hath the dominion and power of two natures
"joined together, which be not of one substance,
"but each of them hath his properties distinct
"from the other. And therefore remaineth there
"two natures, distinct, and not confounded. For
"as before the consecration of the bread, we call
"it bread, but *when God's grace hath sanctified it
"by the priest, it is delivered from the name of
"bread, and is exalted to the name of the body of
"the Lord, although the nature of the bread remain
"still in it,* and it is not called two bodies, but one
"body of God's son; so likewise here the divine
"nature resteth in the body of Christ, and these
"two make one son and one person."

These words of St. Chrysostome declare, and
that not in obscure terms but in plain words, that
after the consecration the nature of bread remaineth still, although it have an higher name,
and be called the body of Christ, to signify unto
the godly eaters of that bread, that they spiritually
eat the supernatural bread of the body of Christ,

who spiritually is there present, and dwelleth in them and they in him, although corporally he sitteth in heaven at the right hand of his Father.

CHAP. V.

Hereunto accordeth also Gelasius[y], writing against Eutyches and Nestorius, of whom the one said, that Christ was a perfect man, but not God; and the other affirmed clean contrary, that he was very God, but not man. But against these two heinous heresies Gelasius proveth by most manifest scriptures, that Christ is both God and man; and that after his incarnation remained in him as well the nature of his Godhead, as the nature of his manhood; so that he hath in him two natures with their natural properties, and yet is he but one Christ[z].

Pope Gelasius.

[y] Gelasius, *Contra Eutychen et Nestorium.*

[z] Dicens, " Sacramenta quæ sumimus corporis et sanguinis " Christi, divina res est, propter quod et per eadem divinæ " efficimur consortes naturæ, et tamen esse non desinit sub- " stantia vel natura panis et vini. Et certe imago et similitudo " corporis et sanguinis Christi in actione mysteriorum cele- " brantur. Satis ergo nobis evidenter ostenditur, hoc nobis " in ipso Christo Domino sentiendum, quod in ejus imagine " profitemur, celebramus, et sumimus: ut sicut in hanc scilicet " divinam transeant (Spiritu Sancto perficiente) substantiam, " permanent tamen in suæ proprietate naturæ: sic illud ipsum " mysterium principale, (cujus nobis efficientiam virtutemque " veraciter repræsentant,) his ex quibus constat proprie per- " manentibus, unum Christum (quia integrum verumque) per- " manere demonstrant." EMBD. [The writers of the Church of Rome have laboured hard to prove that the author of this work was not Gelasius the Pope, but either Gelasius of Cyzicus or Gelasius of Cæsarea. But, as Cave says, "frustra omnes: " magna enim est veritas et prævaluit. Tandem vi veritatis " adactus, manus dedit ipse Labbæus. Dissert. de Script. Eccl. " tom. 1. p. 342." Cave, *Hist. Liter.—Jenkyns*]

And for the more evident declaration hereof, he bringeth two examples; the one is of man, who being but one, yet he is made of two parts, and hath in him two natures, remaining both together in him, that is to say, the body and the soul with their natural properties.

The other example is of the sacrament of the body and blood of Christ; which, saith he, " is a " godly thing, and yet *the substance or nature of* " *bread and wine do not cease to be there still.*"

Note well these words against all the papists of our time, that Gelasius, which was Bishop of Rome[a] more than a thousand years past, writeth of this sacrament, that the bread and wine cease not to be there still; as Christ ceased not to be God after his incarnation, but remained still perfect God as he was before[b].

Theodoretus[c] also affirmeth the same, both in his first and in his second Dialogue. In the first he saith thus : " He that called his natural body " wheat and bread, and also called himself a vine, " the selfsame *called bread and wine his body and* " *blood, and yet changed not their natures.*"

And in his second Dialogue he saith more plainly : " For," saith he, " as *the bread and wine* " *after the consecration lose not their proper nature,* " *but keep their former substance, form, and figure,*

[a] [A.D. 492.]
[b] Et Leo, ut habetur, *De Consecrat.* dist. 2. " Incarnationis " quoque exemplo astruamus mysterii veritatem." Idem habet Ambrosius, *De iis qui initiuntur Mysteriis,* cap. ult.
[c] Theodoretus *in Dialogis.*

"which they had before; even so the body of "Christ after his ascension was changed into the "godly substance."

Now let the papists choose which of these two they will grant, for one of them they must needs grant, either that the nature and substance of bread and wine remain still in the sacrament after the consecration, (and then must they recant their doctrine of transubstantiation,) or else that they be of the error of Nestorius and other, which did say that the nature of the Godhead remained not in Christ after his incarnation. For all these old authors agree that it is in the one, as it is in the other.

Now forasmuch as it is proved sufficiently, as well by the holy Scripture, as by natural operation, by natural reason, by all our senses, and by the most old and best learned authors and holy martyrs of Christ's Church, that the substance of bread and wine do remain, and be received of faithful people in the blessed sacrament, or Supper of the Lord; it is a thing worthy to be considered and well weighed, what moved the school authors of late years to defend the contrary opinion, not only so far from all experience of our senses, and so far from all reason, but also clean contrary to the old Church of Christ and

CHAP. V.

CHAP. VI.
Transubstantiation came from Rome.

to God's most holy word. Surely nothing moved them thereto so much, as did the vain faith which they had in the Church and see of Rome.

For Johannes Scotus[d], otherwise called Duns, the subtlest of all the school authors, in treating of this matter of transubstantiation, showeth plainly the cause thereof: "For," saith he, "*the* "*words of the Scripture might be expounded more* "*easily and more plainly without transubstantia-* "*tion;* but the Church did choose this sense, " which is more hard, being moved thereto, as it " seemeth, chiefly *because that of the sacraments* " *men ought to hold as the holy Church of Rome* " *holdeth.* But it holdeth that bread is transub- " stantiate or turned into the body, and wine into " the blood, as it is showed *De summa Trinitate* " *et Fide Catholica.* 'Firmiter credimus.'"

Gabriel. And Gabriel also, who of all other wrote most largely upon the canon of the Mass, saith thus[e]: " It is to be noted, that although it be taught in " the Scripture, that the body of Christ is truly " contained and received of Christian people " under the kinds of bread and wine; yet how " the body of Christ is there, whether by con- " version of any thing into it, or without conver- " sion the body is there with the bread, both the " substance and accidents of bread remaining " there still, *it is not found expressed in the Bible.* " Yet *forasmuch as of the sacraments men must*

[d] Scotus, *Super* 4. *Sent.* distinct. 11.
[e] Gabriel, *Super Canonem Missæ*, lect. 40. [1580.]

CHAP. VI.

"*hold as the holy Church of Rome holdeth, as it*
"*is written, De Hæreticis, 'Ad abolendam;' and*
"*that Church holdeth and hath determined, that*
"*the bread is transubstantiated into the body of*
"*Christ, and the wine into his blood; therefore is*
"*this opinion received of all them that be catholic,*
"*that the substance of bread remaineth not, but*
"*really and truly is turned, transubstantiated,*
"*and changed into the substance of the body of*
"*Christ.*"

CHAP. VII.

Thus you have heard the cause, wherefore this opinion of transubstantiation at this present is holden and defended among Christian people; that is to say, because the Church of Rome hath so determined; although the contrary, by the papists' own confession, appear to be more easy, more true, and more according to the Scripture[f].

But because our English papists (who speak more grossly herein than the Pope himself, affirming that the natural body of Christ is naturally in the bread and wine) cannot nor dare not ground their faith concerning transubstantiation

---

[f] "Quoniam autem Ecclesia Romana transubstantionem esse "declaravit, ideo eligitur hic intellectus (ut inquit Scotus) ita "difficilis, cum verba Scripturæ possent salvari secundum in- "tellectum facilem et veriorem secundum apparentiam." EMBD. [See *Disputation at Oxford with Chedsey.*]

Strong views of the Romish Church.

upon the Church of Rome; which although in name it be called most holy, yet indeed it is the most stinking dunghill of all wickedness that is under heaven, and the very synagogue of the Devil, which whosoever followeth cannot but stumble, and fall into a pit full of errors; because, I say, the English papists dare not now stablish their faith upon that foundation of Rome, therefore they seek fig-leaves, that is to say, vain reasons gathered of their own brains, and authorities wrested from the intent and mind of the authors, wherewith to cover and hide their shameful errors. Wherefore I thought it good somewhat to travail herein, to take away those fig-leaves, that their shameful errors may plainly to every man appear.

CHAP. VIII.

The first reason of the papists to prove their transubstantiation. Matt. xxvi. Mark xiv. Luke xxii. The answer.

The greatest reason and of most importance, and of such strength, as they think or at the least as they pretend, that all the world cannot answer thereto, is this: *Our Saviour Christ taking the bread, brake it, and gave it to his disciples, saying,* This is my body. Now, say they, as soon as Christ had spoken these words, the bread was straightway altered and changed, and the substance thereof was converted into the substance of his precious body.

But what Christian ears can patiently hear this doctrine, that Christ is every day made anew, and made[g] of another substance than he was made of in his mother's womb? For whereas, at his incarnation, he was made of the nature and substance of his blessed mother ; now, by these papists' opinion, he is made every day of the nature and substance of bread and wine, which, as they say, be turned into the substance of his body and blood. O what a marvellous metamorphosis and abominable heresy is this, to say that Christ is daily made anew, and of a new matter! whereof it followeth necessarily, that they make us every day a new Christ, and not the same that was born of the Virgin Mary, nor that was crucified upon the cross, as it shall be plainly proved by these arguments following.

First, thus : If Christ's body that was crucified was not made of bread, but the body that was eaten in the supper was made of bread, as the papists say, then Christ's body that was eaten was not the same that was crucified.

And again : If Christ's body that was crucified was not made of bread, and Christ's body that was crucified was the same that was eaten at his last supper, then Christ's body that was eaten was not made of bread.

And moreover ; If Christ's body that was eaten at the last supper was the same that was crucified, and Christ's body that was eaten at the supper

[g] Roffens. *Contra Œcolampadium*, lib. ii. cap. 20. [1580.]

was made of bread, as the papists feign, then Christ's body that was crucified was made of bread.

And in like manner it followeth : If the body of Christ in the sacrament be made of the substance of bread and wine, and the same body was conceived in the Virgin's womb, then the body of Christ in the Virgin's womb was made of bread and wine.

Or else turn the argument thus : The body of Christ in the Virgin's womb was not made of bread and wine; but this body of Christ in the sacrament is made of bread and wine; then this body of Christ is not the same that was conceived in the Virgin's womb.

Another argument : Christ that was born in the Virgin's womb, as concerning his body, was made of none other substance but of the substance of his blessed mother ; but Christ in the sacrament is made of another substance : then he is another Christ.

And so the Antichrist of Rome, the chief author of all idolatry, would bring faithful Christian people from the true worshipping of Christ, that was made and born of the blessed Virgin Mary through the operation of the Holy Ghost, and suffered for us upon the cross, to worship another Christ made of bread and wine through the consecration of a popish priest.

And thus the popish priests make themselves the makers of God. For, say they, the priest by the words of consecration maketh that thing

TRANSUBSTANTIATION.

which is eaten and drunken in the Lord's Supper; and that, say they, is Christ himself, both God and man; and so they take upon them to make both God and man.

CHAP. VIII.

But let all true worshippers worship one God, one Christ, once corporally made, of one only corporal substance, that is to say, of the blessed Virgin Mary; that once died, and rose once again, once ascended into heaven, and there sitteth and shall sit at the right hand of his Father evermore, although spiritually he be every day amongst us, and whosoever come together in his name, he is in the midst among them. And he is the spiritual pasture and food of our souls, as meat and drink is of our bodies; which he signifieth unto us by the institution of his most holy supper in bread and wine declaring that as the bread and wine corporally comfort and feed our bodies, so doth he with his flesh and blood spiritually comfort and feed our souls.

And now may be easily answered the papists' argument, whereof they do so much boast. For brag they never so much of their conversion of bread and wine into the body and blood of Christ, yet that conversion is spiritual, and putteth not away the corporal presence of the material bread and wine. But forasmuch as the same is a most holy sacrament of our spiritual nourishment, which we have by the body and blood of our Saviour Christ, there must needs remain the sensible element, that is to say, bread and wine, without the which there can be no sacrament.

The answer more directly.

As in our spiritual regeneration there can be no sacrament of baptism, if there be no water. For as baptism is no perfect sacrament of spiritual regeneration, without there be as well the element of water, as the Holy Ghost spiritually regenerating the person that is baptized, (which is signified by the said water,) even so the Supper of our Lord can be no perfect sacrament of spiritual food, except there be as well bread and wine, as the body and blood of our Saviour Christ, spiritually feeding us, which by the said bread and wine is signified.

And howsoever the body and blood of our Saviour Christ be there present, they may as well be present there with the substance of bread and wine, as with the accidents of the same; as the school authors do confess themselves, and it shall be well proved if the adversaries will deny it. Thus you see the strongest argument of the papists answered unto, and the chief foundation whereupon they build their error of transubstantiation, utterly subverted and overthrown.

CHAP. IX.

The second argument for transubstantiation.

Another reason have they of like strength. If the bread should remain, say they, then should follow many absurdities, and chiefly, that Christ hath taken the nature of bread, as he took the nature of man, and so joined it to his substance.

And then as we have God verily incarnate for our redemption, so should we have him impanate.

The answer.

Thou mayest consider, good reader, that the rest of their reasons be very weak and feeble, when these be the chief and strongest. Truth it is indeed, that Christ should have been impanate, if he had joined the bread unto his substance in unity of person, that is to say, if he had joined the bread unto him in such sort, that he had made the bread one person with himself. But forasmuch as he is joined to the bread but sacramentally, there followeth no impanation thereof, no more than the Holy Ghost is inaquate, that is to say, made water, being sacramentally joined to the water in baptism. Nor he was not made a dove, when he took upon him the form of a dove, to signify that he whom St. John did baptize was very Christ.

*Matt. iii.
Mark i.
Luke iii.*

But rather of the error of the papists themselves, (as one error draweth another after it,) should follow the great absurdity which they speak upon, that is to say, that Christ should be impanate and invinate. For if Christ do use the bread in such wise that he doth not annihilate and make nothing of it, as the papists say, but maketh of it his own body, then is the bread joined to his body in a greater unity, than is his humanity to his Godhead. For his Godhead is adjoined unto his humanity in unity of person, and not of nature: but our Saviour Christ, by their saying, adjoineth bread unto his body in unity both of nature and person. So that the bread and the body of Christ be but one thing, both in nature and person. And so is there a more entire union between Christ and bread, than between his Godhead and manhood, or between his soul and his body. And thus these arguments of the papists return, like rivetted nails, upon their own heads.

CHAP. X.

The third reason. John vi.

Yet a third reason they have, which they gather out of the sixth of John, where Christ saith: *I am lively bread, which came from heaven. If any man eat of this bread, he shall live for ever. And the bread which I will give is my flesh, which I will give for the life of the world.*

Then reason they after this fashion. If the bread which Christ gave be his flesh, then it cannot also be material bread; and so it must needs follow, that the material bread is gone, and that none other substance remaineth but the flesh of Christ only.

The answer.

To this is soon made answer, that Christ in that place of John spake not of the material and sacramental bread, nor of the sacramental eating, (for that was spoken two or three years before the sacrament was first ordained,) but he spake of

John vi

spiritual bread, many times repeating, *I am the bread of life which came from heaven,* and of

TRANSUBSTANTIATION. 73

spiritual eating by faith, after which sort he was at the same present time eaten of as many as believed on him, although the sacrament was not at that time made and instituted. And therefore he said : *Your fathers did eat manna in the desert, and died; but he that eateth this bread shall live for ever.* Therefore this place of St. John can in no wise be understand of the sacramental bread, which neither came from heaven, neither giveth life to all that eat it. Nor of such bread Christ could have then presently said, *This is my flesh*, except they will say that Christ did then consecrate, so many years before the institution of his holy Supper. [See pp. 47 and 48.]

CHAP. X.

Now that I have made a full, direct, and plain answer to the vain reasons and cavillations of the papists, order requireth to make likewise answer unto their sophistical allegations and wresting of authors unto their phantastical purposes. There be chiefly three places, which at the first show seem much to make for their intent, but when they shall be thoroughly weighed, they make nothing for them at all.

CHAP. XI.
Authors wrested by the papists for their transubstantiation

The first is a place of Cyprian[h], in his Sermon of the Lord's Supper, where he saith, as is alleged

[h] Cyprianus, *De Cœna Domini.* [This Sermon, as has been already stated, pp. 48 and 49, is now held to be spurious.]

BOOK II.

The answer.

in the Detection of the Devil's Sophistry[i], "This "bread, which our Lord gave to his disciples, "changed in nature, but not in outward form, is, "by the omnipotency of God's word, made flesh." Here the papists stick tooth and nail to these words, "*changed in nature.*" Ergo, say they, the nature of the bread is changed. Here is one chief point of the Devil's sophistry used, who in allegation of Scripture useth ever either to add thereto, or to take away from it, or to alter the sense thereof. And so have they in this author left out those words which would open plainly all the whole matter. For next the words which be here before of them recited, do follow these words: "As in the person of Christ the humanity was "seen and the divinity was hid, even so did the "divinity ineffably put itself into the visible "sacrament[k]." Which words of Cyprian do manifestly show, that the sacrament doth still remain

[i] [Cranmer here refers to a work published by Gardyner in 1546, entitled, *A Detection of the Devil's Sophistrie, wherwith he robbeth the unlearned people of the true byleef in the most blessed Sacrament of the aulter.*]

[k] "Ut esset religioni circa sacramenta devotio, et ad verita- "tem cujus corpus sacramenta sunt sincerior pateret accessus, "usque ad participationem spiritus; non quod usque ad con- "substantialitatem Christi, sed usque ad societatem germanissi- "mam ejus hæc unitas perveniret." Et ibidem: "Ex con- "sueto rerum effectu fidei nostræ adjuta infirmitas, sensibili "argumento edocta est, visibilibus sacramentis inesse vitæ "æternæ effectum; et non tam corporali quam spirituali transi- "tione, Christo nos uniri." Et mox: "Nostra vero et ipsius "conjunctio, nec miscet personas, nec unit substantias, sed "affectus consociat et confœderat voluntates." EMBD.

with the divinity; and that sacramentally the divinity is poured into the bread and wine, the same bread and wine still remaining: like as the same divinity by unity of person was in the humanity of Christ, the same humanity still remaining with the divinity.

And yet the bread is changed, not in shape, nor substance, but in nature, as Cyprian truly saith, not meaning that the natural substance of bread is clean gone, but that by God's word there is added thereto another higher property, nature, and condition, far passing the nature and condition of common bread, that is to say, that the bread doth show unto us, as the same Cyprian saith, that we be partakers of the Spirit of God, and most purely joined unto Christ, and spiritually fed with his flesh and blood; so that now the said mystical bread is both a corporal food for the body, and a spiritual food for the soul.

And likewise is the nature of the water changed in baptism; forasmuch as beside his common nature, (which is to wash and make clean the body,) it declareth unto us, that our souls be also washed and made clean by the Holy Ghost[1]. And thus is answered the chief authority

[1] Augustinus, *In Joan.* xv. tract. 80. "*Jam vos mundi estis, propter verbum quod locutus sum vobis.* Quare non ait, "'Mundi estis propter baptismum quo loti estis,' sed ait, 'prop-"'ter verbum quod loquutus sum vobis?' Nisi quia et in aqua "verbum mundat. Detrahe verbum: quid est aqua nisi aqua? "Accedit verbum ad elementum, et fit sacramentum: etiam "ipsum tanquam visibile verbum." Et mox: "Unde ista tanta

of the doctors, which the papists take for the principal defence of their error. But for further declaration of St. Cyprian's mind herein, read the place of him before recited, pp. 47, 48.

CHAP. XII.

Chrysostomus.

Another authority they have of St. John Chrysostome, which they boast also to be invincible. Chrysostome, say they, writeth thus, in a certain Homily *De Eucharistia*[m]: "Dost thou see "bread? Dost thou see wine? Do they avoid "beneath, as other meats do? God forbid; think "not so. For as wax, if it be put into the fire, it "is made like the fire, no substance remaineth, "nothing is left: so here also think thou, that *the* "*mysteries be consumed by the substance of the* "*body.*"

At these words of Chrysostome the papists do triumph, as though they had won the field. Lo, say they, doth not Chrysostomus, the great clerk, say most plainly, that we see neither bread nor wine? but that, as wax in the fire, they be consumed to nothing, so that no substance remaineth?

The answer.

But if they had rehearsed no more but the very

"virtus aquæ, ut corpus tangat, et cor abluat, nisi faciente "verbo? Non quia dicitur, sed quia creditur. Nam et in "ipso verbo, aliud est sonus transiens, aliud virtus remanens: "*Hoc est verbum fidei quod prædicamus.*" EMBD.

[m] [Entitled in the Benedictine edition, *De Pœnitentia*, Hom. ix. See *Authorities* in Mr. Jenkyns' Appendix.]

TRANSUBSTANTIATION. 77

next sentence that followeth in Chrysostome, (which craftily and maliciously they leave out,) the meaning of St. John Chrysostome would easily have appeared, and yet will make them blush, if they be not utterly past shame. For after the foresaid words of Chrysostome immediately follow these words : "Wherefore," saith he, "when " ye come to these mysteries, *do not think that* " *you receive by a man the body of God*, but that " with tongues you receive fire by the angels " Seraphin." And straight after it followeth thus : " Think that the blood of salvation floweth " out of the pure and godly side of Christ, and so " coming to it receive it with pure lips. Where- " fore, brethren, I pray you and beseech you, let " us not be from the church, nor let us not be " occupied there with vain communication, but let " us stand fearful and trembling, casting down our " eyes, lifting up our minds, mourning privily " without speech, and rejoicing in our hearts."

These words of Chrysostome do follow immediately after the other words, which the papists before rehearsed. Therefore if the papists will gather of the words by them recited, that there is neither bread nor wine in the sacrament, I may as well gather of the words that follow, that there is neither priest nor Christ's body.

For as in the former sentence Chrysostome saith, that we may not think that we see bread and wine ; so in the second sentence he saith, that we may not think that we receive the body of

Christ of the priest's hands. Wherefore if upon the second sentence, as the papists themselves will say, it cannot be truly gathered, that in the holy communion there is not the body of Christ ministered by the priest; then must they confess also, that it cannot be well and truly gathered upon the first sentence, that there is no bread nor wine.

But there be all these things together in the holy communion · Christ himself spiritually eaten and drunken, and nourishing the right believers; the bread and wine as a sacrament declaring the same; and the priest as a minister thereof. Wherefore St. John Chrysostome meant not absolutely to deny that there is bread and wine, or to deny utterly the priest and the body of Christ to be there; but he useth a speech which is no pure negative, but a negative by comparison.

Negatives by comparison.

Which fashion of speech is commonly used, not only in the Scripture, and among all good authors, but also in all manner of languages. For when two things be compared together, in the extolling of the more excellent or abasing of the more vile is many times used a negative by comparison, which nevertheless is no pure negative, but only in the respect of the more excellent or the more base.

As by example: when the people, rejecting the Prophet Samuel, desired to have a king, Almighty God said to Samuel, *They have not rejected thee, but me.* Not meaning by this negative absolutely that they had not rejected Samuel, (in whose place they desired to have a king,) but by that one

1 Sam. viii.

TRANSUBSTANTIATION. 79

negative by comparison he understood two affirmatives, that is to say, that they had rejected Samuel, and not him alone, but also that they had chiefly rejected God.

CHAP. XII.

And when the prophet David said in the person of Christ, *I am a worm, and not a man;* by this negative he denied not utterly that Christ was a man, but the more vehemently to express the great humiliation of Christ, he said that he was not abased only to the nature of man, but was brought so low, that he might rather be called a worm than a man.

Psal xxii.

This manner of speech was familiar and usual to St. Paul, as when he said, *It is not I that do it, but it is the sin that dwelleth in me.* And in another place he saith, *Christ sent me not to baptize, but to preach the Gospel.* And again he saith, *My speech and preaching was not in words of man's persuasion, but in manifest declaration of the Spirit and power.* And he saith also, *Neither he that grafteth, nor he that watereth, is any thing; but God that giveth the increase.* And he saith moreover, *It is not I that live, but Christ liveth within me.* And, *God forbid that I should rejoice in any thing, but in the cross of our Lord Jesu Christ.* And further, *We do not wrestle against flesh and blood, but against the spirits of darkness.*

Rom. vii.

1 Cor. i.

Ibid

1 Cor. iii.

Gal. ii.
Gal. vi.

Ephes. vi.

In all these sentences and many other like, although they be negatives, nevertheless St. Paul meant not clearly to deny that he did that evil whereof he spake, or utterly to say that he was not sent to baptize, (who indeed did baptize at certain times, and was sent to do all things that pertained to salvation,) or that in his office of setting forth of God's word he used no witty persuasions, (which indeed he used most discreetly,) or that the grafter and waterer be nothing, (which be God's creatures made to his similitude, and without whose work there should be no increase,) or to say that he was not alive, (who both lived and ran from country to country, to set forth God's glory,) or clearly to affirm that he gloried and rejoiced in no other thing than in Christ's cross, (who rejoiced with all men that were in joy, and sorrowed with all that were in sorrow,) or to deny utterly that we wrestle against flesh and blood, (which cease not daily to wrestle and war against our enemies, the world, the flesh, and the devil.) In all these sentences, St. Paul, as I said, meant not clearly to deny these things, which undoubtedly were all true, but he meant, that in comparison of other greater things, these smaller were not much to be esteemed; but that the greater things were the chief things to be considered: as that sin committed by his infirmity, was rather to be imputed to original sin or corruption of nature, which lay lurking within him, than to his own will and consent. And that although he was sent to baptize, yet he was chiefly sent to preach God's word. And that although he used wise and discreet persuasions therein, yet the success thereof came principally of the power of God, and of the working of the Holy Spirit. And that although the grafter and waterer of the garden be some things, and do not a little in their offices, yet it is God chiefly that giveth the increase. And that although he lived in this world, yet his chief life, concerning God, was by Christ, whom he had living within him. And that although he gloried in many other things, yea, in his own infirmities, yet his greatest joy was in the redemption by the cross of Christ. And that although our spirit daily fighteth against our flesh, yet our chief and principal fight is against our ghostly enemies, the subtle and puissant wicked spirits and devils.

CHAP. XII.
Gal. ii.
2 Cor. xi.
xii. Gal. vi.
Gal. v.
Ephes vi.

The same manner of speech used also St. Peter in his first Epistle, saying, *That the apparel of women should not be outwardly with braided hair and setting on of gold, nor in putting on of gorgeous apparel, but that the inward man of the heart should be without corruption.*

1 Pet iii.

In which manner of speech he intended not utterly to forbid all braiding of hair, all gold and costly apparel to all women; for every one must be apparelled according to their condition, state, and degree; but he meant hereby clearly to condemn all pride and excess in apparel, and to move all women that they should study to deck their souls inwardly with all virtues, and not to be curious outwardly to deck and adorn their bodies with sumptuous apparel.

<small>BOOK II.
Matt. vi.</small>

And our Saviour Christ himself was full of such manner of speeches. *Gather not unto you,* saith he, *treasure-upon earth:* willing us thereby rather to set our minds upon heavenly treasure which ever endureth, than upon earthly treasure, which by many sundry occasions perisheth and is taken away from us. And yet worldly treasure must needs be had and possessed of some men, as the person, time, and occasion doth serve.

<small>Matt. x</small>

Likewise he said, *When you be brought before kings and princes, think not what and how you shall answer:* not willing us by this negative, that we should negligently and unadvisedly answer we care not what, but that we should depend of our heavenly Father, trusting that by his Holy Spirit he will sufficiently instruct us of answer, rather than to trust of any answer to be devised by our own wit and study.

<small>Matt. x.</small>

And in the same manner he spake, when he said, *It is not you that speak, but it is the Spirit of God that speaketh within you.* For the Spirit of God is he that principally putteth godly words into our mouths, and yet nevertheless we do speak according to his moving.

<small>Matt xxiii.
Ibid.
Matt. x.
Ibid.
Matt. xx.
John iv.
John v.</small>

And to be short, in all these sentences following, that is to say, *Call no man your father upon earth.—Let no man call you lord or master.—Fear not them that kill the body.—I came not to send peace upon earth.—It is not in me to set you at my right hand or left hand.—You shall not worship the Father neither in this mount, nor in Jerusalem.*

—*I take no witness at no man.*—*My doctrine is not mine.*—*I seek not my glory.* In all these negatives, our Saviour Christ spake not precisely and utterly to deny all the foresaid things, but in comparison of them to prefer other things: as to prefer our Father and Lord in heaven above any worldly father, lord, or master in earth, and his fear above the fear of any creature, and his word and Gospel above all worldly peace: also to prefer spiritual and inward honouring of God in pure heart and mind, above local, corporal, and outward honour; and that Christ preferred his Father's glory above his own.

CHAP. XII.
John vii.
John viii.

Now forasmuch as I have declared at length the nature and kind of these negative speeches, (which be no pure negatives but by comparison,) it is easy hereby to make answer to St. John Chrysostome, who used this phrase of speech most of any author. For his meaning in his foresaid Homily was not that in the celebration of the Lord's Supper is neither bread nor wine, neither priest, nor the body of Christ, (which the papists themselves must needs confess,) but his intent was to draw our minds upward to heaven, that we should not consider so much the bread, wine, priest, and body of Christ, as we should consider his divinity and Holy Spirit given unto us to our eternal salvation.

And therefore in the same place he useth so many times these words, "Think, and think not;" willing us by those words that we should not fix our thoughts and minds upon the bread, wine, priest, nor Christ's body; but to lift up our hearts higher unto his spirit and divinity, without the which his body availeth nothing, as he said himself: *It is the spirit that giveth life, the flesh availeth nothing.*

And as the same Chrysostome in many places moveth us not to consider the water in baptism, but rather to have respect to the Holy Ghost, received in baptism, and represented by the water: even so doth he in this Homily of the holy communion move us to lift up our minds from all visible and corporal things to things invisible and spiritual[n].

Insomuch that although Christ was but once crucified, yet would Chrysostome have us to think that we see him daily whipped and scourged before our eyes, and his body hanging upon the cross, and the spear thrust into his side, and the most holy blood to flow out of his side into our mouths. After which manner St. Paul wrote to the Galatians, that Christ *was painted and crucified before their eyes.*

Therefore, saith Chrysostome, in the same Homily, a little before the place rehearsed,

[n] Chrysostomus, *In* 1 *Cor.* ii. "Infidelis cum baptismatis "lavacrum audit, simpliciter aquam esse sibi persuadet. Ego "verno non simpliciter video quod video, sed animæ per Spiritum "purgationem, necnon sepulturam, resurrectionem, justitiam, "adoptionem, hæreditatem, regnum cœlorum, Spiritûs societa- "tem considero. Non enim aspectu judico quæ videntur, sed "mentis oculis." Hac loquendi forma usus est Chrysostomus, cum non solum de Eucharistia sed de Baptismo quoque dicit: "Nihil sensibile traditum nobis a Christo."

"What dost thou, O man? didst not thou promise to the priest which said, Lift up your minds and hearts; and thou didst answer, We lift them up unto the Lord? Art not thou ashamed and afraid, being at that same hour found a liar? A wonderful thing: the table is set forth, furnished with God's mysteries, the Lamb of God is offered for thee, the priest is careful for thee, spiritual fire cometh out of that heavenly table, the angels Seraphin be there present, covering their faces with six wings; all the angelical powers with the priest be means and intercessors for thee, a spiritual fire cometh down from heaven, blood in the cup is drunk out of the most pure side unto thy purification. And art thou not ashamed, afraid, and abashed, not endeavouring thyself to purchase God's mercy? O man, doth not thine own conscience condemn thee? There be in the week one hundred and sixty-eight hours, and God asketh but one of them to be given wholly unto him, and thou consumest that in worldly business, in trifling and talking; with what boldness then shalt thou come to these holy mysteries, O corrupt conscience?"

Hitherto I have rehearsed St. John Chrysostome's words, which do show, how our minds should be occupied at this holy table of our Lord, that is to say, withdrawn from the consideration of sensible things, unto the contemplation of most heavenly and godly things. And thus is answered this place of Chrysostome, which the papists took

CHAP. XIII.

Yet there is another place of St. Ambrose[o], which the papists think maketh much for their purpose; but after due examination it shall plainly appear how much they be deceived. They allege these words of St. Ambrose, in a book entitled, *De iis qui initiantur Mysteriis:* "Let us prove "that *there is not that thing which nature formed,* "*but which benediction did consecrate, and that* "*benediction is of more strength than nature.* "*For by the blessing, nature itself is also changed.* "Moses held a rod, he cast it from him, and it "was made a serpent. Again he took the serpent "by the tail, and it was turned again into the "nature of a rod. Wherefore thou seest, that by "the grace of the Prophet, the nature of the "serpent and rod was twice changed. The floods "of Egypt ran pure water and suddenly blood "began to burst out of the veins of the springs, "so that men could not drink of the flood; but, at "the prayer of the Prophet, the blood of the flood "went away, and the nature of water came again. "The people of the Hebrews were compassed "about on the one side with the Egyptians, and

Exod. iv.

Exod. vii.

[o] Ambros. *De iis qui Mysteriis initiantur.*

" on the other side with the sea. Moses lifted up CHAP
" his rod, the water divideth itself and stood up XIII.
                                                  ─────
                                                  Exod. xiv.
" like a wall, and between the waters was left a way
" for them to pass on foot. And Jordan, against Josh. iii
" nature, turned back to the head of his spring.
" Doth it not appear now that the nature of the
" sea floods, or of the course of fresh water, was
" changed? The people was dry, Moses touched Exod. xvii.
" a stone, and water came out of the stone. Did
" not grace here work above nature, to make the
" stone to bring forth water, which it had not of
" nature? Marath [Marah] was a most bitter Exod. xv.
" flood, so that the people being dry could not
" drink thereof. Moses put wood into the
" water, and the nature of the water lost his
" bitterness, which grace infused did suddenly 2 Kings vi.
" moderate. In the time of Heliseus [Elisha]
" the Prophet, an axe-head fell from one of
" the Prophet's servants into the water; he that
" lost the iron, desired the Prophet Heliseus' help,
" who put the helve into the water, and the iron
" swam above. Which thing we know was done
" above nature, for iron is heavier than the liquor
" of water. Thus we perceive that grace is of
" more force than nature, and yet hitherto we
" have rehearsed but the grace of the blessing
" of the prophets. *Now if the blessing of a*
" *man be of such value that it may change nature,*
" *what do we say of the consecration of God,*
" *wherein is the operation of the words of our*
" *Saviour Christ?* For this sacrament which thou

88 DEFENCE, &c.

BOOK II.

Psalm cxlviii.

"receivest is done by the word of Christ. Then "if the word of Helias [Elijah] was of such power "that it could bring fire down from heaven, *shall* "*not the word of Christ be of that power to change* "*the kinds of the elements?* Of the making of the "whole world thou hast read, that *God spake, and* "*the things were done; he commanded, and they* "*were created. The word then of Christ that* "*could of no things make things that were not, can* "*it not change those things that be, into that thing* "*which before they were not? For it is no less* "*matter to give to things new natures, than to* "*alter natures*[q]."

Thus far have I rehearsed the words of St. Ambrose, if the said book be his, (which they that be of greatest learning and judgment do not think[r],) by which words the papists would prove, that in the Supper of the Lord after the words of consecration, as they be commonly called, there remaineth neither bread nor wine, because that St. Ambrose saith in this place, that the nature of bread and wine is changed.

The answer.

But to satisfy their minds, let us grant for their pleasure, that the foresaid book was St. Ambrose's own work; yet the same book maketh

[q] "Vera utique caro Christi, quæ crucifixa est, quæ sepulta "est, vere ergo carnis illius sacramentum est. Ipse clamat "Dominus Jesus, *Hoc est corpus meum.* Ante benedictionem "verborum cœlestium alia species nominatur: post consecra- "tionem corpus Christi significatur." EMBD.

[r] [Respecting the spuriousness of this work, and of that which is quoted shortly afterwards *De Sacramentis*, see note, pp. 53, 54.

nothing for their purpose, but quite against them. For he saith not that the substance of bread and wine is gone, but he saith that their nature is changed; that is to say, that in the holy communion we ought not to receive the bread and wine as other common meats and drinks, but as things clean changed into a higher estate, nature, and condition, to be taken as holy meats and drinks, whereby we receive spiritual feeding and supernatural nourishment from heaven, of the very true body and blood of our Saviour Christ, through the omnipotent power of God and the wonderful working of the Holy Ghost. Which so well agreeth with the substance of bread and wine still remaining, that if they were gone away, and not there, this our spiritual feeding could not be taught unto us by them.

And therefore in the most part of the examples which St. Ambrose allegeth for the wonderful alteration of natures, the substances did still remain, after the natures and properties were changed. As when the water of Jordan, contrary to his nature, stood still like a wall, or flowed against the stream towards the head and spring, yet the substance of the water remained the same that it was before. Likewise the stone, that above his nature and kind flowed water, was the self-same stone that it was before. And the flood of Marath [Marah], that changed his nature of bitterness, changed, for all that, no part of his substance. No more did that iron, which contrary to his nature swam upon the water, lose thereby any part of the substance thereof. Therefore as in these alterations of natures the substances nevertheless remained the same that they were before the alterations; even so doth the substance of bread and wine remain in the Lord's Supper, and be naturally received and digested into the body, notwithstanding the sacramental mutation of the same into the body and blood of Christ. Which sacramental mutation declareth the supernatural, spiritual, and inexplicable eating and drinking, feeding and digesting, of the same body and blood of Christ, in all them that godly and according to their duty, do receive the said sacramental bread and wine.

And that St. Ambrose thus meant, that the substance of bread and wine remain still after the consecration, it is most clear by three other examples of the same matter, following in the same chapter. One is of them that be regenerated, in whom after their regeneration doth still remain their former natural substance. Another is of the incarnation of our Saviour Christ, in the which perished no substance, but remained as well the substance of his Godhead, as the substance which he took of the blessed Virgin Mary. The third example is of the water in baptism, where the water still remaineth water, although the Holy Ghost come upon the water, or rather upon him that is baptized therein.

And although the same St. Ambrose, in

TRANSUBSTANTIATION. 91

another book, entitled *De Sacramentis*, doth say, "That the bread is bread before the words of "consecration; but *when the consecration is done, "of bread is made the body of Christ*[r]*:*" yet in the same book, and in the same chapter, he telleth in what manner and form the same is done by the words of Christ; not by taking away the substance of the bread, but adding to the bread the grace of Christ's body, and so calling it the body of Christ.

And hereof he bringeth four examples; the first, of the regeneration of a man; the second is of the standing of the water of the Red Sea; the third is of the bitter water of Marath [Marah]; and the fourth is of the iron that swam above the water. In every of the which examples, the former substance remained still, notwithstanding alteration of the natures. And he concludeth the whole matter in these few words: "If there be "so much strength in the words of the Lord Jesu, "that things had their beginning which never were "before, how much more be they able to work, "that those things that were before should re- "main, and also be changed into other things!" Which words do show manifestly, that notwithstanding this wonderful sacramental and spiritual changing of the bread into the body of Christ, yet the substance of the bread remaineth the same that it was before.

Thus is a sufficient answer made unto three principal authorities, which the papists use to

[r] Lib. 4. *De Sacramentis*, cap. 4.

BOOK II. allege to stablish their error of transubstantiation: the first of Cyprian, the second of St. John Chrysostome, and the third of St. Ambrose. Other authorities and reasons some of them do bring for the same purpose; but forasmuch as they be of small moment and weight and easy to be answered unto, I will pass them over at this time, and not trouble the reader with them, but leave them to be weighed by his discretion.

CHAP. XIV.

Absurdities that follow of transubstantiation.

ᵃAnd now I will rehearse divers difficulties, absurdities, and inconveniences, which must needs follow upon this error of transubstantiation; whereof not one doth follow of the true and right faith which is according to God's word.

First, if the papists be demanded, what thing it is that is broken, what is eaten, what is drunken, and what is chawed [chewed] with the teeth, lips, and mouth in this sacrament, they have nothing to answer but the accidents. For, as they say, bread and wine be not the visible elements in this sacrament, but only their accidents; and so they be forced to say, that accidents be broken, eaten, drunken, chawen [chewed], and swallowed, without any substance at all: which is not only against all reason, but also against the doctrine of all ancient authors.

ᵃ See above, chap. iii.

TRANSUBSTANTIATION. 93

Secondly, these transubstantiators do say, contrary to all learning, that the accidents of bread and wine do hang alone in the air without any substance wherein they may be stayed. And what can be be said more foolishly?

Thirdly, that the substance of Christ's body is there really, corporally, and naturally present, without any accidents of the same. And so the papists make accidents to be without substances, and substances to be without accidents.

Fourthly, they say, that the place where the bread and wine be, hath no substance there to fill that place, and so must they needs grant *vacuum*, which nature utterly abhorreth.

Fifthly, they are not ashamed to say, that substance is made of accidents, when the bread mouldeth, or is turned into worms, or when the wine soureth.

Sixthly, that substance is nourished without substance by accidents only, if it chance any cat, mouse, dog, or any other thing, to eat the sacramental bread, or drink the sacramental wine.

These inconveniences and absurdities do follow of the fond papistical transubstantiation, with a number of other errors as evil or worse than these, whereunto they be never able to answer, as many of them have confessed themselves.

And it is a wonder to see, how in many of the foresaid things they vary among themselves. Whereas the other doctrine of the Scripture, and of the old catholic Church, (but not of the lately corrupted Romish Church,) is plain and easy, as well to be understood, as to answer to all the foresaid questions, without any absurdity or inconvenience following thereof: so that every answer shall agree with God's word, with the old Church, and also with all reason and true philosophy.

For as touching the first point, what is broken, what is eaten, what drunken, and what chawen [chewed] in this sacrament, it is easy to answer, The bread and wine, as St. Paul saith: *The bread which we break.*

And as concerning the second and third points, neither is the substance of bread and wine without their proper accidents, nor their accidents hang alone in the air without any substance, but according to all learning the substances of the bread and wine reserve their own accidents, and the accidents do rest in their own substances.

And also as concerning the fourth point, there is no place left void after consecration, as the papists dream, but bread and wine fulfil their places, as they did before.

And as touching the fifth point, whereof the worms or moulding is engendered, and whereof the vinegar cometh, the answer is easy to make, according to all learning and experience, that they come according to the course of nature of the substance of the bread and wine too long kept, and not of the accidents alone, as the papists do fondly phantasy.

And likewise the substances of bread and wine do feed and nourish the body of them that eat the same, and not only the accidents.

In these answers is no absurdity nor inconvenience, nothing spoken either contrary to holy Scripture, or to natural reason, philosophy, or experience, or against any old ancient author, or the primitive or catholic Church; but only against the malignant and papistical Church of Rome. Whereas on the other side, that cursed synagogue of Antichrist hath defined and determined in this matter many things contrary to Christ's words, contrary to the old catholic Church and the holy martyrs and doctors of the same, and contrary to all natural reason, learning, and philosophy.

And the final end of all this Antichrist's doctrine is none other, but by subtlety and craft to bring Christian people from the true honouring of Christ, unto the greatest idolatry that ever was in this world devised: as, by God's grace, shall be plainly set forth hereafter.

THUS ENDETH THE SECOND BOOK.

The Third Book teacheth the manner how Christ is present in his Supper.

CHAP. I.

The presence of Christ in the sacrament.

Now this matter of transubstantiation being, as I trust, sufficiently resolved, which is the first part before rehearsed, wherein the papistical doctrine varieth from the catholic truth, order requireth next to intreat of the second part, which is of the manner of the presence of the body and blood of our Saviour Christ in the sacrament thereof, wherein is no less contention than in the first part.

For a plain explication whereof, it is not unknown to all true faithful Christian people, that our Saviour Christ, being perfect God, and in all things equal and coeternal with his Father, for our sakes became also a perfect man, taking flesh and blood of his blessed mother and Virgin Mary, and, saving sin, being in all things like unto us, adjoining unto his divinity a most perfect soul and a most perfect body; his soul being endued with life, sense, will, reason, wisdom, memory, and all other things required to the perfect soul of man; and his body being made of very flesh and bones, not only having all members of a perfect man's body in due order and proportion, but also being subject to hunger, thirst, labour, sweat, weariness, cold, heat, and all other like infirmities and passions of man, and unto death also, and that the most vile and painful upon the cross. And after his death he rose again with the selfsame visible and palpable body, and appeared therewith, and showed the same unto his Apostles, and specially to Thomas, making him to put his hands into his side and to feel his wounds. And with the selfsame body he forsook this world, and ascended into heaven, (the Apostles seeing and beholding his body when it ascended,) and now sitteth at the right hand of his Father, and there shall remain until the last day, when he shall come to judge the quick and the dead.

CHAP. I.

Christ corporally is ascended into heaven

Acts iii.

This is the true catholic faith which the Scripture teacheth, and the universal Church of Christ hath ever believed from the beginning, until within these four or five hundred years last past that the Bishop of Rome, with the assistance of his papists, hath set up a new faith and belief of their own devising, that the same body really, corporally, naturally, and sensibly is in this world still, and that in an hundred thousand places at one time, being enclosed in every pix and bread consecrated.

And although we do affirm according to God's word, that Christ is in all persons that truly believe in him, in such sort, that with his flesh and blood he doth spiritually nourish them and feed

CHAP. II

The difference between the true and

98 DEFENCE, &c.

BOOK III.

The papistical doctrine concerning the presence of Christ's body.

them, and giveth them everlasting life, and doth assure them thereof, as well by the promise of his word, as by the sacramental bread and wine in his holy Supper, which he did institute for the same purpose, yet we do not a little vary from the heinous errors of the papists.

The first comparison.

For they teach, that Christ is in the bread and wine[a]: but we say, according to the truth, that he is in them that worthily eat and drink the bread and wine.

The second comparison.

They say, that when any man eateth the bread and drinketh the cup, Christ goeth into his mouth or stomach with the bread and wine, and no further: but we say, that Christ is in the whole man, both in the body and soul of him that worthily eateth the bread and drinketh the cup and not in his mouth or stomach only.

The third comparison.

They say, that Christ is received in the mouth, and entereth in with the bread and wine: we say, that he is received in the heart, and entereth in by faith.

The fourth comparison.

They say, that Christ is really in the sacramental bread, being reserved an whole year, or so long as the form of bread remaineth; but after the receiving thereof, he flyeth up, say they, from the receiver unto heaven, as soon as the bread is chawed in the mouth, or changed in the stomach: but we say, that Christ remaineth in the man that worthily receiveth it, so long as the man remaineth a member of Christ.

[a] Id est, sub speciebus panis et vini. EMBD.

THE PRESENCE OF CHRIST.

They say, that in the sacrament, the corporal members of Christ be not distant in place one from another, but that wheresoever the head is, there be the feet, and wheresoever the arms be, there be the legs; so that in every part of the bread and wine is altogether whole head, whole feet, whole flesh, whole blood, whole heart, whole lungs, whole breast, whole back, and altogether whole, confused and mixed without distinction or diversity. O, what a foolish and an abominable invention is this, to make of the most pure and perfect body of Christ such a confused and monstrous body! And yet can the papists imagine nothing so foolish, but all Christian people must receive the same as an oracle of God, and as a most certain article of their faith, without whispering to the contrary.

The fifth comparison.

Furthermore the papists say, that a dog or a cat eateth the body of Christ, if they by chance do eat the sacramental bread: we say, that no earthly creature can eat the body of Christ nor drink his blood, but only man.

The sixth comparison.

They say, that every man, good and evil, eateth the body of Christ: we say, that both do eat the sacramental bread and drink the wine, but none do eat the very body of Christ and drink his blood, but only they that be lively members of his body.

The seventh comparison.

They say, that good men eat the body of Christ and drink his blood, only at that time when they receive the sacrament: we say, that they eat,

The eighth comparison.

drink, and feed of Christ continually, so long as they be members of his body.

The ninth comparison. They say, that the body of Christ that is in the sacrament, hath his own proper form and quantity: we say, that Christ is there sacramentally and spiritually, without form or quantity.

The tenth comparison. They say, that the fathers and prophets of the Old Testament did not eat the body nor drink the blood of Christ: we say, that they did eat his body and drink his blood, although he was not yet born nor incarnated.

The eleventh comparison. They say, that the body of Christ is every day many times made, as often as there be masses said, and that then and there he is made of bread and wine: we say, that Christ's body was never but once made, and then not of the nature and substance of bread and wine, but of the substance of his blessed mother.

The twelfth comparison. They say, that the mass is a sacrifice satisfactory for sin, by the devotion of the priest that offereth, and not by the thing that is offered: but we say, that their saying is a most heinous lie and detestable error against the glory of Christ. For the satisfaction for our sins is not the devotion nor offering of the priest; but the only host and satisfaction for all the sins of the world is the death of Christ, and the oblation of his body upon the cross, that is to say, the oblation that Christ himself offered once upon the cross, and never but once, nor never none but he. And therefore that oblation, which the priests make

THE PRESENCE OF CHRIST. 101

daily in their papistical masses, cannot be a satisfaction for other men's sins by the priest's devotion, but it is a mere elusion and subtle craft of the Devil, whereby Antichrist hath many years blinded and deceived the world.

They say, that Christ is corporally in many places at one time, affirming that his body is corporally and really present in as many places as there be hosts consecrated : we say, that as the sun corporally is ever in heaven, and no where else ; and yet by his operation and virtue the sun is here in earth, by whose influence and virtue all things in the world be corporally regenerated, increased, and grow to their perfect state ; so likewise our Saviour Christ bodily and corporally is in heaven, sitting at the right hand of his Father, although spiritually he hath promised to be present with us upon earth unto the world's end. And whensoever two or three be gathered together in his name, he is there in the midst among them, by whose supernal grace all godly men be first by him spiritually regenerated, and after increase and grow to their spiritual perfection in God, spiritually by faith eating his flesh and drinking his blood, although the same corporally be in heaven, far distant from our sight.

CHAP. II.

The thirteenth comparison.

BOOK III.
CHAP. III.
Christ corporally is in heaven and not in earth [1580.]

Now to return to the principal matter, lest it might be thought a new device of us, that Christ as concerning his body and his human nature is in heaven, and not in earth: therefore by God's grace, it shall be evidently proved, that this is no new devised matter, but that it was ever the old faith of the catholic Church, until the papists invented a new faith, that Christ really, corporally, naturally, and sensibly is here still with us in earth, shut up in a box or within the compass of bread and wine.

The proof thereof by our profession in our common Creed.

This needeth no better nor stronger proof, than that which the old authors bring for the same, that is to say, the general profession of all Christian people in the common Creed, wherein, as concerning Christ's humanity, they be taught to believe after this sort: that he was conceived by the Holy Ghost, born of the Virgin Mary; that he suffered under Pontius Pilate, was crucified, dead, and buried; that he descended into hell, and rose again the third day; that *he ascended into heaven, and sitteth at the right hand of his almighty Father*, and from thence shall come to judge the quick and the dead.

This hath been ever the catholic faith of Christian people, that Christ, as concerning his body and his manhood, is in heaven, and shall there continue until he come down at the last judgment.

And forasmuch as the Creed maketh so express mention of the article of his ascension and departing hence from us; if it had been another article CHAP. of our faith, that his body tarrieth also here with us in earth, surely in this place of the Creed was so urgent an occasion given to make some mention thereof, that doubtless it would not have been passed over in our Creed with silence. For if Christ, as concerning his humanity, be both here and gone hence, and both those two be articles of our faith, when mention was made of the one in the Creed, it was necessary to make mention of the other, lest, by professing the one, we should be dissuaded from believing the other, being so contrary the one to the other.

To this article of our Creed accordeth holy CHAP. IV. Scripture, and all the old ancient doctors of Christ's Church. For Christ himself said, I *hereof by the Scrip-* leave the world, *and go to my Father.* And also *ture.* he said, *You shall ever have poor folks with you, but* you shall not ever have me with you. And he gave warning of this error beforehand, saying, *That the time would come when many deceivers* John xvi. Matt.xxvi. *should be in the world, and* say, Here is Christ, Matt.xxiv. *and there is Christ; but believe them not,* said Christ. And St. Mark writeth in the last chapter of his Gospel, *That the Lord Jesus* was taken up Mark xvi. into heaven, and sitteth at the right hand of his Father. And St. Paul exhorteth all men *to seek* Coloss. iii.

for things that be above in heaven, where Christ, saith he, sitteth at the right hand of God his Father. Also he saith, *That we have such a bishop, that sitteth in heaven at the right hand of the throne of God's majesty.* And *that he having offered one sacrifice for sins, sitteth continually at the right hand of God, until his enemies be put under his feet as a footstool*[b].

And hereunto consent all the old doctors of the Church.

CHAP. V.

The proof thereof by ancient authors.

First, Origen[c] upon Matthew reasoneth this matter, how Christ may be called a stranger that is departed into another country, seeing that he is with us alway unto the world's end, and is among all them that be gathered together in his name, and also in the midst of them that know him not. And thus he reasoneth: If he be here among us still, how can he be gone hence as a stranger departed into another country? Whereunto he answereth, that Christ is both God and man, having in him two natures. And *as a man, he is not with us unto the world's end, nor is present with all his faithful that be gathered to-*

[b] *Quem oportet cœlum suscipere usque ad tempus restitutionis omnium.* Acts iii EMBD.

[c] Origen. *in Mat.* cap. 25. tract. 33.

THE PRESENCE OF CHRIST. 105

gether in his name; but his divine power and spirit is ever with us. Paul, saith he, was absent from the Corinthians in his body, when he was present with them in his spirit. *So is Christ,* saith he, *gone hence and absent in his humanity,* which in his divine nature is every where. And in this saying, saith Origen, we divide not his humanity; for St. John writeth, that *no spirit that divideth* [1John iv] *Jesus can be* of God; but we reserve to both his natures their own properties.

In these words Origen hath plainly declared his mind, that Christ's body is not both present here with us, and also gone hence and estranged from us. For that were to make two natures of one body, and to divide the body of Jesus; forasmuch as one nature cannot at one time be both with us and absent from us. And therefore, saith Origen, that the presence must be understood of his divinity, and the absence of his humanity.

And according hereunto, St. Augustine writeth thus, in an epistle *Ad Dardanum*[d]. "Doubt not
" but *Jesus Christ, as concerning the nature of*
" *his manhood, is now there from whence he shall*
" *come;* and remember well and believe the pro-
" fession of a Christian man, that he rose from
" death, ascended into heaven, sitteth at the right
" hand of his Father, and from that place and
" none other, shall he come to judge the quick and
" the dead. And he shall come, as the angels
" said, as he was seen go into heaven, that is to

[d] August. *Ad Dardanum, Epist.* 57.

"say, in the same form and *substance, unto the* "*which he gave immortality, but changed not nature.*

" After this form," saith he, meaning his man's nature, " *we may not think that he is every where.* " *For we must beware, that we do not so stablish* " *his divinity, that we take away the verity of his* " *body*[e]*.*"

These be St. Augustine's plain words.

And by and by after, he addeth these words: " The Lord Jesus as God is every where, and *as* " *man is in heaven.*" And, finally, he concludeth this matter in these few words: " Doubt not but " our Lord Jesus Christ is every where as God; " and as a dweller he is in man that is the temple " of God, and *he is in a certain place in heaven,* " *because of the measure of a very body.*"

And again St. Augustine writeth upon the Gospel of St. John[f]: " Our Saviour Jesus Christ," saith St. Augustine, " is above, but yet his truth is " here. *His body wherein he arose is in one* " *place,* but the truth of his word is spread every " where."

And in another place of the same book[g], St Augustine, expounding these words of Christ, *You shall ever have poor men with you, but me you shall not ever have,* saith, " That *Christ spake* " *these words of the presence of his body.* For,"

[e] Hunc locum citat Leo, Epistola ultima, ad probandum in Christo veram formam humanam. Et in tota Epistola, forma accipitur pro substantia. EMBD.

[f] *In Joan. Tract.* 30.   [g] *In Joan. Tract.* 50.

saith he, "as concerning his Divine Majesty, as "concerning his providence, as concerning his "infallible and invisible grace, these words be "fulfilled which he spake, *I am with you unto* "*the world's end.* But *as concerning the flesh* "which he took in his incarnation, as concerning "that which was born of the Virgin, as concern-"ing that which was apprehended by the Jews, "and crucified upon a tree, and taken down from "the cross, lapped in linen clothes, and buried, "and rose again, and appeared after his resurrec-"tion; as concerning that flesh he said, *You shall* "*not ever have me with you.* Wherefore seeing "that as concerning his flesh, he was conversant "with his disciples forty days, and they ac-"companying, seeing, and following him, he went "up into heaven, both *he is not here, (for he sit-*"*teth at the right hand of his Father,)* and yet he "is here, for he departed not hence, as concerning "the presence of his Divine Majesty. As con-"cerning the presence of his Majesty, we have "Christ ever with us; *but as concerning the* "*presence of his flesh, he said truly to his dis-*"*ciples, Ye shall not ever have me with you.* For "as concerning the presence of his flesh, the "Church had Christ but a few days; yet now it "holdeth him fast by faith, though it see him "not with eyes[h]."

All these be St. Augustine's words.

Matt. xxviii.

[h] "Ergo, si ita dictum est; *Me autem non semper habebitis,*
"quæstio, sicut arbitrior, jam nulla est, quæ duobus modis
"soluta est." EMBD.

Also in another book[i], entitled to St. Augustine, is written thus: "We must believe and confess "that the Son of God, as concerning his divinity, "is invisible, without a body, immortal, and in-"circumscriptible; but, *as concerning his human-*"*ity*, we ought to believe and confess that he is "visible, hath a body, and *is contained in a cer-*"*tain place, and hath truly all the members of a* "*man*[k]."

Of these words of St. Augustine it is most clear, that the profession of the catholic faith is, that Christ, as concerning his bodily substance and nature of man, is in heaven, and not present here with us in earth. For the nature and property of a very body is to be in one place, and to occupy one place, and not to be every where or in many places at one time. And though the body of Christ, after his resurrection and ascension, was made immortal, yet the nature thereof

[i] *De Essentia Divinitatis.* [This work is considered spurious by the Benedictine editors.]

[k] Augustinus, *De verbis Domini Sermone* 53. "In cœlis "Christus erat et persecutori dicebat: 'Quid me persequeris?' "Ubi Dominus expressit sic et hic se esse in nobis. Sic totus "crescit, quia quemadmodum ille in nobis hic, sic et nos ibi in "illo sumus." Idem, *In Joan. tract.* 50. "Quomodo tenebo "absentem? Quomodo in cœlum manum mittam, ut ibi seden-"tem teneam? Fidem mitte, et tenuisti: Parentes tui ten-"uerunt carne, tu tene corde, quoniam Christus absens, etiam "præsens est. Nisi præsens esset, a nobis teneri non posset: "sed quoniam verum est quod ait: *Ecce ego vobiscum sum, &c.*, "et abiit et hic est, et rediit et nos deseruit. Corpus suum "intulit cœlo, majestatem non abstulit mundo." Et mox: "*Me autem non semper habebitis*. Quid est enim 'non sem-"per?' Si bonus es, si ad corpus Christi pertines (quod signifi-

was not changed; for then, as St. Augustine saith, it were no very body. And further, St. Augustine showeth both the manner and form, how Christ is here present with us in earth, and how he is absent, saying, that he is present by his divine nature and majesty, by his providence, and by his grace; but by his human nature and very body, he is absent from this world, and present in heaven.

Cyrillus[1] likewise, upon the Gospel of St. John, agreeth fully with St. Augustine, saying, "Al-"though *Christ took away from hence the presence* "*of his body*, yet in the majesty of his Godhead "he is ever here, as he promised to his disciples "at his departing, saying, *I am with you ever unto* "*the world's end.*"

And in another place[m] of the same book, St.

"cat Petrus) habes Christum et in præsenti et in futuro. In "præsenti per fidem, in præsenti per signum, in præsenti per "baptismi sacramentum, in præsenti per altaris cibum et potum." Idem, *In Joan. tract.* 102. super illis verbis: *Relinquo mundum* &c. "Reliquit mundum corporali discessione, perrexit ad Pat-"rem hominis ascensione, nec mundum deseruit præsentiæ "gubernatione."

Idem, *De Symbolo ad Catechumenos*, lib. ii. "Quis est iste "sponsus, absens et præsens? Quis est iste sponsus præsens et "latens? quem sponsa Ecclesia fide tantum concipit, et sine ullo "amplexu membra ejus quotidie parit?" Et mox: "Ipsa est "virtus omnipotentiæ tuæ, ut plus possis in ipsis fidelibus, "quando absens ab eis in homine illo suscepto sentiris. "Cæterum præsentia tuæ majestatis de cordibus fidelium "tuorum nunquam discedis." Et mox: "Accepit Petrus, ut "moreretur pro absente, quem desperando negaverat præsen-"tem." EMBD.

[1] Cyrillus, *In Joan.* lib. ix. cap. 14.   [m] Lib. ix. cap. 21.

Cyril saith thus: "Christian people must believe, "that although *Christ be absent from us as concerning his body,* yet by his power he governeth "us and all things, and is present with all them "that love him. Therefore he said, *Truly, truly,* "*I say unto you, wheresoever there be two or* "*three gathered together in my name, there* "*am I in the midst of them.* For like as when "he was conversant here in earth as a man, "yet then he filled heaven, and did not leave "the company of angels: even so *being now in* "*heaven with his flesh,* yet he filleth the earth, "and is in them that love him. And it is to "be marked, that although *Christ should go* "*away only as concerning his flesh,* (for he is "ever present in the power of his divinity,) *yet* "*for a little time he said he would be with his* "*disciples.*" These be the words of St. Cyril.

St Ambrose also saith[n], "That we must not seek "Christ upon earth, *nor in earth, but in heaven,* "*where he sitteth at the right hand of his Father.*"

And likewise St. Gregory[o] writeth thus: "Christ," saith he, "*is not here by the presence* "*of his flesh,* and yet he is absent no where by "the presence of his majesty."

[n] Ambrosius, *In Lucam,* lib. x. cap. 24.
[o] Gregorius in *Hom. Paschatis.*
[p] Beda in *Homil. Paschali quadam* super illis verbis: *Ecce ego vobis. cum sum.* "Ipse Deus et homo assumptus est "humanitate quam de terra susceperat, manet cum sanctis in "terra divinitate qua terram pariter implet et cœlum." Idem super illis verbis: *Modicum jam, et non videbitis me.* "Ac si "aperte diceret: Propterea me suscitatum a mortuis modico "tempore videbitis, quia non semper in terra corporaliter mansu- "rus, sed per humilitatem quam assumpsi, jam sum ascensurus

What subtlety thinkest thou, good reader, can the papists now imagine, to defend their pernicious error, that Christ in his human nature is bodily here in earth, in the consecrated bread and wine; seeing that all the old Church of Christ believed the contrary, and all the old authors wrote the contrary.

For they all affirmed and believed that Christ being one person, hath nevertheless in him two natures or substances, that is to say, the nature of his Godhead, and the nature of his manhood. They say furthermore, that Christ is both gone hence from us unto heaven, and is also here with us in earth, but not in his human nature, as the papists would have us to believe; but the old authors say, that he is in heaven, as concerning his manhood, and nevertheless both here, and there, and everywhere, as concerning his Godhead. For although his Divinity be such that it is infinite, without measure, compass, or place : so that, as concerning that nature, he is circumscribed with no place, but is everywhere, and filleth all the world; yet, as concerning his human nature, he hath measure, compass, and place; so that when he was here upon earth, he was not at the same time in heaven; and now that he is ascended into heaven, as concerning that nature he hath now forsaken the earth, and is only in heaven.

"in cœlum." Idem in *Homil. in Vigilia Pentecostes:* "Ille
"post resurrectionem ascendens in cœlum, eos corporaliter de-
"seruit, quibus tamen divinæ præsentia majestatis nunquam
"defuit, ideo recte de hoc paracleto subjunxit: Ut maneat vo-
"biscum in æternum." EMBD. [This quotation from Bede is not in the Parker's Society edition.—C.H.H.W.]

For one nature that is circumscribed, compassed, and measured, cannot be in divers places at one time. This is the faith of the old catholic Church, as appeareth as well by the authors before rehearsed, as by these that hereafter follow.

St. Augustine speaking that a body must needs be in some place, saith, "That *if it be not within* "*the compass of a place, it is no where.* And if " *it be no where, then it is not*[q]."

And St. Cyril, considering the proper nature of a very body, said, "That *if the nature of the* "*Godhead were a body, it must needs be in a* "*place, and have quantity, greatness, and cir-* "*cumscription*[r]."

If then the nature of the Godhead must needs be circumscribed if it were a body, much more must the nature of Christ's manhood be circumscribed and contained within the compass of a certain place.

Didymus also[s], in his book *De Spiritu Sancto,* (which St. Hierome did translate,) proveth, that the Holy Ghost is very God, because he is in many places at one time, which no creature can be. For, saith he, *all creatures, visible and invisible, be circumscribed and environed either within one place,* (as corporal and visible things be,) *or within the property of their own substance,*

---

[q] *Ad Dardanum Epist.* 57.
[r] Cyrillus, *De Trin.* lib. ii.
[s] Didymus, *De Spiritu Sancto*, lib. i. cap. 1.

(as angels and invisible creatures be,) so that *no angel*, saith he, *can be at one time in two places.* And forasmuch as *the Holy Ghost is in many men at one time, therefore,* saith he, *the Holy Ghost must needs be God.*

The same affirmeth also St. Basil[t], "That the "angel which was with Cornelius was not at the "same time with Philip; nor the angel which "spake to Zachary in the altar was not the same "time in his proper place in heaven. But *the "Holy Ghost was at one time in Habakkuk, and in "Daniel in Babylon, and with Jeeremy in prison, "and with Ezekiel in Chebar; whereby he proveth "that the Holy Ghost is God.*"

Wherefore the papists, which say that the body of Christ is in an infinite number of places at one time, do make his body to be God, and so confound the two natures of Christ, attributing to his human nature that thing which belongeth only to his divinity, which is a most heinous and detestable heresy.

Against whom writeth Fulgentius[u] in this wise, speaking of the distinction and diversity of the two natures in Christ: "One and the selfsame "Christ," saith he, "of mankind was made a man "*compassed in a place*, who of his Father is God "without measure or place. One and the self- "same person, as concerning his man's substance, "was not in heaven when he was in earth, and

---

[t] Basilius, *De Spiritu Sancto*, cap. 22.
[u] Fulgentius, *Ad Trasimundum Regem*, lib. ii.

"*forsook the earth when he ascended into heaven:* "*but as concerning his godly substance, which is* "*above all measure, he neither left heaven when* "*he came from heaven, nor he left not the earth* "*when he ascended into heaven, which may be* "*known by the most certain word of Christ him-* "*self,* who to show *the placing of his humanity,* "*said to his disciples, I ascend up to my Father* "*and your Father, to my God and your God.*

"Also when he had said of Lazarus, that he was "dead, he added, saying, *I am glad for your* "*sakes, that you may believe; for* I *was not there.*

"But to show the unmeasurable compass of his "divinity, he said to his disciples, *Behold, I am* "*with you always unto the world's end.* Now "how did he go up into heaven, but because *he is* "*a very man, contained within a place?* Or *how* "*is he present with faithful people, but because he* "*is very God, being without measure*[x]*?*"

Of these words of Fulgentius it is declared most certainly, that Christ is not here with us in earth, but by his Godhead, and that his humanity is in heaven only, and absent from us.

Yet the same is more plainly showed, (if more plainly can be spoken,) by Vigilius[y], a bishop and an holy martyr. He writeth thus against the

[x] Et lib. iii. "Idem atque inseparabilis Christus secundum "solam carnem de sepulchro surrexit, secundum totum hominem "quem accepit, terram localiter deserens, ad cœlum ascendit et "in dextris Dei sedet: secundum eundem totum hominem ven- "turus est ad judicandum vivos et mortuos." EMBD.

[y] Vigilius. *Contra Eutychen,* lib. i.

heretic Eutyches, which denied the humanity of Christ, holding opinion that he was only God and not man. Whose error Vigilius confuting, proveth that Christ had in him two natures joined together in one person, the nature of his Godhead and the nature of his manhood. Thus he writeth: " Christ said to his disciples, *If you loved me, you* " *would be glad, for I go unto my Father.* And " again he said, *It is expedient for you that I go,* " *for if I go not, the Comforter shall not come to* " *you.* And yet surely the eternal word of God, " the virtue of God, the wisdom of God, was ever " with his Father and in his Father, yea even at " the same time when he was with us and in us. " For when he did mercifully dwell in this world, " he left not his habitation in heaven, for he is " every where whole with his Father equal in " Divinity, whom no place can contain, for the " Son filleth all things, and there is no place that " lacketh the presence of his Divinity. From " whence then and whither did he say that he " would go? Or how did he say that he went to " his Father, from whom doubtless he never de-" parted? But *that to go to his Father, and from* " *us, was to take from this world that nature* " *which he received of us.* Thou seest, therefore, " that it was the property of that nature to be " taken away and go from us, which in the end of " the world shall be rendered again to us, as the " angels witnessed, saying, *This Jesus, which is* " *taken from you, shall come again, like as you* "*saw him going up into heaven.* For look upon "the miracle, look upon the mystery of both the "natures. The Son of God, *as concerning his* "*humanity, went from us;* as concerning his "Divinity, he said unto us, *Behold I am with you* "*all the days unto the world's end.*"

Thus far have I rehearsed the words of Vigilius, and by and by he concludeth thus: "He is with "us, and not with us. For *those whom he left* "*and went from them, as concerning his humanity,* "those he left not nor forsook them not, as "touching his Divinity. For *as touching the* "*form of a servant, which he took away from us* "*into heavvn, he is absent from us;* but by the "form of God, which goeth not from us, he is "present with us in earth: and nevertheless both "present and absent, he is all one Christ."

Hitherto you have heard Vigilius speak, that Christ as concerning his bodily presence, and the nature of his manhood, is gone from us, taken from us, is gone up into heaven, is not with us, hath left us, hath forsaken us. But as concerning the other nature of his Deity, he is still with us; so that he is both with us, and not with us: with us in the nature of his Deity, and not with us in the nature of his humanity.

And yet more clearly doth the same Vigilius declare the same thing in another place[a], saying, "If the Word and the flesh were both of one "nature, seeing that the Word is every where,

[a] *Contra Eutychen,* lib. iv.

"why is not the flesh then everywhere? For
" *when it was in earth, then verily it was not in*
" *heaven; and now when it is in heaven, it is not*
" *surely in earth.* And it is *so sure that it is not*
" *in earth*, that as concerning it we look for him
" to come from heaven, whom, as concerning his
" eternal Word, we believe to be with us in earth.
" Therefore by your doctrine," saith Vigilius unto
Eutyches, who defended that the Divinity and
humanity in Christ was but one nature, " either
" the Word is contained in a place with his flesh,
" or else the flesh is everywhere with the Word.
" For *one nature cannot receive in itself two divers*
" *and contrary things.* But these two things be
" divers and far unlike, that is to say, to be con-
" tained in a place, and to be everywhere. There-
" fore inasmuch as the Word is everywhere,
" and the flesh is not everywhere, it appeareth
" plainly, that one Christ himself hath in him two
" natures; and that by his divine nature he is
" everywhere, and *by his human nature he is con-*
" *tained in a place;* that he is created, and hath
" no beginning; that he is subject to death, and
" cannot die. Whereof one he hath by the nature
" of his Word, whereby he is God, and the other
" he hath by the nature of his flesh, whereby the
" same God is man also. Therefore one Son of
" God, the self-same was made the Son of man, and
" he hath a beginning by the nature of his flesh,
" and no beginning by the nature of his Godhead.
" He is created by the nature of his flesh, and not

"created by the nature of his Godhead. *He is* "*comprehended in a place by the nature of his* "*flesh*, and not comprehended in a place by the "nature of his Godhead. He is inferior to angels "in the nature of his flesh, and is equal to his "Father in the nature of his Godhead. He died "by the nature of his flesh, and died not by the "nature of his Godhead. This is the faith and "catholic confession which the Apostles taught, "the martyrs did corroborate, and faithful people "keep unto this day."

All these be the sayings of Vigilius, who according to all the other authors before rehearsed, and to the faith and catholic confession of the Apostles, martyrs, and all faithful people unto his time, saith, that as concerning Christ's humanity, when he was here on earth, he was not in heaven; and now when he is in heaven, he is not in earth. For one nature cannot be both contained in a place in heaven, and be also here in earth at one time. And forasmuch as Christ is here with us in earth, and also is contained in a place in heaven, he proveth thereby, that Christ hath two natures in him, the nature of a man, whereby he is gone from us and ascended into heaven; and the nature of his Godhead, whereby he is here with us in earth. So that it is not one nature that is here with us, and that is gone from us, that is ascended into heaven and there contained, and that is permanent here with us on earth.

Wherefore the papists, which now of late years

THE PRESENCE OF CHRIST. 119

have made a new faith, that Christ's natural body is really and naturally present both with us here in earth, and sitteth at the right hand of his Father in heaven, do err in two very horrible heresies.

CHAP. VI.

The one, that they confound his two natures, his Godhead and his manhood, attributing unto his humanity that thing which appertaineth only to his Divinity, that is to say, to be in heaven and earth and in many places at one time.

The other is, that they divide and separate his human nature or his body, making of one body of Christ two bodies and two natures; one, which is in heaven, visible and palpable, having all members and proportions of a most perfect natural man: and another, which they say is in earth here with us, in every bread and wine that is consecrated, having no distinction, form, nor proportion of members: which contrarieties and diversities, as this holy martyr Vigilius saith, cannot be together in one nature.

But now seeing that it is so evident a matter, both by the express words of Scripture, and also by all the old authors of the same, that our Saviour Christ, as concerning his bodily presence, is ascended into heaven, and is not here in earth; and seeing that this hath been the true confession

CHAP. VII.

An answer to the papists, alleging for them these words, "This is my body."

of the catholic faith ever since Christ's ascension; it is now to be considered, what moved the papists to make a new and contrary faith, and what Scriptures they have for their purpose. What moved them I know not, but their own iniquity, or the nature and condition of the see of Rome, which is of all other most contrary to Christ, and therefore most worthy to be called the see of Antichrist. And as for Scripture, they alledge none but only one, and that not truly understanded; but, to serve their purpose, wrested out of tune, whereby they make it to jar, and sound contrary to all other Scriptures pertaining to that matter.

The argument of the papists Christ took bread, say they, blessed and brake it, and gave it to his disciples, saying, *This is my body*. These words they ever still repeat and beat upon, that Christ said, *This is my body*. And this saying they make their sheet-anchor, to prove thereby as well the real and natural presence of Christ's body in the sacrament, as their imagined transubstantiation. For these words of Christ, say they, be most plain and most true. Then forasmuch as he said, *This is my body*, it must needs be true, that that thing which the priest holdeth in his hands is Christ's body. And if it be Christ's body, then can it not be bread; whereof they gather by their reasoning, that there is Christ's body really present, and no bread.

The answer. Now forasmuch as all their proof hangeth only

THE PRESENCE OF CHRIST.

upon these words, *This is my body,* the true sense and meaning of these words must be examined. But, say they, what need they any examination? What words can be more plain than to say, *This is my body?*

Truth it is indeed, that the words be as plain as may be spoken; but that the sense is not so plain, it is manifest to every man that weigheth substantially the circumstances of the place. For when Christ gave bread to his disciples, and said, *This is my body,* there is no man of any discretion, that understandeth the English tongue, but he may well know by the order of the speech, that Christ spake those words of the bread, calling it his body, as all the old authors also do affirm, although some of the papists deny the same. Wherefore this sentence cannot mean as the words seem and purport, but there must needs be some figure or mystery in this speech, more than appeareth in the plain words. For by this manner of speech plainly understand without any figure as the words lie, can be gathered none other sense, but that bread is Christ's body, and that Christ's body is bread, which all Christian ears do abhor to hear. Wherefore in these words must needs be sought out another sense and meaning than the words of themselves do bear[b].

Marginal notes: CHAP. VII. — The interpretation of these words, 'This is my body.'

[b] Hilarius, *De Trin.* lib. iv. "Intelligentia dictorum ex "causis est assumenda dicendi: quia non sermoni res, sed "rei est sermo subjectus." Et lib. ix. "Dictorum intelligen- "tia, aut ex præpositis aut ex sequentibus est expectanda." EMBD.

BOOK III.
CHAP. VIII.
Christ called bread his body, and wine his blood.

And although the true sense and understanding of these words be sufficiently declared before, when I spake of transubstantiation; yet to make the matter so plain that no scruple or doubt shall remain, here is occasion given more fully to intreat thereof. In which process shall be showed that these sentences of Christ, *This is my body, This is my blood*, be figurative speeches. And although it be manifest enough by the plain words of the Gospel, and proved before in the process of transubstantiation, that Christ spake of bread when he said, *This is my body;* likewise that it was very wine which he called his blood; yet lest the papists should say that we suck this out of our own fingers, the same shall be proved, by testimony of the old authors, to be the true and old faith of the catholic Church. Whereas the school authors and papists shall not be able to show so much as one word of any ancient author to the contrary[c].

[c] Ac primum Clemens in *Pædagogo*, lib. i. cap. 6. "Dominus dixit: '*Comedite carnes meas, et bibite sanguinem meum*, evidenter fidei et promissionis quod est esculentum et poculentum dicens allegorice, per quæ Ecclesia tanquam homo ex multis constans membris irrigatur et augetur."

Justin. in *Apol.* ii.. "Hoc alimentum apud nos Eucharistia dicitur, cujus participem esse nemini licet, nisi qui crediderit vera esse, quæ a nobis docentur, et lavacro regenerationis in remissione peccatorum lotus fuerit, et ad eum modum, quem Christus tradidit, vitam instituerit. Non enim ut communen panem aut communem potum, hæc accipimus, sed quemadmodum Jesus Christus Servator noster, per verbum Dei factus caro, et carnem et sanguinem nostræ salutis causa habuit, sic etiam, cibum illum, postquam per precationem verbi illius fuerit benedictus, ex quo sanguis et carnes nostræ per muta-

First, Irenæus writing against the Valentinians, in his fourth book saith, that "*Christ confessed* "*bread which is a creature, to be his body, and* "*the cup to be his blood.*" And in the same book he writeth thus also : "*The bread, wherein the* "*thanks be given, is the body of the Lord.*" And yet again in the same book[d] he saith, that "Christ "*taking bread of the same sort that our bread is* "*of,* confessed that *it was his body.*" And that "*that thing which was tempered in the chalice* "*was his blood.*"

And in the fifth book[e] he writeth further, that "*of the chalice,* which is his blood, *a man is* "*nourished, and doth grow by the bread,* which is "*his body*[f].*"

"tionem nutriuntur, edocti sumus esse carnem et sanguinem "illius Jesu qui pro nobis fuerit incarnatus. Apostoli enim in "commentariis ab eis factis (quæ dicuntur Evangelia) sic tradi- "derunt, præcepisse illis Jesum, cum accepisset panem, gratias "agentem dixisse : *Hoc facite in mei commemorationem, Hoc est* "*corpus meum, Hic est sanguis meus,* et solis ipsis impartisse." Deinde Irenæus, *Contra Valent.* lib. iv. cap. 32. " Christus "suis discipulis dans consilium, primitias Deo offerre de suis "creaturis, (non quasi indigenti, sed ut ipsi nec infructuosi nec "ingrati sint) eum qui ex creatura panis est accepit, et gratias "egit, dicens : *Hoc est corpus meum.* Et calicem similiter, qui "est ex ea creatura quæ est secundum nos, suum sanguinem con- "fessus est, et novi testamenti novam docuit oblationem." Et cap. 34 : " Panis in quo gratiæ actæ sunt, qui est a terra, perci- "piens vocationem Dei, jam non communis panis est, sed "Eucharistia, ex duabus rebus constans, terrena et cœlesti." EMBD.

[d] Irenæus, *Contra Valent.* lib. iv. cap. 57.

[e] Lib. v. cap. 2.

[f] Et *ibidem :* " Quando mixtus calix, et fractus panis, percipit "verbum Dei, fit Eucharistia corporis et sanguinis Christi ex "quibus augetur et consistit carnis nostræ substantia." EMBD.

These words of Irenæus be most plain, that Christ taking very material bread, a creature of God, and of such sort as other bread is which we do use, called that his body, when he said, *This is my body.* And the wine also which doth feed and nourish us, he called his blood.

Tertullian likewise, in his book written against the Jews[k], saith, that "*Christ called bread his body*" And in his book against Marcion, he oftentimes repeateth the selfsame words.

And St. Cyprian in the first book of his Epistles[l], saith the same thing, that "*Christ called* "*such bread as is made of many corns joined to-* "*gether, his body: and such wine he named his* "*blood, as is pressed out of many grapes,* and "made into wine."

And in his second book[m], he saith these words, "*Water is not the blood of Christ, but wine.*" And again, in the same Epistle, he saith, that "*it was wine which Christ called his blood;*" and that "*if wine be not in the chalice,* then we drink "not of the fruit of the vine." And in the same Epistle he saith, that "*meal alone, or water alone,* "*is not the body of Christ, except they be both* "*joined together to make thereof bread.*"

Epiphanius also saith[n], that "Christ, speaking "of *a loaf which is round in fashion, and cannot* "*see, hear, nor feel,* said of it, This is my body."

[k] Tertullianus, *Adversus Judæos.*
[l] Cyprianus, *Ad Magnum*, lib. i. Epist. 6.
[m] Cyprianus, *Ad Cæcilium*, lib. ii. Epist. 3.
[n] Epiphan. in *Ancorato.*

THE PRESENCE OF CHRIST.

And St. Hierome writing *Ad Hedibiam*, saith these words[o], "Let us mark, that *the bread* "*which the Lord brake* and gave to his dis- "ciples, *was the body of our Saviour Christ*, as "he said unto them, *Take and eat, this is my* "*body*[p]."

And St. Augustine also saith[q], that "although "we may set forth Christ by mouth, by writing, "and by the sacrament of his body and blood, yet "we call neither our tongue, nor words, nor ink, "letters, nor paper, the body and blood of Christ; "but *that we call the body and blood of Christ,* "*which is taken of the fruit of the earth, and con-* "*secrated by mystical prayer.*" And also he saith[r], "*Jesus called meat his body, and drink his* "*blood*[s]."

Moreover Cyril upon St. John saith[t], that "Christ gave to his disciples *pieces of bread,* "saying, *Take, eat, this is my body.*"

Likewise Theodoretus saith[u], "When Christ "gave the holy mysteries, *he called bread his*

[o] Hieron. *Ad Hedibiam.*

[p] "Et calicem illum esse de quo item locutus est, *Bibite ex* "*hoc omnes; Hic est sanguis meus novi testamenti, qui pro* "*multis effunditur, &c.* Iste est calix de quo in Propheta legi- "mus, *Calicem salutaris accipiam;* et alibi: *Calix tuus* "*inebrians quam præclarus est.*" EMBD.

[q] August. *De Trinit.* lib. iii. cap. 4.

[r] *De Verbis Apostoli,* Serm. 2.

[s] Idem, *De Trin.* lib. xii. cap. 58. "Fractum panem dis- "tribuebat dicens: *Hoc est corpus meum.*" EMBD.

[t] Cyrillus, *In Joannem.* lib. iv. cap. 14.

[u] Theodoretus in *Dialogo.* 1.

"*body*, and *the cup mixt with wine and water he called his blood*[x]."

By all these foresaid authors and places, with many mo, it is plainly proved, that when our Saviour Christ gave bread unto his disciples, saying, *Take and eat, this is my body;* and likewise when he gave them the cup, saying, *Divide this among you, and drink you all of this, for this is my blood;* he called then the very material bread his body, and the very wine his blood.

That bread, I say, that is one of the creatures here in earth among us, and that groweth out of the earth, and is made of many grains of corn beaten into flour, and mixt with water, and so baken and made into bread, of such sort as other our bread is, that hath neither sense nor reason, and finally, that feedeth and nourisheth our bodies; such bread Christ called his body, when he said, *This is my body;* and such wine as is made of grapes pressed together and thereof is made drink which nourisheth the body, such wine be called his blood.

This is the true doctrine, confirmed as well by holy Scripture, as by all ancient authors of Christ's Church, both Greeks and Latins, that is to say, that when our Saviour Christ gave bread and wine to his disciples, and spake these words, *This*

---

[x] Rabanus, lib. i. cap. 31. "Quia panis corporalis cor con-"firmat, ideo ille corpus Christi congruenter nuncupatur." "Vinum autem, quia sanguinem operatur in carne, ideo ad "sanguinem Christi refertur." EMBD.

is my body, This is my blood, it was very bread and wine which he called his body and blood.

Now let the papists show some authority for their opinion, either of Scripture, or of some ancient author. And let them not constrain all men to follow their fond devices, only because they say it is so, without any other ground or authority but their own bare words. For in such wise credit is to be given to God's word only, and not to the word of any man.

As many of them as I have read (the Bishop of Winchester only excepted) do say, that Christ called not the bread his body, nor wine his blood, when he said, *This is my body, This is my blood.* And yet in expounding these words they vary among themselves; which is a token that they be uncertain of their own doctrine.

For some of them say, that by this pronoun demonstrative, "*this,*" Christ understood not the bread nor wine, but his body and blood.

And other some say, that by the pronoun, "*this,*" he meant neither the bread nor wine, nor his body nor blood, but that he meant a particular thing uncertain, which they call *individuum vagum,* or *individuum in genere,* I trow some mathematical quiddity, they cannot tell what.

But let all these papists together show any one authority, either of Scripture, or of ancient author, either Greek or Latin, that saith as they say, that Christ called not bread and wine his body and blood, but *individuum vagum;* and for my part I shall give them place, and confess that they say true.

And if they can show nothing for them of antiquity, but only their own bare words, then it is reason that they give place to the truth confirmed by so many authorities, both of Scripture and of ancient writers, which is, that Christ called very material bread his body, and very wine made of grapes his blood.

CHAP. IX.
"Bread is my body." "Wine is my blood," be figurative speeches.

Now this being fully proved, it must needs follow consequently, that this manner of speaking is a figurative speech : for in plain and proper speech it is not true to say, that bread is Christ's body, or wine his blood. For Christ's body hath a soul, life, sense, and reason : but bread hath neither soul, life, sense, nor reason.

Likewise in plain speech it is not true, that we eat Christ's body, and drink his blood. For eating and drinking, in their proper and usual signification, is with the tongue, teeth, and lips to swallow, divide, and chaw in pieces : which thing to do to the flesh and blood of Christ, is horrible to be heard of any Christian.

THE PRESENCE OF CHRIST. 129

So that these speeches, "To eat Christ's body," "and drink his blood," "To call bread his body," "or wine his blood," be speeches not taken in the proper signification of every word, but by translation of these words, "*eating*" and "*drinking*," from the signification of a corporal thing to signify a spiritual thing; and by calling a thing that signifieth, by the name of the thing which is signified thereby: which is no rare nor strange thing, but an usual manner and phrase in common speech. And yet lest this fault should be imputed unto us, that we do feign things of our own heads without authority, (as the papists be accustomed to do,) here shall be cited sufficient authority, as well of Scripture as of old ancient authors, to approve the same.

CHAP. X.

"To eat Christ's flesh, and drink his blood," be figurative speeches.

First, when our Saviour Christ, in the sixth of John, said, *That he was the bread of life, the which whosoever did eat, should not die, but live for ever; and that the bread which he would give us was his flesh; and, therefore, whosoever should eat his flesh, and drink his blood, should have everlasting life; and they that should not eat his flesh and drink his blood, should not have everlasting life:* when Christ had spoken these words with many mo of the eating of his flesh and drinking of his blood, both the Jews, and many also of his disciples, were offended with his words, and said, *This is an hard saying: for how can he give us his flesh to be eaten?* Christ perceiving their murmuring hearts, (because they knew none

John vi.

other eating of his flesh, but by chawing [chewing] and swallowing,) to declare that they should not eat his body after that sort, nor that he meant of any such carnal eating, he said thus unto them, *What if you see the Son of man ascend up where he was before? It is the spirit that giveth life, the flesh availeth nothing. The words which I spake unto you, be spirit and life.*

These words our Saviour Christ spake, to lift up their minds from earth to heaven, and from carnal to spiritual eating, that they should not phantasy that they should with their teeth eat him present here in earth, for his flesh so eaten, saith he, should nothing profit them. And yet so they should not eat him, for he would take his body away from them, and ascend with it into heaven; and there by faith and not with teeth, they should spiritually eat him, sitting at the right hand of his Father. And therefore saith he, *The words which I do speak be spirit and life:* that is to say, are not to be understand, that we shall eat Christ with our teeth grossly and carnally, but that we shall spiritually and ghostly with our faith eat him, being carnally absent from us in heaven; and in such wise as Abraham and other holy fathers did eat him, many years before he was incarnated and born. As St. Paul saith, that *they all did eat the same spiritual meat that we do, and drank the same spiritual drink, that is to say, Christ.* For they spiritually by their faith were fed and nourished with Christ's body and blood, and had eternal life by him, before he was born, as we have now, that come after his ascension.

Thus have you heard, by the declaration of Christ himself and of St Paul, that the eating and drinking of Christ's flesh and blood is not taken in the common signification, with mouth and teeth to eat and chaw [chew] a thing being present, but by a lively faith in heart and mind to chaw and digest a thing being absent, either ascended hence into heaven, or else not yet born upon earth.

And Origen[x], declaring the said eating of Christ's flesh and drinking of his blood, not to be understand as the words do sound, but figuratively, writeth thus upon these words of Christ, *Except you eat my flesh and drink my blood, you shall not have life in you:* "Consider," saith Origen, "that *these things,* written in God's "books, *are figures;* and therefore examine and "understand them, as spiritual and not as carnal "men. For *if you understand them as carnal* "*men, they hurt you, and feed you not.* For even "in the Gospels is there found letter that killeth; "and not only in the Old Testament, but also in "the New, is there found letter that slayeth him "that doth not spiritually understand that which "is spoken. For *if thou follow the letter or words* "*of this that Christ said,* Except you eat my "flesh and drink my blood, *this letter killeth.*"

[x] Origen. *In Levit. Hom.* 7.

Who can more plainly express in any words, that the eating and drinking of Christ's flesh and blood are not to be taken in common signification, as the words pretend and sound, than Origen doth in this place?

And St. John Chryostome affirmeth the same, saying, [y]that "*if any man understand the words* "*of Christ carnally, he shall surely profit nothing* "*thereby.* For what mean these words, *The flesh* "*availeth nothing? He meant not of his flesh, God* "*forbid, but he meant of them that fleshly and* "*carnally understood those things that Christ* "*spake.* But what is *carnal understanding? To* "*understand the words simply as they be spoken,* "*and nothing else.* For we ought not so to "understand the things which we see, but all "mysteries must be considered with inward eyes, "*and that is spiritually to understand them.*"

In these words St. John Chrysostome showeth plainly, that the words of Christ concerning the eating of his flesh and drinking of his blood, are not to be understand simply as they be spoken, but spiritually and figuratively.

And yet most plainly of all other, St. Augustine doth declare this matter in his book *De Doctrina Christiana*[z], in which book he instructeth Christian people how they should understand those places of Scripture, which seem hard and obscure.

"Seldom," saith he, " is any difficulty in proper " words, but either the circumstance of the place,

[y] Chrysost. *In Joan. Hom.* 46.
[z] Augustinus, *De Doctrina Christ.* lib. iii. cap. 4 et 5.

THE PRESENCE OF CHRIST. 133

"or the conferring of divers translations, or else "the original tongue wherein it was written, will "make the sense plain. But in words that be "altered from their proper signification, there is "great diligence and heed to be taken. And " *specially we must beware, that we take not literally* " *any thing that is spoken figuratively*[a]. Nor con- "trariwise, we must not take for a figure, any "thing that is spoken properly. Therefore must "be declared," saith St. Augustine, "the manner " *how to discern a proper speech from a figura-* " *tive;* wherein," saith he," must be observed this "rule, that if the thing which is spoken be to "the furtherance of charity, then it is a proper "speech, and no figure. So that if it be a com- "mandment that forbiddeth any evil or wicked 'act, or commandeth any good or beneficial "thing, then it is no figure. But *if it command* " *any ill or wicked thing, or forbid any thing that* " *is good and beneficial, then it is a figurative* " *speech.* Now *this saying of Christ,* Except "you eat the flesh of the Son of man and "drink his blood, you shall have no life in you,

[a] "Et ad hoc etiam pertinet quod ait Apostolus: *Litera* "*occidit, spiritus autem vivificat.* Cum enim figurate dictum " sic accipitur, tanquam proprie dictum sit, carnaliter sapitur. " Neque ulla mors animæ congruentius appellatur, quam cum " id etiam, quod in ea bestiis antecellit (hoc est intelligentia) " carni subjicitur sequendo literam. Qui enim sequitur literam, "translata verba sicut propria tenet," &c. Et mox: "Ea " demum est miserabilis animæ servitus, signa pro rebus acci- " pere, et supra creaturam corpoream oculum mentis ad haurien- " dum æternum lumen levare non posse." August. *De Doctr. Christ.* lib. iii. cap. 5. EMBD.

CHAP. X.

134 DEFENCE, &c.

"*seemeth to command an heinous and a wicked
"thing ; therefore it is a figure*, commanding
"us to be partakers of Christ's passion, keeping
"in our minds to our great comfort and profit,
"that his flesh was crucified and wounded for us."
This is briefly the sentence of St. Augustine,
in his book *De Doctrina Christiana*.
And the like he writeth in his book *De Catechizandis Rudibus*[b], and in his book *Contra Adversarium Legis et Prophetarum*[c], and in divers
other places, which for tediousness I pass over.
For if I should rehearse all the authorities of St.
Augustine and other which make mention of this
matter, it would weary the reader too much[d].

[b] *De Catech. Rudib.* cap. 26.
[c] *Contra Advers. Legis et Prophet.* lib. ii. cap. 9.
[d] Aug. *de Catechizandis Rudibus*, cap. 26. "De Sacra-
"mento quod accepit, cum ei bene commendatum fuerit, signa-
"cula quidem rerum divinarum esse visibilia, sed res ipsas in-
"visibiles in eis honorari ; nec sic habendam esse speciem illam
"benedictione sanctificatam, quemadmodum habetur in usu
"quolibet : dicendum etiam quid significet et sermo ille quem
"audivit, quid in illo condatur, cujus illa res similitudinem
"gerit. Deinde monendus est [Catechizandus] ut si quid in
"Scripturis audiat, quod carnaliter sonat, etiamsi non intelli-
"git, credat tamen spirituale aliquid significari, quod ad
"sanctos mores futuramque vitam pertineat. Hoc autem
"breviter discet, ut quicquid audierit ex libris canonicis, quod
"ad dilectionem æternitatis et veritatis et sanctitatis, et
"ad dilectionem proximi referre non possit, figurate dictum
"vel gestum esse credat, atque ita conetnr intelligere ut ad illam
"geminam referat dilectionem."
Idem, *Contra Adversarium Legis et Prophetarum*, lib. ii.
cap. 9. "Mediatorem Dei et hominum, hominem Christum
"Jesum carnem suam nobis manducandam, bibendumque san-
"guinem dantem, fideli corde atque ore suscipimus, quamvis
"horribilius videatur humanam carnem manducare quam peri-

Wherefore to all them that by any reasonable means will be satisfied, these things before rehearsed are sufficient to prove, that the eating of Christ's flesh and drinking of his blood, is not to be understand simply and plainly, as the words do properly signify, that we do eat and drink him with our mouths; but it is a figurative speech spiritually to be understand, that we must deeply print and fruitfully believe in our hearts, that his flesh was crucified and his blood shed, for our redemption. And this our belief in him, is to eat his flesh and to drink his blood, although they be not present here with us, but be ascended into heaven. As our forefathers, before Christ's time,

"mere, et humanum sanguinem potare quam fundere. Atqui in "omnibus sanctis Scripturis secundum sanæ fidei regulam, "figuratè dictum vel factum si quid exponitur, de quibuslibet "rebus vel verbis, quæ sacris paginis continentur, expositio illa "ducatur, non aspernanter sed sapienter audiamus."

Justinus *in* 2. *Apol. ad Gentes.* "Deinde profertur illi qui "fratribus præest, panis et poculum aqua et vino mixtum, quæ "cum is acceperit, laudem et gloriam ei qui Pater est omnium "per nomen Filii et Spiritus Sancti destinat, et gratiarum "actionem, quod ab illo dignus his sit habitus, prolixe facit. "Quibus rite peractis precibus cum gratiarum actione, populus "omnis qui adest benedicit, dicens, Amen. Illud autem, "Amen, Hebraica linguâ significat, Fiat. Cum autem is qui "præest gratias egerit, et totus populus benedixerit, hi qui "apud nos vocantur Diaconi, distribuunt unicuique præsentium "ut participent de pane, in quo gratiæ actæ sunt, et de vino et "aquâ, et his qui non sunt præsentes deferunt. Atque hoc "alimentum vocatur apud nos Eucharistia," &c. ut supra cap. 8.

Bonaventura, lib. iv. dist. 9. "Manducatio primo et proprie "in corporalibus invenitur, et ab illis ad spiritualia est trans- "lata. Et ideo si volumus accipere rectam illam manduca- "tionem spiritualem, necesse habemus a propria acceptione "vocabuli nos transferre." EMBD.

BOOK III. did likewise eat his flesh and drink his blood, which was so far from them, that he was not yet then born.

CHAP. XI.

"This is my body" "This is my blood," be figurative speeches.

The same authors did say also, that when Christ called the bread his body and the wine his blood, it was no proper speech that he then used; but as all sacraments be figures of other things, and yet have the very names of the things which they do signify: so Christ, instituting the sacrament of his most precious body and blood, did use figurative speeches, calling the bread by the name of his body, because it signified his body; and the wine he called his blood, because it represented his blood.

The bread representeth Christ's body, and the wine his blood.

Tertullian[e], herein writing against Marcion, saith these words: "Christ did not reprove *bread*, "*whereby he did represent his very body.*" And in the same book he saith, that "Jesus taking "bread, and distributing it amongst his disciples, "made it his body, saying, This is my body; "*that is to say,*" saith Tertullian, "*a figure of my* "*body.* And therefore," saith Tertullian, "*Christ* "*called bread his body and wine his blood,* because "that in the Old Testament bread and wine were "figures of his body and blood."

[e] Tertullianus *Contra Marcionem* lib. i.

And St. Cyprian, the holy martyr[f], saith of this matter, that "Christ's blood *is showed* in the "wine, and the people in the water that is mixt "with the wine: so that *the mixture of the water* "*to the wine signifieth the spiritual commixtion and* "*joining of us unto Christ.*"

By which similitude Cyprian meant not that the blood of Christ is wine, or the people water; but as the water doth signify and represent the people, so doth the wine signify and represent Christ's blood: and the uniting of the water and wine together signifieth the uniting of Christian people unto Christ himself.

And the same St. Cyprian in another place[g], writing hereof, saith, that "Christ, in his last "supper, *gave to his apostles with his own hands* "*bread and wine, which he called his flesh and* "*blood;* but in the cross he gave his very body to "be wounded with the hands of the soldiers, that "the Apostles might declare to the world how "and in what manner bread and wine may be the "flesh and blood of Christ." And the manner he straightways declareth thus: that "those things "which do signify, and those things which be "signified by them, may be both called by one "name."

Here it is certain by St. Cyprian's mind, wherefore and in what wise bread is called Christ's flesh, and wine his blood; that is to say, because that

[f] Cyprianus, lib. ii. Epist. 3.
[g] *De Unctione Chrismatis.* [A spurious work.]

every thing that representeth and signifieth another thing, may be called by the name of the thing which it signifieth.

And therefore St. John Chrysostome saith[h], that "Christ ordained the table of his holy supper "for this purpose, that in that sacrament he "should daily show unto us *bread and wine for a* "*similitude of his body and blood.*"

St. Hierome likewise saith[i], upon the Gospel of Matthew, that "Christ took bread which "comforteth man's heart, that he might *represent* "thereby his very body and blood[k]."

Also St. Ambrose[l] (if the book be his that is entitled *De iis qui Mysteriis initiantur*[m]) saith, that "before the consecration another kind is "named; but after the consecration the body of "Christ *is signified.* Christ said his blood; before "the consecration it is called another thing; but, "after the consecration, *is signified* the blood of "Christ."

And in his book *De Sacramentis*[n], (if that be also his,) he writeth thus : " Thou dost receive "the sacrament for *a similitude* of the flesh and "blood of Christ ; but thou dost obtain the grace

[h] Chrysost. *In Psal.* xxii.   [i] Hieronym. *In Matt.* xxvi.

[k] " Postquam typicum Pascha fuerat impletum, et agni carnes "cum Apostolis comederat, assumit panem qui comfortat cor "hominis, et ad verum Paschæ transgreditur sacramentum, ut "quo modo in præfiguratione ejus Melchisedek summi Dei "sacerdos offerens fecerat, ipse quoque veritatem sui corporis et "sanguinis repræsentaret." EMBD.

[l] Ambros. *De iis qui Msyteriis initiantur,* cap. ult.
[m] [See note, p. 326.]   [n] *De Sacramentis,* lib. vi. cap. 1.

THE PRESENCE OF CHRIST.

"and virtue of his true nature; and, receiving the
"bread, in that food thou art partaker of his godly
"substance." And in the same book[o] he saith,
"As thou hast in baptism received *the similitude*
"*of death*, so likewise dost thou in this sacrament
"drink *the similitude of Christ's precious blood*[p]."
And again he saith in the said book[q], "The priest
"saith, Make unto us this oblation to be accept-
"able, which is *the figure of the body and blood of*
"*our Lord Jesu Christ.*"

And upon the Epistle of St. Paul to the Co- rinthians, he saith, that "in eating and drinking
"the bread and wine, we do *signify* the flesh and
"blood which were offered for us. And the Old
"Testament," he saith, "was instituted in blood,
"because that blood was a witness of God's benefit;
"*in signification and figure whereof, we take the*
"*mystical cup of his blood*, to the tuition of our
"body and soul."

Of these places of St. Chrysostome, St. Hierome,
and St. Ambrose, it is clear, that in the sacramental bread and wine, is not really and corporally
the very natural substance of the flesh and blood
of Christ, but that the bread and wine be similitudes, mysteries, and representations, significations,
sacraments, figures and signs of his body and
blood; and therefore be called and have the name
of his very flesh and blood.

Marginal: CHAP. XI. — 1 Cor. xi. — Signs and figures have the names of the things which they signify.

[o] *De Sacramentis*, lib. iv. cap. 4.

[p] "Ut nullus horror cruoris sit; et pretium tamen operetur redemptionis." EMBD.

[q] *De Sacramentis*, lib. iv. cap. 5.

And yet St. Augustine showeth this matter more clearly and fully than any of the rest, especially in an epistle which he wrote *Ad Bonifacium*[r], where he saith, that "a day or two "before Good Friday, we use in common speech "to say thus: To-morrow, or this day two days, "Christ suffered his passion: where in very deed "he never suffered his passion but once, and that "was many years passed. Likewise upon Easter-"day we say, This day Christ rose from death, "where in very deed it is many hundred years "sithence he rose from death. Why then do not "men reprove us as liars, when we speak in this "sort, but because we call these days so, by a "similitude of those days wherein these things "were done in deed? And so it is called that "day, which is not that day in deed, but by the "course of the year it is a like day, and such "things be said to be done that day, for the "solemn celebration of the sacrament, which "things in deed were not done that day, but "long before. Was Christ offered any more but "once? And he offered himself, and yet in a "sacrament or representation, not only every "solemn feast of Easter, but every day, he is "offered to the people; so that he doth not lie "that saith, He is every day offered. For if "sacraments had not some similitude or likeness "of those things whereof they be sacraments, "they could in no wise be sacraments. And for

[r] August. *Ad Bonifacium*, Epist. 23.

"their similitude and likeness, commonly they
" have the name of the things whereof they be
" sacraments. Therefore, as *after a certain man-*
"*ner of speech, the sacrament of Christ's body is*
" *Christ's body, the sacrament of Christ's blood is*
" *Christ's blood :* so likewise the sacrament of faith
" is faith. And to believe is nothing else but to
" have faith : and therefore, when we answer for
" young children in their baptism, that they
" believe which have not yet the mind to believe,
" we answer that they have faith, because they
" have the sacrament of faith. And we say also,
" that they turn unto God, because of the sacra-
" ment of conversion unto God ; for that answer
" pertaineth to the celebration of the sacrament.
" And likewise speaketh the Apostle of baptism,
" saying, that *by baptism we be buried with him*
" *into death :* he saith not, that ' we signify
" burial ;' but he saith plainly, that ' we be buried.'
" So that the sacrament of so great a thing is not
" called but by the name of the thing itself."

Hitherto I have rehearsed the answer of St. Augustine unto Boniface, a learned bishop, who asked of him, how the parents and friends could answer for a young babe in baptism, and say in his person, that he believeth and converteth unto God, when the child can neither do nor think any such thing.

Whereunto the answer of St. Augustine is this : that forasmuch as baptism is the sacrament of the profession of our faith, and of our conversion unto God, it becometh us so to answer for young children coming thereunto, as to that sacrament appertaineth, although the children indeed have no knowledge of such things.

And yet in our said answers we ought not to be reprehended as vain men or liars; forasmuch as in common speech we use daily to call sacraments and figures by the names of the things that be signified by them, although they be not the same thing indeed. As every Good Friday, as often as it returneth from year to year, we call it the day of Christ's passion; and every Easter-day we call the day of his resurrection; and every day in the year we say that Christ is offered, and the sacrament of his body, we call it his body, and the sacrament of his blood, we call it his blood; and our baptism St. Paul calleth our burial with Christ. And yet in very deed Christ never suffered but once, never arose but once, never was offered but once; nor in very deed in baptism we be not buried, nor the sacrament of Christ's body is not his body, nor the sacrament of his blood is not his blood. But so they be called, because they be figures, sacraments, and representations of the things themselves which they signify, and whereof they bear the names.

Thus doth St. Augustine most plainly open this matter in his Epistle to Bonifacius.

Of this manner of speech, (wherein a sign is called by the name of the thing which it signifieth,) speaketh St. Augustine also right largely in his questions *Super Leviticum,* and *Contra Adamantium,* declaring how blood in Scripture is called the soul. "*A thing which signifieth,*" saith he[s], "*is wont to be called by the name of the thing which it signifieth,* as it is written in the Scripture : *The seven ears be seven years,* the Scripture saith not signifieth seven years ; and *seven kine be seven years,* and many other like. And so said Paul, that *the stone* was *Christ* and not that it signified Christ ; but even as it had been he in deed, which nevertheless *was not Christ by substance, but by signification.* Even so," saith St. Augustine, "because the blood signifieth and representeth the soul, therefore in a sacrament or signification it is called the soul."

CHAP. XI.

Gen. xli.

1 Cor. x.

And *Contra Adamantium*[t], he writeth much like, saying, "In such wise is blood the soul, as *the stone was Christ* ; and yet *the Apostle saith not, that the stone signified Christ, but saith it was Christ.* And this sentence, *blood is the soul,* may be understood to be spoken in a sign or figure. For *Christ did not stick to say,* This is my body, *when he gave the sign of his body.*"

Here St. Augustine rehearsing divers sentences, which were spoken figuratively, that is to say, when one thing was called by the name of another, and yet was not the other in substance, but in signification ; as, The blood is the soul,

[s] *Super Lev.* quest. 57.
[t] *Contra Adamantium,* cap. 12.

Seven kine be seven years, Seven ears be seven years, The stone was Christ; among such manner of speeches, he rehearseth those words which Christ spake at his last supper, *This is my body:* which declareth plainly St. Augustine's mind that Christ spake those words figuratively, not meaning that the bread was his body by substance, but by signification.

And therefore St. Augustine saith, *Contra Maximinum*[u], that "in sacraments we must not "consider what they be, but what they signify. "For they be signs of things, being one thing, "and signifying another." Which he doth show specially of this sacrament, saying, "*The heavenly* "*bread, which is Christ's flesh, by some manner of* "*speech is called Christ's body, when in very deed* "*it is the sacrament of his body.* And that offer-"ing of the flesh, which is done by the priest's "hands, is called Christ's passion, death, and "crucifying, not in very deed, but in a mystical "signification[x]."

[u] *Contra Maximinum,* lib. iii. cap. 22.
[x] *In Lib. Sententiarum Prosperi. De Consecr.* dist. 2. "Hoc est." [See p. 328. note.]
Gloss. ibidem. " Cœlestis panis, id est, cœleste sacramentum, "quod vere repræsentat Christi carnem, dicitur corpus Christi, "sed improprie: unde dicitur suo modo, sed non rei veritate, "sed significante mysterio. Ut sit sensus, vocatur Christi corpus, "id est, significatur."
Aug. *in Psalm.* 3. "Dominus Judam adhibuit in convivium, "in quo corporis et sanguinis sui figuram discipulis com-"mendavit et tradidit."
Idem, *Contra Faustum,* lib. xx. cap. 21. "Nostri sacrificii

THE PRESENCE OF CHRIST.

And to this purpose it is both pleasant, comfortable, and profitable, to read Theodoretus in his Dialogues[y], where he disputeth and showeth at length, how the names of things be changed in Scripture, and yet the things remain still. And for example he proveth, that the flesh of Christ is in the Scripture sometime called a veil of covering, sometime a cloth, sometimes a vestment, and sometime a stole: and the blood of the grape is called Christ's blood, and the names of bread and wine, and of his flesh and blood, Christ doth so change, that sometime he calleth his body corn or bread; and sometime contrary, he calleth bread his body. And likewise his blood sometime he calleth wine, and sometime contrary, he calleth wine his blood.

For the more plain understanding whereof, it shall not be amiss to recite his own sayings in his foresaid Dialogues, touching this matter of the holy sacrament of Christ's flesh and blood. The speakers in these Dialogues be *Orthodoxus* the right believer, and *Eranistes* his companion, but not understanding the right faith.

Orthodoxus saith to his companion[z], "Dost thou not know that God *calleth bread his flesh?*

"*Eranistes.* I know that.

"caro et sanguis ante adventum Christi per victimas similitudinum promittebatur, in passione Christi per ipsam veritatem reddebatur, post ascensum Christi per sacramentum memoriæ celebratur." EMBD.

[y] Theodoret. in *Dialogis*.   [z] In the first Dialogue.

"*Orthodoxus.* And in another place he *calleth* "*his body corn?*

"*Eran.* I know that also; for I have heard "him say, *The hour is come that the Son of man* "*shall be glorified;* and, *Except the grain of corn* "*that falleth in the ground die, it remaineth sole;* "*but if it die, then it bringeth forth much* "*fruit.*

"*Orth.* When he gave the mysteries or sacra-"ments, *he called bread his body; and that which* "*was mixt in the cup, he called blood.*

"*Eran.* So he called them.

"*Orth.* But that also which was his natural "body, may well be called his body; and his very "blood also, may be called his blood.

"*Eran.* It is plain.

"*Orth. But our Saviour without doubt changed* "*the names, and gave to the body the name of the* "*sign or token, and to the token he gave the name* "*of the body.* And so when he called himself a. "vine, he called blood that which was the token "of blood.

"*Eran.* Surely thou hast spoken the truth; but "I would know *the cause wherefore the names* "*were changed.*

"*Orth.* The cause is manifest to them that be "expert in true religion. *For he would that they* "*which be partakers of the godly sacraments,* "*should not set their minds upon the nature of the* "*things which they see, but by the changing of the* "*names, should believe the things which be wrought*

THE PRESENCE OF CHRIST.

"*in them by grace.* For he that called that which "*is his natural body corn and bread, and also called* "*himself a vine, he did honour the visible tokens* "*and signs with the names of his body and blood,* "*not changing the nature, but adding grace to* "*nature.*

CHAP. XI.
John xii.
Matt. xxvi.
John xv.

"*Eran.* Sacraments be spoken of sacramentally, "and also by them be manifestly declared things "which all men know not.

"*Orth.* Seeing then that it is certain that the "Patriarch called the Lord's body *a vestment and* "*apparel,* and that now we be entered to speak of "godly sacraments, tell me truly of what thing "thinkest thou *this holy meat to be a token and* "*figure?* Of Christ's Divinity, or of his body "and blood?

Gen. xlvi.

"*Eran.* It is clear that it is the figure of those "things whereof it beareth the name.

"*Orth.* Meanest thou of his body and blood?

"*Eran.* Even so I mean.

"*Orth.* Thou hast spoken as one that loveth "the truth; for the Lord, *when he took the token* "*or sign, he said not, This is my Divinity, but,* "*This is my body, and, This is my blood.* And "in another place, *The bread which I will give is* "*my flesh, which I will give for the life of the* "*world.*

John vi.

"*Eran.* These things be true, for they be God's "words[z]."

[z] "*Ortho.* Porro si sunt vera, corpus utique habebat Dominus.
"*Eran.* Et ego incorporeum illum esse dico.
"*Ortho.* Sed fateris illum habuisse corpus." EMBD.

All this writeth Theodoretus in his first Dialogue.

And in the second he writeth the same in effect, and yet in some things more plainly, against such heretics as affirmed, that after Christ's resurrection and ascension his humanity was changed from the very nature of a man, and turned into his divinity. Against whom thus he writeth.

"*Orth.* Corruption, health, sickness, and death, "be accidents; for they go and come.

"*Eran.* It is meet they be so called.

"*Orth.* Men's bodies after their resurrection be "delivered from corruption, death, and mortality, "and yet they lose not their proper nature.

"*Eran.* Truth it is.

Christ's body glorified hath his form, bigness, and quantity.

"*Orth. The body of Christ* therefore did rise "quite clean from all corruption and death, and is "impassible, immortal, *glorified* with the glory of "God, and is honoured of the powers of heaven; "and yet *it is a body, and hath the same bigness* "*that it had before.*

"*Eran.* Thy sayings seem true and according "to reason; but after he was ascended up into "heaven, I think thou wilt not say, that his body "was not turned into the nature of the Godhead.

"*Orth.* I would not so say for the persuasion of "man's reason; nor *I am not so arrogant and* "*presumptuous to affirm any thing which Scripture* "*passeth over in silence;* but I have heard St. "Paul cry, that *God hath ordained a day, when* "*he will judge all the world in justice by that man* "*which he appointed before, performing his* "*promise to all men, and raising him from death.* "I have learned also of the holy angels, that he "will come after that fashion, as his disciples saw "him go to heaven. *But they saw a nature of a* "*certain bigness, not a nature which had no big-* "*ness.* I heard furthermore the Lord say, *You* "*shall see the Son of man come in the clouds of* "*heaven.* And I know that every thing that men "see hath a certain bigness. *For that nature that* "*hath no bigness cannot be seen.* Moreover to *sit* "in the throne of glory, and to set the lambs upon "his *right hand*, and the goats upon his *left hand*, "signifieth a thing that hath quantity and bigness."

Hitherto have I rehearsed Theodoretus' words, and shortly after *Eranistes* saith:

" *Eran.* We must turn every stone, (as the "proverb saith,) to seek out the truth, but specially "when godly matters be propounded.

" *Orth.* Tell me then, *the sacramental signs*, "which be offered to God by his priests, *whereof* "*be they signs, sayest thou?*

" *Eran.* Of the Lord's body and blood.

" *Orth.* Of a very body, or not of a very body?

" *Eran.* Of a very body.

" *Orth.* Very well, for an image must be made "after a true pattern; for painters follow nature, "and paint the images of such things as we see "with our eyes.

" *Eran.* Truth it is.

" *Orth.* If therefore the godly sacraments *repre-*

"*sent* a true body, then is the Lord's body yet still
"a body, not converted into the nature of his
"Godhead, but replenished with God's glory.

"*Eran.* It cometh in good time that thou
"makest mention of God's sacraments; for by the
"same I shall prove, that Christ's body is turned
"into another nature. Answer, therefore, unto
"my questions.

"*Orth.* I shall answer.

"*Eran.* What callest thou that which is offered,
"before the invocation of the priest?

"*Orth.* We must not speak plainly, for it is
"like that some be present which have not pro-
"fessed Christ.

"*Eran.* Answer covertly.

"*Orth. It is a nourishment made of seeds that
"be like.*

"*Eran.* Then how call we the other sign?

"*Orth.* It is also a common name, that signi-
"fieth *a kind of drink.*

"*Eran.* But *how dost thou call them after the
"sanctification?*

"*Orth. The body of Christ, and the blood of
"Christ.*

"*Eran.* And dost thou believe that thou art
"made partaker of Christ's body and blood?·

"*Orth.* I believe so.

"*Eran.* Therefore *as the tokens of God's body
"and blood* be other things before the priest's
"invocation, but *after the invocation they be
"changed,* and be other things: *so also the body*

THE PRESENCE OF CHRIST.

"*of Christ, after his assumption, is changed into*
"*his divine substance.*

"*Orth.* Thou art taken with thine own net.
"For *the sacramental signs go not from their own*
"*nature after the sanctification, but continue in*
"*their former substance, form, and figure, and*
"*may be seen and touched as well as before; yet*
"*in our minds we do consider what they be made,*
"*and do repute and esteem them, and have them*
"*in reverence, according to the same things that*
"*they be taken for.* Therefore compare the images
"to the pattern, and thou shalt see them like.
"For a figure must be like to the thing itself.
"For *Christ's body hath his former fashion,*
"*figure, and bigness;* and, to speak at one word,
"the same substance of his body. But after his
"resurrection, it was made immortal, and of such
"power, that no corruption nor death could come
"unto it; and it was exalted to that dignity, that
"it was set at the right hand of the Father, and
"honoured of all creatures, as the body of him
"that is the Lord of nature.

"*Eran.* But *the sacramental token changeth his*
"*former name;* for it is no more called as it was
"before, but *is called Christ's body.* Therefore
"must his body, after his ascension, be called God,
"and not a body.

"*Orth.* Thou seemest to me ignorant; for *it is*
"*not called his body only, but also the bread of life,*
"as the Lord called it. So the body of Christ we
"call a godly body, a body that giveth life, God's

"body, the Lord's body, our Master's body, mean-
"ing that it is not a common body, as other men's
"bodies be, but that it is the body of our Lord
"Jesu Christ, both God and man[a]."

This have I rehearsed of the great clerk and holy bishop Theodoretus, whom some of the papists perceiving to make so plainly against them have defamed, saying that he was infected with the error of Nestorius.

Not flattering to the papists

Here the papists show their old accustomed nature and condition, which is, even in a manifest manner, rather to lie without shame, than to give place unto the truth, and confess their own error. And although his adversaries falsely bruited such a fame against him when he was yet alive, nevertheless he was purged thereof by the holy council of Calcedon, about eleven hundred years ago[b].

And furthermore, in his book which he wrote against heresies he specially condemneth Nestorius by name. And also all his three books of his Dialogues, before rehearsed, he wrote chiefly against Nestorius, and was never herein noted of error this thousand year, but hath ever been reputed and taken for a holy bishop, a great learned man, and a grave author, until now at this present time, when the papists have nothing to answer unto him, they begin in excusing of themselves to defame him.

[a] *Jesus enim Christus heri et hodie, ille ipse et in æternum.* EMBD.
[b] Quem Leo primus (Epist. 61.) "charissimum fratrem" appellat. EMBD.

THE PRESENCE OF CHRIST.

Thus much have I spoken for Theodoretus, which I pray thee be not weary to read, good reader, but often and with delectation, deliberation, and good advertisement to read. For it containeth plainly and briefly the true instruction of a Christian man, concerning the matter which in this book we treat upon.

First, that our Saviour Christ in his last supper, when he gave bread and wine to his Apostles, saying, *This is my body, This is my blood*, it was bread which he called his body, and wine mixed in the cup which he called his blood: so that he changed the names of the bread and wine, which were the mysteries, sacraments, signs, figures, and tokens of Christ's flesh and blood, and called them by the names of the things which they did represent and signify, that is to say, the bread he called by the name of his very flesh, and the wine by the name of his blood.

Second, that although the names of bread and wine were changed after sanctification, yet nevertheless the things themselves remained the selfsame that they were before the sanctification, that is to say, the same bread and wine in nature, substance, form, and fashion.

The third, seeing that the substance of the bread and wine be not changed, why be then their names changed, and the bread called Christ's flesh, and the wine his blood? Theodoretus showeth, that the cause thereof was this, that we should not have so much respect to the bread and wine,

CHAP. XI.

Five principal things to be noted in Theodoretus.

After consecration.

which we see with our eyes and taste with our mouths, as we should have to Christ himself, in whom we believe with our hearts, and feel and taste him by our faith, and with whose flesh and blood, by his grace, we believe that we be spiritually fed and nourished.

These things we ought to remember and revolve in our minds, and to lift up our hearts from the bread and wine unto Christ that sitteth above. And because we should so do, therefore after the consecration they be no more called bread and wine, but the body and blood of Christ.

The fourth. It is in these sacraments of bread and wine, as it is in the very body of Christ. For as the body of Christ before his resurrection and after, is all one in nature, substance, bigness, form, and fashion, and yet it is not called as another common body, but with addition, for the dignity of his exaltation, it is called a heavenly, a godly, an immortal, and the Lord's body : so likewise the bread and wine, before the consecration and after, is all one in nature, substance, bigness, form, and fashion, and yet it is not called as other common bread, but for the dignity whereunto it is taken, it is called with addition, heavenly bread, the bread of life, and the bread of thanksgiving.

Papists. The fifth, that no man ought to be so arrogant and presumptuous to affirm for a certain truth in religion, any thing which is not spoken of in holy Scripture. And this is spoken to the great and utter condemnation of the papists, which make and unmake new articles of our faith from time to time, at their pleasure, without any Scripture at all, yea quite and clean contrary to Scripture. And yet will they have all men bound to believe whatsoever they invent, upon peril of damnation and everlasting fire.

And they would constrain with fire and fagot all men to consent, contrary to the manifest words of God, to these their errors in this matter of the holy sacrament of Christ's body and blood.

First, that there remaineth no bread nor wine after the consecration, but that Christ's flesh and blood is made of them.

Papists view of Christ in the sacrament.

Second, that Christ's body is really, corporally, substantially, sensibly, and naturally in the bread and wine.

Thirdly, that wicked persons do eat and drink Christ's very body and blood.

Fourthly, that priests offer Christ every day, and make of him a new sacrifice propitiatory for sin.

Thus, for shortness of time, I do make an end of Theodoretus, with other old ancient writers, which do most clearly affirm, that "to eat Christ's body," and "to drink his blood," be figurative speeches. And so be these sentences likewise, which Christ spake at his supper, *This is my body, This is my blood.*

And marvel not, good reader, that Christ at that time spake in figures, when he did institute that sacrament, seeing that it is the nature of all sacraments to be figures. And although the Scripture be full of schemes, tropes, and figures, yet specially it useth them when it speaketh of sacraments.

When the ark, which represented God's majesty, was come into the army of the Israelites, the Philistines said, that *God was come into the army.* And God himself said by his prophet Nathan, that *from the time that he had brought the children of Israel out of Egypt, he dwelled not in houses, but that he was carried about in tents and tabernacles.* And yet was not God himself so carried about, or went in tents or tabernacles, but because the ark, which was a figure of God, was so removed from place to place, he spake of himself that thing, which was to be understand of the ark.

And Christ himself oftentimes spake in similitudes, parables and figures, as when he said, *The field is the world, the enemy is the Devil, the seed is the word of God.— John is Elias.— I am a vine, and you be the branches.— I am bread of life.— My father is an husbandman, and he hath his fan in his hand, and will make clean his floor, and gather the wheat into his barn; but the chaff he will cast into everlasting fire.— I have a meat to eat which you know not. — Work not meat that perisheth, but that endureth unto everlasting life.— I am a good shepherd. – The Son of man will set*

THE PRESENCE OF CHRIST. 157

the sheep at his right hand, and the goats at his CHAP. XII.
left hand.—I am a door.—One of you is the Devil.
Whosoever doeth my Father's will, he is my brother, John vi.
sister, and mother. And when he said to his Matt. xii.
John xix.
mother and John, *This is thy son, this is thy mother.*

These, with an infinite number of like sentences, Christ spake in parables, metaphors, tropes, and figures. But chiefly when he spake of the sacraments, he used figurative speeches.

As when of baptism he said, that *we must be* Acts i. *baptized with the Holy Ghost;* meaning of spiritual baptism. And like speech used St. John the Baptist, saying of Christ, that *he should baptize* Matt. iii. *with the Holy Ghost and fire.* And Christ said, John iii. that *we must be born again, or else we cannot see* John iv. *the kingdom of God.* And said also, *Whosoever shall drink of that water which I shall give him, he shall never be dry again. But the water which I shall give him, shall be made within him a well, which shall spring into everlasting life.*

And St. Paul saith, that *in baptism we clothe* Rom. vi. *us with Christ, and be buried with him.* This Gal. iii. baptism and washing by the fire and the Holy Ghost, this new birth, this water that springeth in a man and floweth into everlasting life, cannot be understand of any material baptism, material washing, material birth, clothing, and burial, but by translation of things, visible into things invisible, they must be understand spiritually and figuratively.

After the same sort the mystery of our redemption, and the passion of our Saviour Christ upon the cross, as well in the New as the Old Testament, is expressed and declared by many figures and figurative speeches.

The Paschal lamb. As the pure Paschal lamb without spot, signified Christ. The effusion of the lamb's blood signified the effusion of Christ's blood. And the salvation of the children of Israel from temporal death by the lamb's blood, signified our salvation from eternal death by Christ's blood. And as Almighty God, passing through Egypt, killed all the Egyptians' heirs in every house, and left not one alive; and nevertheless he passed by the children of Israel's houses, where he saw the lamb's blood upon the doors, and hurted none of them, but saved them all by the means of the lamb's blood: so likewise at the last judgment of the whole world, none shall be passed over and saved, but that shall be found marked with the blood of the most pure and immaculate Lamb Jesus Christ.

The Lord's Supper. And forasmuch as the shedding of that lamb's blood, was a token and figure of the shedding of Christ's blood then to come; and forasmuch also as all the sacraments and figures of the Old Testament ceased and had an end in Christ: lest by our great unkindness we should peradventure be forgetful of the great benefit of Christ, therefore at his last supper, when he took his leave of his Apostles to depart out of the world, he did make a new will and testament, wherein he

THE PRESENCE OF CHRIST.

bequeathed unto us clean remission of all our sins, and the everlasting inheritance of heaven. And the same he confirmed the next day with his own blood and death.

And lest we should forget the same, he ordained not a yearly memory, (as the Paschal lamb was eaten but once every year,) but a daily remembrance he ordained thereof in bread and wine, sanctified and dedicated to that purpose, saying, *This is my body; this cup is my blood, which is shed for the remission of sins. Do this in remembrance of me:* Admonishing us by these words, spoken at the making of his last will and testament, and at his departing out of the world, (because they should be the better remembered,) that whensoever we do eat the bread in his holy Supper, and drink of that cup, we should remember how much Christ hath done for us, and how he died for our sakes. Therefore, saith St. Paul, *As often as ye shall eat this bread and drink the cup, ye shall show forth the Lord's death until he come.*

And forasmuch as this holy bread broken, and the wine divided, do represent unto us the death of Christ now passed, as the killing of the Paschal lamb did represent the same yet to come: therefore our Saviour Christ used the same manner of speech of the bread and wine, as God before used of the Paschal lamb.

For as in the Old Testament God said, *This is the Lord's pass-by, or passover*, even so saith Christ in the New Testament, *This is my body,*

[Side notes: CHAP. XII. — Matt. xxvi. Mark xiv. — 1 Cor. xi. — Exod. xii. — Matt xxvi.]

This is my blood. But in the old mystery and sacrament, the lamb was not the Lord's very passover or passing-by, but it was a figure which represented his passing by. So likewise in the New Testament, the bread and wine be not Christ's very body and blood, but they be figures, which by Christ's institution be unto the godly receivers thereof sacraments, tokens, significations, and representations of his very flesh and blood: instructing their faith, that as the bread and wine feed them corporally, and continue this temporal life; so the very flesh and blood of Christ feedeth them spiritually, and giveth them everlasting life.

What figurative speeches were used at Christ's last supper

And why should any man think it strange to admit a figure in these speeches, *This is my body, This is my blood?* seeing that the communication the same night, by the papists' own confessions, was so full of figurative speeches? For the Apostles spake figuratively when they asked Christ where he would eat his passover or pass-by. And Christ himself used the same figure when he said, *I have much desired to eat this passover with you.*

Matt. xxvi.
Mark xiv.
Luke xxii.

Also to eat Christ's body and to drink his blood, I am sure they will not say that it is taken properly, to eat and drink as we do eat other meats and drinks.

And when Christ said, *This cup is a new testament in my blood;* here, in one sentence, be two figures, one in this word *cup*, which is not taken for the cup itself, but for the thing contained in the cup: another is in this word *testament;* for neither the cup, nor the wine contained in the cup, is Christ's testament, but is a token, sign, and figure, whereby is represented unto us his testament, confirmed by his blood.

And if the papists will say, as they say indeed, that by this cup is neither meant the cup nor the wine contained in the cup, but that thereby is meant Christ's blood contained in the cup; yet must they needs grant that there is a figure. For Christ's blood is not in proper speech the new testament, but it is the thing that confirmed the new testament. And yet by this strange interpretation the papists make a very strange speech, more strange than any figurative speech is. For this they make the sentence: This blood is a new testament in my blood. Which saying is so fond, and so far from all reason, that the foolishness thereof is evident to every man.

CHAP. XII.

Now forasmuch as it is plainly declared and manifestly proved, that Christ called bread his body, and wine his blood, and that these sentences be figurative speeches; and that Christ, as concerning his humanity and bodily presence, is ascended into heaven with his whole flesh and blood, and is not here upon earth; and that the

CHAP. XIII.

Answer to the authorities and arguments of the papists.

substance of bread and wine do remain still, and be received in the sacrament; and that although they remain, yet they have changed their names, so that the bread is called Christ's body, and the wine his blood; and that the cause why their names be changed is this, that we should lift up our hearts and minds from the things which we see unto the things which we believe, and be above in heaven, whereof the bread and wine have the names, although they be not the very same things in deed: these things well considered and weighed, all the authorities and arguments, which the papists feign to serve for their purpose, be clean wiped away.

CHAP. XIV.

One brief answer to all.

For whether the authors which they allege say, that we do eat Christ's flesh and drink his blood; or that the bread and wine is converted into the substance of his flesh and blood; or that we be turned into his flesh; or that in the Lord's Supper we do receive his very flesh and blood; or that in the bread and wine is received that which did hang upon the cross; or that Christ hath left his flesh with us; or that Christ is in us, and we in him; or that he is whole here and whole in heaven; or that the same thing is in the chalice which flowed out of his side; or that the same thing is received with our mouth which is believed with our faith;

or that the bread and wine, after the consecration, be the body and blood of Christ; or that we be nourished with the body and blood of Christ; or that Christ is both gone hence and is still here; or that Christ at his last supper bare himself in his own hands:

These and all other like sentences may not be understanded of Christ's humanity literally and carnally, as the words in common speech do properly signify: for so doth no man eat Christ's flesh, nor drink his blood; nor so is not the bread and wine turned into his flesh and blood, nor we into him; nor so is the bread and wine after the consecration his flesh and blood; nor so is not his flesh and blood whole here in earth, eaten with our mouths; nor so did not Christ take himself in his own hands.

But these and all other like sentences, which declare Christ to be here in earth, and to be eaten and drunken of Christian people, are to be understanded either of his divine nature, whereby he is every where, or else they must be understanded figuratively or spiritually. For figuratively he is in the bread and wine, and spiritually he is in them that worthily eat and drink the bread and wine; but really, carnally, and corporally he is only in heaven, from whence he shall come to judge the quick and dead.

This brief answer will suffice for all that the papists can bring for their purpose, if it be aptly applied. And for the more evidence hereof, I shall apply the same to some such places as the papists think do make most for them: that by the answer to those places, the rest may be the more easily answered unto.

CHAP. XV.

The answer to Clemens, Epistola 2.

They allege St. Clement, whose words be these, as they report: "The sacraments of God's secrets " are committed to three degrees, to a priest, a " deacon, and a minister; which with fear and " trembling ought to keep *the leavings of the* " *broken pieces of the Lord's body,* that no cor- " ruption be found in the holy place, lest by neg- " ligence great injury be done *to the portion of the* " *Lord's body.*" And by and by followeth : " *So* " *many hosts must be offered in the altar as will* " *suffice for the people* ; and if any remain, *they* " *must not be kept until the morning,* but be spent " and consumed of the clerks with fear and trem- " bling. And they that consume *the residue of* " *the Lord's body,* may not by and by take other " common meats, lest they should mix that holy " portion with the meat which is digested by the " belly, and avoided by the fundament. Therefore " if *the Lord's portion* be eaten in the morning, " the ministers that consume it must fast unto six " of the clock; and if they do take it at three or " four of the clock, the minister must fast until " the evening."

Thus much writeth Clement of this matter, if the Epistle which they allege were Clement's, as indeed it is not[a]. But they have feigned many things in other men's names, thereby to stablish their feigned purposes. Nevertheless whose soever the Epistle was, if it be thoroughly considered, it maketh much more against the papists than for their purpose. For by the same Epistle appeareth evidently three special things against the errors of the papists.

The first is, that the bread in the sacrament is called the Lord's body, and the pieces of the broken bread be called the pieces and fragments of the Lord's body, which cannot be understand but figuratively.

The second is, that the bread ought not to be reserved and hanged up, as the papists every where do use.

The third is, that the priests ought not to receive the sacrament alone, (as the papists commonly do, making a sale thereof unto the people,) but they ought to communicate with the people.

And here is diligently to be noted, that we ought not unreverently and unadvisedly to approach unto the meat of the Lord's table, as we do to other common meats and drinks, but with great fear and dread, lest we should come to that holy table unworthily, wherein is not only represented, but also spiritually given unto us, very Christ himself.

[a] [See *Answer to Gardyner,* book iii. chap. 15.]

And therefore we ought to come to that board of the Lord with all reverence, faith, love and charity, fear and dread, according to the same.

Here I pass over Ignatius[b] and Irenæus[c], which make nothing for the papists' opinions, but stand in the commendation of the holy communion, and in exhortation of all men to the often and godly receiving thereof. And yet neither they, nor no man else, can extol and commend the same sufficiently, according to the dignity thereof, if it be godly used as it ought to be.

The answer to Dionysius De Eccles. Hier. cap. 3.

Dionysius also [d], whom they allege to praise and extol this sacrament, (as indeed it is most worthy, being a sacrament of most high dignity and perfection, representing unto us our most perfect spiritual conjunction unto Christ, and our continual nourishing, feeding, comfort, and spiritual life in him,) yet he never said that the flesh and blood of Christ was in the bread and wine really, corporally, sensibly, and naturally, (as the papists would bear us in hand,) but he calleth ever the bread and wine signs, pledges, and tokens, declaring unto the faithful receivers

[b] Ignatius in *Epist. ad Ephesianos.* [See Smythe, *Assertion of the Sacrament.*]

[c] Irenæus, lib. v. *Contra Valentin.* [See p. 321 and 373; and *Answer to Gardyner,* book ii. chap. 5.]

[d] [That Dionysius the Areopagite was not the author of the works attributed to him, is now generally admitted; but the question, who *did* write them, is still undecided. The most prevailing opinion seems to be, that they were composed by an Apollinarian in the fourth century. See Cave, *Hist. Lit.* Fabricius, *Biblioth, Græc.* ed. Harles.]

of the same, that they receive Christ spiritually, and that they spiritually eat his flesh and drink his blood. And although the bread and wine be figures, signs, and tokens of Christ's flesh and blood, (as St. Dionyse calleth them both before the consecration and after,) yet the Greek annotations upon the same Dionyse do say, that the very things themselves be above in heaven.

And as the same Dionyse maketh nothing for the papists' opinions in this point of Christ's real and corporal presence, so in divers other things he maketh quite and clean against them, and that specially in three points; in transubstantiation, in reservation of the sacrament, and in the receiving of the same by the priest alone.

Furthermore, they do allege Tertullian, that he constantly affirmeth, that in the sacrament of the altar we do eat the body and drink the blood of our Saviour Christ. To whom we grant that our flesh eateth and drinketh the bread and wine, which be called the body and blood of Christ, because, as Tertullian saith, they do represent his body and blood, although they be not really the same in very deed. And we grant also, that our souls by faith do eat his very body and drink his blood; but that is, spiritually, sucking out of the same everlasting life. But we deny that unto this spiritual feeding is required any real and corporal presence.

And therefore this Tertullian speaketh nothing against the truth of our catholic doctrine, but he

The answer to Tertullianus De Resurrectione Carnis.

speaketh many things most plainly for us, and against the papists, and specially in three points. First, in that he saith that Christ called bread his body. The second, that Christ called it so, because it representeth his body. The third, in that he saith, that by these words of Christ, *This is my body,* is meant, This is a figure of my body.

The answer to Origenes In Numer. Hom. 7. Moreover they allege for them Origen, because they would seem to have many ancient authors favourers of their erroneous doctrine; which Origen is most clearly against them. For although he do say, as they allege, that those things which before were signified by obscure figures, be now truly, *in deed, and in their very nature and kind* accomplished and fulfilled; and for the declaration thereof, he bringeth forth three examples; one of the stone that floweth water, another of the sea and cloud, and the third of manna, which in the Old Testament did signify Christ to come, who is now come indeed, and is manifested and exhibited unto us, as it were, face to face and sensibly, *in his word, in the sacrament of regeneration, and in the sacraments of bread and wine;* yet Origen meant not, that Christ is corporally either in his word, or in the water of baptism, or in the bread and wine, nor that we carnally and corporally be regenerated and born again, or eat Christ's flesh and blood. For our regeneration in Christ is spiritual, and our eating and drinking is a spiritual feeding, which kind of regeneration and feeding requireth no real and corporal presence of Christ, but only his presence in spirit, grace, and effectual operation.

And that Origen thus meant, that Christ's flesh is a spiritual meat, and his blood a spiritual drink; and that the eating and drinking of his flesh and blood may not be understand literally, but spiritually; it is manifested by Origen's own words, in his seventh Homily upon the book called Leviticus, where he showeth, that those words must be understand figuratively, and whosoever understandeth them otherwise, they be deceived, and take harm by their own gross understanding[e].

And likewise meant Cyprian, in those places which the adversaries of the truth allege of him, concerning the true eating of Christ's very flesh and drinking of his blood.

The answer to Cyprianus, lib. 2. Epist. 3

For Cyprian spake of no gross and carnal eating with the mouth, but of an inward, spiritual, and pure eating with heart and mind; which is to believe in our hearts, that his flesh was rent and torn for us upon the cross, and his blood shed for our redemption, and that the same flesh and blood now sitteth at the right hand of the Father, making continual intercession for us; and to imprint and digest this in our minds, putting our whole affiance and trust in him, as touching our salvation, and offering ourselves clearly unto him, to love and serve him all the days of our life. This

Spiritual feeding.

[e] *In Levit.* Hom. 7.

is truly, sincerely, and spiritually to eat his flesh and to drink his blood.

And this sacrifice of Christ upon the cross was that oblation, which, Cyprian saith, was figured and signified, before it was done, by the wine which Noe drank, and by the bread and wine which Melchisedech gave to Abraham, and by many other figures which St. Cyprian there rehearseth.

And now when Christ is come, and hath accomplished that sacrifice, the same is figured, signified, and represented unto us by that bread and wine, which faithful people receive daily in the holy communion: wherein like as with their mouths carnally they eat the bread and drink the wine, so by their faith spiritually they eat Christ's very flesh, and drink his very blood. And hereby it appeareth that St. Cyprian clearly affirmeth the most true doctrine, and is wholly upon our side.

And against the papists he teacheth most plainly, that the communion ought to be received of all men under both kinds, and that Christ called bread his body and wine his blood, and that there is not transubstantiation, but that bread remaineth there as a figure to represent Christ's body, and wine to represent his blood; and that those which be not the lively members of Christ, do eat the bread and drink the wine, and be nourished by them, but the very flesh and blood of Christ they neither eat nor drink.

Thus have you heard declared the mind of St. Cyprian.

<small>CHAP. XV.</small>

But Hilarius, think they, is plainest for them in this matter, whose words they translate thus: "If "the Word was made verily flesh, and we verily "receive the Word being flesh in our Lord's meat, "how shall not Christ be thought to dwell naturally "*in us?* who, being born man, hath taken unto "him the nature of our flesh, that cannot be "severed, and hath put together the nature of his "flesh to the nature of his eternity, under the "sacrament of the communion of his flesh unto "us. For so we be all one, because the Father is "in Christ, and *Christ in us.* Wherefore whoso-"ever will deny the Father to be naturally in "Christ, he must deny first either himself to be "naturally in Christ, or *Christ to be naturally in* "*him.* For the being of the Father in Christ, and "*the being of Christ in us*, maketh us to be one in "them. And therefore if Christ have taken verily "the flesh of our body, and the man that was "verily born of the Virgin Mary is Christ, and "also *we receive under the* [1]*true mystery the flesh* "*of his body*, by means whereof we shall be one, "(for the Father is in Christ, and *Christ in us,*)

<small>The answer to Hilarius De Trinitate.</small>

[1] [The translation of this clause is not correct, and furnished grounds to Cranmer's adversaries at Oxford for charging him with falsifying Hilary designedly. But the error seems to have originated in his copying the citation from Gardyner's *Detection of the Devil's Sophistry*, where "*vero* sub mysterio" is read instead of "*vere* sub mysterio." See *Answer to Gardyner*, book iii. chap. 15. and *Disputation at Oxford with Chedsey.*]

"how shall that be called the unity of will, when "*the natural property, brought to pass by the* "*sacrament*, is the sacrament of unity?"

Thus doth the papists, the adversaries of God's word and of his truth, allege the authority of Hilarius, either perversely and purposely, as it seemeth, untruly citing him, and wresting his words to their purpose, or else not truly understanding him.

For although he saith that Christ is naturally in us, yet he saith also that we be naturally in him. And nevertheless in so saying, he meant not of the natural and corporal presence of the substance of Christ's body and of ours; for as our bodies be not after that sort within his body, so is not his body after that sort within our bodies; but he meant that Christ in his incarnation received of us a mortal nature, and united the same unto his Divinity, and so be we naturally in him.

And the sacraments of baptism and of his holy Supper, if we rightly use the same, do most assuredly certify us, that we be partakers of his godly nature, having given unto us by him immortality and life everlasting, and so is Christ naturally in us. And so be we one with Christ, and Christ with us, not only in will and mind, but also in very natural properties.

And so concludeth Hilarius against Arius, that Christ is one with his Father, not in purpose and will only, but also in very nature.

And as the union between Christ and us in

THE PRESENCE OF CHRIST. 173

baptism is spiritual, and requireth no real and corporal presence; so likewise our union with Christ in his holy Supper is spiritual, and therefore requireth no real and corporal presence. And therefore Hilarius, speaking there of both the sacraments, maketh no difference between our union with Christ in baptism, and our union with him in his holy Supper; and saith further, that as Christ is in us, so be we in him; which the papists cannot understand corporally and really, except they will say, that all our bodies be corporally within Christ's body. Thus is Hilarius answered unto both plainly and shortly [g].

[g] Idem Hilarius *De Trin.* lib. viii. [ed. Bened. p. 218.]
"Quorum anima una et cor unum omnium erat, quæro utrum
"per fidem Dei unum erat? utique per fidem. Et interrogo,
"utrum fides una, anne altera sit? una certe. Si ergo per
"fidem, id est, per unius fidei naturam, utique unum omnes
"erant: quomodo non naturalem in his intelligis unitatem,
"qui per naturam unius fidei unum sunt? Omnes enim renati
"erant ad innocentiam, ad immortalitatem, &c. Sin vero
"regenerati in unius vitæ atque æternitatis naturam sunt, per
"quod anima eorum et cor unum est; cessat in his assensus
"unitas, qui unum sunt in ejusdem regeneratione naturæ, &c.
"Docet Apostolus ex natura sacramentorum esse hanc fidelium
"unitatem, ad Galatas scribens: *Quotquot enim in Christo
"baptizati estis, Christum induistis, &c.* Quod unum sunt
"in tanta gentium, conditionum, sexuum diversitate, nunquid ex
"assensu voluntatis est, aut ex sacramenti unitate, quia his et
"baptisma sit unum, et unum Christum induti omnes sunt?
"Quid ergo hic animorum concordia faciet, cum per id unum
"sint, quod uno Christo per naturam unius baptismi induantur?
"&c. Itaque, qui per rem eandem unum sunt, natura etiam
"unum sunt, non tantum voluntate, &c. Dominus Patrem orat,
"ut qui in se credituri sint, unum sint, et sicut ipse in Patre
"est, et Pater in eo est, ita omnes in his unum sint, &c. Primum precatio est, *Ut omnes unum sint,* tum deinde unitatis Joan xvii.

174   DEFENCE, &c.

BOOK III.
The answer to Cyrillus.

And this answer to Hilarius will serve also unto Cyril, whom they allege to speak after the

"profectus exemplo uñitatis ostenditur, cum ait: *Sicut tu Pater*
"*in me, et ego in te, ut et ipsi unum sint in nobis:* ut sicut
"Pater in Filio, et Filius in Patre est, ita per hujus unitatis for-
"mam in Patre et Filio unum omnes essent, &c. Per id ergo
"mundus crediturus est Filium a Patre missum esse, quod
"omnes qui credituri in eum sunt, unum in Patre et Filio
"erunt: et quomodo erunt, mox docemur. *Et ego honorem*
"*quem dedisti mihi, dedi eis.* Et nunc interrogo, utrum id
"ipsum sit honor quod voluntas; (cum voluntas motus mentis
"sit,) an vero honor naturæ, aut species, aut dignitas? Honorem
"ergo acceptum a Patre, Filius omnibus qui in se credituri
"sunt, dedit, non utique voluntatem, &c. Et cum per honorem
"datum Filio, et a Filio præstitum credentibus, omnes unum
"sunt: quæro, quomodo Filius diversi honoris a Patre sit?
"Cum credentes omnes honor Filii ad unitatem paterni honoris
"assumat, &c. Fidem teneo, atque causam unitatis accipio,
"sed nondum apprehendo rationem, quomodo datus honor unum
"omnes esse perficiat. Sed Dominus nihil conscientiæ fidelium
"incertum relinquens, ipsum illum naturalis efficientiæ docuit
"effectum, dicens: *Ut sint unum, sicut et nos unum sumus. Ego*
"*in his, et tu in me, ut sint perfecti in unum.* Eos nunc qui
"inter Patrem et Filium voluntatis ingerunt unitatem, in-
"terrogo, utrumne per naturæ veritatem hodie Christus in
"nobis sit, an per concordiam voluntatis?" [Here follows the passage translated by Cranmer.] "De naturali in nobis Christi veri-
"tate ipse ait: *Caro mea vere est esca, et sanguis meus vere*
"*est potus. Qui edit carnem meam, et bibit sanguinem*
"*meum in me manet, et ego in eo.* De veritate carnis et san-
"guinis non relictus est ambigendi locus: nunc enim et ipsius
"Domini professione et fide nostra, vere caro est, et vere sanguis
"est. Et hæc accepta atque hausta efficiunt, ut et nos in Christo
"et Christus in nobis sit." Et mox. "Est ergo in nobis ipse
"per carnem, et sumus in eo, dum secum hoc quod nos sumus,
"in Deo est. Quod autem in eo per sacramentum communicatæ
"carnis et sanguinis simus, ipse testatur dicens: *Et hic mun-*
"*dus jam me non videt, vos autem me videbitis, quo-*
"*niam ego vivo et vos vivetis, quoniam ego in Patre meo, et vos*
"*in me, et ego in vobis.* Si voluntatis tantum unitatem in-

THE PRESENCE OF CHRIST. 175

same sort that Hilarius doth, that Christ is CHAP. XV.
"telligi vellet, cur gradum quendam atque ordinem consum-
"mandæ unitatis exposuit: nisi ut cum ille in Patre per
"naturam Divinitatis esset, nos contra in eo per corporalem
"ejus nativitatem, et ille rursum in nobis per sacramentorum
"inesse mysterium crederetur, ac sic perfecta per mediatorem
"unitas doceretur? cum nobis in se manentibus, ipse maneret
"in Patre, et in Patre manens ipse maneret in nobis,
"et ita ad unitatem Patris proficeremus, cum qui in eo
"naturaliter secundum nativitatem inest, nos quoque in eo
"naturaliter inessemus, ipso in nobis naturaliter permanente.
"Quod autem in nobis naturalis hæc unitas sit, ipse ita testatus
"est. *Qui edit carnem meam, et bibit sanguinem meum, in me
"manet, et ego in eo.* Non enim quis in eo erit, nisi in quo
"ipse fuerit: ejus tantum in se assumptam habens carnem,
"qui suam sumpserit. Perfectæ autem hujus unitatis sacra-
"mentum superius jam docuerat, dicens: *Sicut me misit vivens
"Pater, et ego vivo per Patrem, et qui manducat meam car-
"nem, et ipse vivet per me.* Vivet ergo per Patrem, et quo
"modo per Patrem vivit, eodem modo nos per carnem ejus vi-
"vemus. Omnis enim comparatio ad intelligentiæ formam
"præsumitur: ut id de quo agitur, secundum propositum exem-
"plum assequamur. Hæc ergo vitæ nostræ causa est, quod
"in nobis carnalibus manentem per carnem Christum habemus;
"victuris nobis per eum ea conditione qua vivit ille per Patrem.
"Si ergo nos naturaliter secundum carnem per eum vivimus, id
"est, naturam carnis suæ adepti; quomodo non naturaliter
"secundum Spiritum in se Patrem habeat, cum vivat ipse per
"Patrem?" Et mox. "Hæc autem idcirco a nobis com-
"memorata sunt, quia voluntatis tantum inter Patrem
"et Filium unitatem hæretici mentientes unitatis nostræ ad
"Deum utebantur exemplo, tanquam nobis ad Filium, et per
"Filium ad Patrem obsequio tantum ac voluntate religionis
"unitis, nulla per sacramentum carnis et sanguinis naturalis
"communionis proprietas indulgeretur; cum et per honorem
"nobis datum Filii, et per manentem in nobis carnaliter
"Filium, et in eo nobis corporaliter et inseparabiliter unitis,
"mysterium veræ ac naturalis unitatis sit prædicandum."
Idem, *lib. eodem,* [ed. Bened. p. 244.] "*Hcc est opus Dei, ut
"credatis ei quem misit ipse.* Sacramentum et corporationis
"et Divinitatis suæ Dominus exponens, fidei quoque nostræ et

176 DEFENCE, &c.

naturally in us. The words which they recite be

"spei doctrinam locutus est; ut escam non pereuntem sed per-
"manentem in vitam æternam operaremur, ut hanc æternitatis
"escam dari nobis a filio hominis meminissemus, ut filium
"hominis signatum a Deo Patre sciremus, ut hoc esse opus
"Dei nosceremus, credere in eum quem misisset. Et quis
"est, quem Pater misit? Nempe quem signavit Deus. Et quis
"est, quem signavit Deus? Filius utique hominis, escam
"scilicet præbens vitæ æternæ. Qui tandem sunt quibus præ-
"bet eam? Illi namque qui operabuntur escam non intereun-
"tem. Atque ita, quæ opera escæ est, eadem operatio Dei est,
"in eum, scilicet, credidisse quem misit."
Idem, *lib. ix.* [ed. Bened. p. 263.] "*Videte ne quis vos decipiat
"per philosophiam, &c.* (Coloss. ii.) *Et non secundum Jesum
"Christum, quia in ipso inhabitat omnis plenitudo Divinitatis
"corporaliter, et estis in illo repleti, &c.* Exposita itaque
"habitantis corporaliter Divinitatis in eo plenitudine, sacra-
"mentum assumptionis nostræ continuo subjecit, dicens: *Et
"estis in eo repleti.* Ut enim in eo Divinitatis est plenitudo,
"ita in eo et nos sumus repleti. Neque sane ait, estis repleti,
"sed, *in eo estis repleti*, quia per fidei spem in vitam æternam
"regenerati et regenerandi omnes, nunc in Christi corpore ma-
"nent, replendis postea ipsis, non jam *in eo*, sed in ipsis, secun-
"dum tempus illud de quo Apostolus ait: *Qui transfigurabit
"corpus humilitatis nostræ, conforme corpori claritatis suæ,
"&c.* Demonstrato autem et naturæ suæ et assumptionis nostræ
"sacramento, cum in eo plenitudine Divinitatis manente, nos in
"eo per id quod homo natus est, repleamur, reliquam dispen-
"sationem humanæ salutis exequitur, dicens: *In quo et circum-
"cisi estis circimcisione non manu facta in despoliatione cor-
"poris carnis, sed in circumcisione Christi, consepulti ei in
"baptismate, in quo et consurrexistis per fidem operationis
"Dei, qui excitavit eum a mortuis, &c.* Regeneratio, bap-
"tismi resurrectionis est virtus, &c. In eo enim resurgimus
"per ejus Dei fidem, qui eum suscitavit a mortuis."
Idem, *lib. ii.* "Virgo, partus, et corpus, postque crux, mors,
"inferi, salus nostræ est. Humani enim generis causa Dei
"Filius natus ex virgine est Spiritu Sancto, ipso sibi in hac
"operatione famulante, et sua videlicet Dei inumbrante virtute,
"corporis sibi initia consevit, et exordia carnis instituit: ut
"homo factus ex virgine, naturam in se carnis acciperet, per-

these: "ʰWe deny not," saith Cyril against the heretic, "but we be spiritually joined to Christ "by faith and sincere charity; but that we should "have no manner of conjunction in our flesh with "Christ, that we utterly deny, and think it "utterly discrepant from God's holy Scriptures. "For who doubteth, that Christ is so the vine "tree and we so the branches, as we get thence "our life. Hear what St. Paul saith, *We be all* "*one body with Christ;* for though we be many, "we be one in him. All we participate in one "food. Thinketh this heretic that we know not "*the strength and virtue of the mystical bene-* "*diction?* *which, when it is made in us, doth it* "*not make Christ by communication of his flesh* "*to dwell corporally in us?* Why be the members "of faithful men's bodies called the members of "Christ? *Know you not,* saith St. Paul, *that* "*your members be the members of Christ? And* "*shall I make the members of Christ part of the* "*whore's body?* God forbid. And our Saviour "also saith, *He that eateth my flesh, and drinketh* "*my blood,* dwelleth in me, *and I in him.*"

CHAP. XV.

1 Cor. vi.

John vi.

"que hujus admixtionis societatem sanctificatum in eo universi "generis humani corpus existeret: ut quemadmodum omnes "in se, per id quod corporeum se esse voluit, conderentur, ita "rursum in omnes ipse per id quod ejus est invisible, referretur." Et mox. "Non ille eguit homo effici, per quem homo factus est, "sed nos eguimus, ut Deus caro fieret, et habitaret in nobis, id "est, assumptione carnis unius, membra universæ carnis in- "coleret. Humilitas ejus nostra nobilitas est, contumelia ejus "honor noster est: quod ille est Deus in carne consistens, hoc "nos vicissim in Deum ex carne renovat." EMBD.

ʰ Cyril, *In Joan.* lib. x. cap. 13.

Although in these words Cyril doth say, that Christ doth dwell corporally in us, when we receive the mystical benediction; yet he neither saith that Christ dwelleth corporally in the bread, nor that he dwelleth in us corporally only at such times as we receive the sacrament, nor that he dwelleth in us, and not we in him; but he saith as well, that we dwell in him, as that he dwelleth in us. Which dwelling is neither corporal nor local, but an heavenly, spiritual and supernatural dwelling, whereby, so long as we dwell in him and he in us, we have by him everlasting life. And therefore Cyril saith in the same place, that Christ is the vine and we the branches, because that by him we have life. For as the branches receive life and nourishment of the body of the vine, so receive we by him the natural property of his body, which is life and immortality: and by that means we, being his members, do live, and are spiritually nourished.

And this meant Cyril by this word *corporally*, when he saith, that Christ dwelleth corporally in us. And the same meant also St. Hilarius by this word *naturally*, when he said that Christ dwelleth naturally in us. And as St. Paul, when he said that *in Christ dwelleth the full Divinity corporally*, by this word *corporally* he meant not that the Divinity is a body, and so by that body dwelleth bodily in Christ: but by this word *corporally*, he meant that the Divinity is not in Christ accidentally, lightly, and slenderly, but

THE PRESENCE OF CHRIST. 179

substantially and perfectly, with all his might and power; so that Christ was not only a mortal man, to suffer for us, but also he was immortal God, able to redeem us.

So St. Cyril, when he said that Christ is in us *corporally*, he meant that we have him in us, not lightly and to small effect and purpose, but that we have him in us substantially, pithily, and effectually, in such wise that we have by him redemption and everlasting life.

And this I suck not out of mine own fingers, but have it of Cyril's own express words, where he saith, "A little benediction draweth the "whole man to God, and filleth him with his "grace; and *after this manner Christ dwelleth in* "*us* and we in Christ.[i]"

But as for corporal eating and drinking with our mouths, and digesting with our bodies, Cyril never meant that Christ doth so dwell in us, as he plainly declareth.

"Our sacrament," said he[k], doth not affirm "the eating of a man, drawing wickedly "Christian people to have gross imaginations and "carnal phantasies of such things as be fine and "pure and received only with a sincere faith."

"But as two waxes that be molten and put "together, they close so in one, that every part "of the one is joined to every part of the other; "even so," saith Cyril[l], "*he that receiveth the flesh*

[i] *In Joan.* lib. iv. cap. 17.   [k] *Anathematismo.* 11
[l] *In Joan* lib. iv. cap. 17.

"*and blood of the Lord must needs be so joined with Christ, that Christ must be in him and he in Christ.*"

By these words of Cyril appeareth his mind plainly, that we may not grossly and rudely think of the eating of Christ with our mouths, but with our faith, by which eating, although he be absent hence bodily, and be in the eternal life and glory with his Father, yet we be made partakers of his nature, to be immortal, and have eternal life and glory with him.

And thus is declared the mind as well of Cyril as of Hilarius.

Basilius, Nyssenus, and Nazianzenus. And here may be well enough passed over Basilius, Gregorius Nyssenus, and Gregorius Nazianzenus, partly because they speak little of this matter, and because they may be easily answered unto by that which is before declared and often repeated, which is, that a figure hath the name of the thing whereof it is the figure, and therefore of the figure may be spoken the same thing that may be spoken of the thing itself.

And as concerning the eating of Christ's flesh and drinking of his blood, they spake of the spiritual eating and drinking thereof by faith, and not of corporal eating and drinking with the mouth and teeth.

The answer to Emissenus. Likewise Eusebius Emissenus is shortly answered unto; for he speaketh not of any real and corporal conversion of bread and wine into Christ's body and blood, nor of any corporal and

THE PRESENCE OF CHRIST. 181

real eating and drinking of the same, but he speaketh of a sacramental conversion of bread and wine, and of a spiritual eating and drinking of the body and blood. After which sort, Christ is as well present in baptism (as the same Eusebius plainly there declareth) as he is in the Lord's table : which is, not carnally and corporally, but by faith and spiritually. But of this author is spoken before more at large in the matter of transubstantiation[1].

And now I will come to the saying of St. Ambrose, which is always in their mouths[m]. "Before the consecration," saith he, as they allege "it is bread; but after the words of consecration" "it is the body of Christ."

For answer hereunto, it must be first known what consecration is.

Consecration is the separation of any thing from a profane and worldly use unto a spiritual and godly use.

And therefore when usual and common water is taken from other uses, and put to the use of baptism, in the name of the Father, and of the Son, and of the Holy Ghost, then it may rightly be called consecrated water, that is to say, water put to an holy use.

Even so when common bread and wine be taken and severed from other bread and wine, to the use of the holy communion, that portion of bread and wine, although it be of the same substance that

CHAP. XV.

The answer to Ambrosius *De Sacramentis,* lib. iv. cap. 4.

Consecration.

[1] See p. 86 and fol. [m] [See note q. p. 88]

the other is from the which it is severed, yet it is now called consecrated or holy bread and holy wine.

Not that the bread and wine have or can have any holiness in them, but that they be used to an holy work, and represent holy and godly things. And therefore St. Dionyse[n] calleth the bread holy bread, and the cup an holy cup, as soon as they be set upon the altar to the use of the holy communion.

But specially they may be called holy and consecrated, when they be separated to that holy use by Christ's own words, which he spake for that purpose, saying of the bread, *This is my body*; and of the wine, *This is my blood.*

So that commonly the authors, before those words be spoken, do take the bread and wine but as other common bread and wine; but after those words be pronounced over them, then they take them for consecrated and holy bread and wine.

Not that the bread and wine can be partakers of any holiness or godliness, or can be the body and blood of Christ; but that they represent the very body and blood of Christ, and the holy food and nourishment which we have by him. And so they be called by the names of the body and blood of Christ, as the sign, token, and figure is called by the name of the very thing which it showeth and signifieth

And therefore as St. Ambrose, in the words

---

[n] *De Eccl. Hierar.* cap. 3.

THE PRESENCE OF CHRIST. 183

before cited by the adversaries, saith, that before the consecration it is bread, and after the consecration it is Christ's body; so in other places he doth more plainly set forth his meaning, saying these words: "Before the benediction of the "heavenly words, it is called another kind of thing; "but *after the consecration is signified* the body "of Christ." Likewise: "Before the consecra-"tion, it is called another thing; but *after the* "*consecration, it is named* the blood of Christ[o]." And again he saith: "When I treated of the "sacraments, I told you, that that thing which "is offered, before the words of Christ is called "bread; but when the words of Christ be pro-"nounced, then it is not called bread, but it is "called by the name of Christ's body[p]."

By which words of St. Ambrose, it appeareth plainly, that the bread is called by the name of Christ's body after the consecration; and although it be still bread, yet after consecration it is dignified by the name of the thing which it representeth, as at length is declared before in the process of transubstantiation, and specially in the words of Theodoretus.

And as the bread is a corporal meat, and corporally eaten, so, saith St. Ambrose[q], is the body of Christ a spiritual meat, and spiritually eaten, and that requireth no corporal presence.

Now let us examine St. John Chrysostome, who, in sound of words, maketh most for the adversaries

CHAP. XV.

The answer to Chrysostomus.

[o] *De iis qui Mysteriis initiantur,* cap. ult.
[p] *De Sacramentis,* lib. v. cap. 4.   [q] Ibid. lib. vi. cap. 1.

of the truth: but they that be familiar and acquainted with Chrysostome's manner of speaking, how in all his writings he is full of allusions, schemes, tropes, and figures, shall soon perceive, that he helpeth nothing their purposes, as it shall well appear by the discussing of those places, which the papists do allege of him; which be specially two: one is, *In Sermone de Eucharistia in Encœniis;* and the other is, *De Proditione Judœ.*

And as touching the first, no man can speak more plainly against them than St. John Chrysostome speaketh in that Sermon. Wherefore it is to be wondered, why they should allege him for their party, unless they be so blind in their opinion that they can see nothing, nor discern what maketh for them, nor what against them. For there he hath these words: " When " you come to these mysteries," speaking of the Lord's board and holy communion, "*do you think* "*that you receive by a man the body of God,*" meaning of Christ[r]. These be St. John Chrysostome's own words in that place.

Then if we receive not the body of Christ at the hands of a man, ergo, the body of Christ is not really, corporally, and naturally in the sacrament, and so given to us by the priest. And then it followeth that all the papists be liars, because they feign and teach the contrary.

But this place of Chrysostome is touched before

[r] *In Sermone de Eucharistia in Encœniis.* [Ed. Bened. *De Pœnitent. Hom.* 9. See above, p. 341, and the *Authorities* in Jenkyns' Appendix.]

THE PRESENCE OF CHRIST. 185

more at length in answering to the papists' transubstantiation.

Wherefore now shall be answered the other place[s], which they allege of Chrysostome in these words: "Here he is present in the sacrament and "doth consecrate, which garnished the table at "the Maundy or last supper. For *it is not man,* "*which maketh of the bread and wine,* being set "forth to be consecrated, *the body and blood of* "*Christ;* but *it is Christ himself,* which for us is "crucified, *that maketh himself to be there present.* "*The words are uttered and pronounced by the* "*mouth of the priest, but the consecration is by the* "*virtue, might, and grace of God himself:* and as "this saying of God, *Increase, be multiplied, and* "*fill the earth,* once spoken by God, took always "effect toward generation: even so *the saying of* "*Christ,* This is my body, *being but once spoken,* "*doth throughout all Churches to this present, and* "*shall to his last coming, give force and strength* "*to this sacrifice.*"

Thus far they rehearse of Chrysostome's words. Which words, although they sound much for their purpose, yet if they be thoroughly considered, and conferred with other places of the same author, it shall well appear, that he meant nothing less than that Christ's body should be corporally and naturally present in the bread and wine; but that in such sort he is in heaven only, and in our minds by faith we ascend up into

[s] *De Proditione Judæ.*

heaven, to eat him there, although sacramentally, as in a sign and figure, he be in the bread and wine; and so is he also in the water of baptism; and in them that rightly receive the bread and wine, he is in a much more perfection than corporally, which should avail them nothing; but in them he is spiritually with his divine power, giving them eternal life.

And as in the first creation of the world all living creatures had their first life by God's only word; for God only spake his word, and all things were created by and by accordingly; and after their creation he spake these words, *Increase and multiply;* and, by the virtue of those words, all things have gendered and increased ever since that time: even so after that Christ said, *Eat, this is my body, and drink, this is my blood, do this hereafter in remembrance of me;* by virtue of these words, and not by virtue of any man, the bread and wine be so consecrated, that whosoever with a lively faith doth eat that bread and drink that wine, doth spiritually eat, drink, and feed upon Christ, sitting in heaven with his Father. And this is the whole meaning of St. Chrysostome.

And therefore doth he often say, that we receive Christ in baptism; and when he hath spoken of the receiving of him in the holy communion, by and by he speaketh of the receiving of him in baptism, without declaring any diversity of his presence in the one from his presence in the other.

He saith also in many places[t], "That *we ascend* "*into heaven, and do eat Christ sitting there* "*above.*"

And where St. Chrysostome and other authors do speak of the wonderful operation of God in his sacraments, passing all man's wit, senses, and reason, they mean not of the working of God in the water, bread, and wine, but of the marvellous working of God in the hearts of them that receive the sacraments, secretly, inwardly, and spiritually transforming them, renewing, feeding, comforting, and nourishing them with his flesh and blood, through his most Holy Spirit, the same flesh and blood still remaining in heaven.

Thus is this place of Chrysostome sufficiently answered unto; and if any man require any more, then let him look what is recited of the same author before, in the matter of transubstantiation.

Yet furthermore they bring for them Theophilus Alexandrinus, who, as they allege, saith thus: "Christ giving thanks did break, (which also we "do), adding thereto prayer: and he gave unto "them, saying, *Take, this is my body;* this that I "do now give, and that which ye now do take.

The answer to Theophilus, In Mark xiv.

[t] *Ad Populum Antiochenum, Hom.* 61. et *In Joan. Hom.* 45. [This reference, though apparently to two Homilies, is in fact to one only: the Sermons, which in the earlier editions of Chrysostom are entitled, *Ad Populum Antiochenum*, being, with the exception of the first twenty-five, mere compilations from his other works. Cave, *Hist. Liter.*]

BOOK III.
John vi.

"For *the bread is not a figure only of Christ's* *body, but it is changed into the very body of* *Christ;* for Christ saith, *The bread which I will* *give you is my flesh.* Nevertheless the flesh of "Christ is not seen for our weakness, but bread "and wine are familiar unto us. And surely if "we should visibly see flesh and blood, we could "not abide in it. And therefore our Lord, bearing "with our weakness, doth retain and keep the "form and appearance of bread and wine; but *he* *doth turn the very bread and wine into the very* *flesh and blood of Christ.*"

These be the words which the papists do cite out of Theophilus upon the Gospel of St. Mark. But by this one place it appeareth evidently, either how negligent the papists be in searching out and examining the sayings of the authors, which they allege for their purpose; or else how false and deceitful they be, which willingly and wittingly have made in this one place, and as it were with one breath, two loud and shameful lies.

The first is, that because they would give the more authority to the words by them alleged, they (like false poticaries that sell *quid pro quo*) falsify the author's name, fathering such sayings upon Theophilus Alexandrinus, an old and ancient author, which were indeed none of his words, but were the words of Theophylactus, who was for many years after Theophilus Alexandrinus[u]. But

[u] [Theophilus was Bishop of Alexandria A.D. 385. Theophylact was Archbishop of Bulgaria A.D. 1077. His Commen-

such hath ever been the papistical subtleties, to set forth their own inventions, dreams, and lies, under the name of antiquity and ancient authors.

The second lie or falsehood is, that they falsify the author's words and meaning, subverting the truth of his doctrine. For where Theophylactus according to the catholic doctrine of ancient authors saith, that Almighty God, condescending to our infirmity, reserveth the kind of bread and wine, and yet turneth them into the virtue of Christ's flesh and blood; they say that he reserveth the forms and appearances of bread and wine, and turneth them into the verity of his flesh and blood, so turning and altering kinds into forms and appearances, and virtue into verity, that of the virtue of the flesh and blood they make the verity of his flesh and blood. And thus they have falsified as well the name as the words of Theophylactus, turning verity into plain and flat falsity.

But to set forth plainly the meaning of Theophylactus in this matter: as hot and burning iron is iron still, and yet hath the force of fire; and as the flesh of Christ, still remaining flesh, giveth life, as the flesh of him that is God; so the sacramental bread and wine remain still in their proper kinds; and yet to them that worthily eat and drink them, they be turned not into the

tary on the Gospels is a compilation from Chrysostom and others. See Fabricius, *Bibl. Gr.* Harles, vol. v. p. 287. Cave, *Hist. Liter.*]

corporal presence, but into the virtue of Christ's flesh and blood.

And although Theophylactus spake of the eating of the very body of Christ, and the drinking of his very blood, (and not only of the figures of them,) and of the conversion of the bread and wine into the body and blood of Christ, yet he meaneth not of a gross, carnal, corporal, and sensible conversion of the bread and wine, nor of a like eating and drinking of his flesh and blood; for so not only our stomachs would yearn and our hearts abhor to eat his flesh and to drink his blood, but also such eating and drinking could nothing profit or avail us: but he spake of the celestial and spiritual eating of Christ, and of a sacramental conversion of the bread, calling the bread not only a figure, but also the body of Christ, giving us by those words to understand, that in the sacrament we do not only eat corporally the bread, which is a sacrament and figure of Christ's body; but spiritually we eat also his very body, and drink his very blood. And this doctrine of Theophylactus is both true, godly, and comfortable.

The answer to Hieronymus, Super Epist. ad Titum.

Besides this, our adversaries do allege St. Hierome upon the Epistle *Ad Titum*, that " there is as great difference between the loaves " called *panes propositionis*, and the body of " Christ, as there is between the shadow of a " body, and the body itself, and as there is " between an image, and the thing itself, and

THE PRESENCE OF CHRIST. 191

CHAP. XV.

"between an example of things to come, and the "things that be prefigured by them."

These words of St. Hierome, truly understand, serve nothing for the intent of the papists. For he meant that the show-bread of the law was but a dark shadow of Christ to come; but the sacrament of Christ's body is a clear testimony that Christ is already come, and that he hath performed that which was promised, and doth presently comfort and feed us spiritually with his precious body and blood, notwithstanding that corporally he is ascended into heaven.

And the same is to be answered unto all that the adversaries bring of St. Augustine, Sedulius, Leo, Fulgentius, Cassiodorus, Gregorius, and other, concerning the eating of Christ in the sacrament. Augustinus, Sedulius, Leo, Fulgentius, Cassiodorus, Gregorius.

Which thing cannot be understood plainly as the words sound, but figuratively and spiritually, as before is sufficiently proved, and hereafter shall be more fully declared in the fourth part of this book.

But here John Damascene[x] may in no wise be passed over, whom for his authority the adversaries of Christ's true natural body do reckon as a stout champion sufficient to defend all the whole matter alone. But neither is the authority of Damascene so great, that they may oppress us thereby, nor his words so plain for them, as they boast and untruly pretend. For he is but a The answer to Damascenus De Fide Orth.

[x] Damascenus, *De Fide Orth.* lib. iv. cap. 14.

young new author in the respect of those which we have brought in for our party. And in divers points he varieth from the most ancient authors, if he mean as they expound him; as when he saith, that the bread and wine be not figures, which all the old authors call figures, and that the bread and wine consume not, nor be avoided downward, which Origen and St. Augustine affirm, or that they be not called the examples of Christ's body after the consecration, which shall manifestly appear false by the Liturgy ascribed unto St. Basil.

And moreover the same Damascene was one of the Bishop of Rome's chief proctors against the emperors, and as it were his right hand, to set abroad all idolatry by his own handwriting. And therefore if he lost his hand, as they say he did, he lost it by God's most righteous judgment, whatsoever they feign and fable of the miraculous restitution of the same[y]. And yet whatsoever the said Damascene writeth in other matters, surely in this place which the adversaries do allege, he writeth spiritually and godly, although the papists either of ignorance mistake him, or else willingly wrest and writhe him to their purpose, clean contrary to his meaning.

The sum of Damascene his doctrine in this matter is this. That as Christ, being both God and man, hath in him two natures; so hath he

[y] [The story of its miraculous restoration is told by Gardyner, *Detection of the Devil's Sophistry*, f. 35.]

two nativities, one eternal and the other temporal. And so likewise we, being as it were double men, or having every one of us two men in us, the new man and the old man, the spiritual man and the carnal man, have a double nativity: one of our first carnal father, Adam, by whom, as by ancient inheritance, cometh unto us malediction and everlasting damnation; and the other of our heavenly Adam, that is to say, of Christ, by whom we be made heirs of celestial benediction and everlasting glory and immortality.

And because this Adam is spiritual, therefore our generation by him must be spiritual, and our feeding must be likewise spiritual. And our spiritual generation by him is plainly set forth in baptism, and our spiritual meat and food is set forth in the holy Communion and Supper of the Lord. And because our sights be so feeble that we cannot see the spiritual water wherewith we be washed in baptism, nor the spiritual meat wherewith we be fed at the Lord's table; therefore to help our infirmities, and to make us the better to see the same with a pure faith, our Saviour Christ hath set forth the same, as it were before our eyes, by sensible signs and tokens, which we be daily used and accustomed unto.

And because the common custom of men is to wash in water, therefore our spiritual regeneration in Christ, or spiritual washing in his blood, is declared unto us in baptism by water. Likewise our spiritual nourishment and feeding in Christ, is set before our eyes by bread and wine, because they be meats and drinks which chiefly and usually we be fed withal; that as they feed the body, so doth Christ with his flesh and blood spiritually feed the soul.

And therefore the bread and wine be called examples of Christ's flesh and blood, and also they be called his very flesh and blood, to signify unto us, that as they feed us carnally so do they admonish us that Christ with his flesh and blood doth feed us spiritually and most truly unto everlasting life.

And as Almighty God by his most mighty word and his Holy Spirit and infinite power brought forth all creatures in the beginning, and ever sithence hath preserved them; even so by the same word and power he worketh in us from time to time this marvellous spiritual generation, and wonderful spiritual nourishment and feeding, which is wrought only by God, and is comprehended and received of us by faith.

And as bread and drink by natural nourishment be changed into a man's body, and yet the body is not changed, but the same that it was before; so although the bread and wine be sacramentally changed into Christ's body, yet his body is the same and in the same place that it was before, that is to say, in heaven, without any alteration of the same.

And the bread and wine be not so changed into the flesh and blood of Christ, that they be made one nature, but they remain still distinct in nature, so that the bread in itself is not his flesh, and the wine his blood, but unto them that worthily eat and drink the bread and wine, to them the bread and wine be his flesh and blood ; that is to say, by things natural and which they be accustomed unto, they be exalted unto things above nature. For the sacramental bread and wine be not bare and naked figures, but so pithy and effectuous, that whosoever worthily eateth them, eateth spiritually Christ's flesh and blood, and hath by them everlasting life.

Wherefore whosoever cometh to the Lord's table must come with all humility, fear, reverence, and purity of life, as to receive not only bread and wine, but also our Saviour Christ both God and man, with all his benefits, to the relief and sustentation both of their bodies and souls.

This is briefly the sum and true meaning of Damascene concerning this matter.

Wherefore they that gather of him either the natural presence of Christ's body in the sacraments of bread and wine, or the adoration of the outward and visible sacrament, or that after the consecration there remaineth no bread nor wine nor other substance, but only the substance of the body and blood of Christ ; either they understand not Damascene, or else of wilful frowardness they will not understand him ; which rather seemeth to be true, by such collections as they have unjustly gathered and noted out of him.

For although he say, that Christ is the spiritual meat, yet as in baptism the Holy Ghost is not in the water, but in him that is unfeignedly baptized; so Damascene meant not, that Christ is in the bread, but in him that worthily eateth the bread.

And though he say, that the bread is Christ's body and the wine his blood, yet he meant not that the bread considered in itself, or the wine in itself being not received, is his flesh and blood; but to such as by unfeigned faith worthily receive the bread and wine, to such the bread and wine are called by Damascene the body and blood of Christ, because that such persons through the working of the Holy Ghost be so knit and united spiritually to Christ's flesh and blood, and to his Divinity also, that they be fed with them unto everlasting life.

Sacrament not to be worshipped. Furthermore Damascene sayeth not, that the sacrament should be worshipped and adored, as the papists term it, which is plainly idolatry, but that we must worship Christ, God and man. And yet we may not worship him in bread and wine, but sitting in heaven with his Father, and being spiritually within ourselves.

Nor he sayeth not, that there remaineth no bread nor wine, nor none other substance, but only the substance of the body and blood of Christ; but he saith plainly, that as a burning coal is not wood only, but fire and wood joined together; so the bread of the communion is not bread only, but bread joined to the Divinity.

THE PRESENCE OF CHRIST.

But those that say, that there is none other substance but the substance of the body and blood of Christ, do not only deny that there is bread and wine, but by force they must deny also that there is either Christ's Divinity or his soul. For if the flesh and blood, the soul and Divinity of Christ be four substances, and in the sacrament be but two of them, that is to say, his flesh and blood, then where is his soul and Divinity? And thus these men divide Jesus, separating his Divinity from his humanity: of whom St. John saith, *Whosoever divideth Jesus is not of God, but he is Antichrist.* [1 John iv.]

And moreover these men do so separate Christ's body from his members in the sacrament, that they leave him no man's body at all. For as Damascene saith, that the distinction of members pertain so much to the nature of a man's body, that where there is no such distinction, there is no perfect man's body[z].

But by these papists' doctrine, there is no such distinction of members in the sacrament; for either there is no head, feet, hands, arms, legs, mouth, eyes, and nose at all; or else all is head, all feet, all hands, all arms, all legs, all mouth, all eyes, and all nose. And so they make of Christ's body no man's body at all.

Thus being confuted the papists' errors as well concerning transubstantiation, as the real, corporal, and natural presence of Christ in the sacrament,

[z] In libro *De duabus in Christo Voluntatibus.*

which were two principal points purposed in the beginning of this work: now it is time something to speak of the third error of the papists, which is concerning the eating of Christ's very body and drinking of his blood.

THUS ENDETH THE THIRD BOOK.

The Fourth Book is of the Eating and Drinking of the Body and Blood of our Saviour Christ.

THE gross error of the papists, is of the carnal eating and drinking of Christ's flesh and blood with our mouths.

For they say, that whosoever eat and drink the sacraments of bread and wine, do eat and drink also with their mouths Christ's very flesh and blood, be they never so ungodly and wicked persons. But Christ himself taught clean contrary in the sixth of John, that we eat not him carnally with our mouths, but spiritually with our faith, saying, *Verily, verily, I say unto you, he that believeth in me, hath everlasting life. I am the bread of life. Your fathers did eat manna in the wilderness, and died. This is the bread that came from heaven, that whosoever shall eat thereof, shall not die. I am the lively bread that came from heaven; if any man eat of this bread, he shall live for ever. And the bread which I will give, is my flesh, which I will give for the life of the world.*

This is the most true doctrine of our Saviour Christ, that whosoever eateth him, shall have everlasting life. And by and by it followeth in the same place of John more clearly: *Verily, verily, I say unto you, Except you eat the flesh of the Son of man, and drink his blood, you shall not*

CHAP I.
Whether evil men do eat and drink Christ.

The godly only eat Christ.

John vi.

John vi.

have life in you. He that eateth my flesh and drinketh my blood, hath life everlasting, *and I will raise him again at the last day: for my flesh is very meat, and my blood is very drink.* He that eateth my flesh, and drinketh my blood, dwelleth in me, and I in him. *As the living Father hath sent me, and I live by the Father; even so he that eateth me, shall live by me. This is the bread which came down from heaven, not as your fathers did eat manna, and are dead;* he that eateth of this bread, shall live for ever.

This taught our Saviour Christ as well his disciples as the Jews at Capernaum, that the eating of his flesh and drinking of his blood was not like to the eating of manna. For both good and bad did eat manna, but none do eat his flesh and drink his blood, but they have everlasting life. For as his Father dwelleth in him, and he in his Father, and so hath life by his Father: so he that eateth Christ's flesh and drinketh his blood, dwelleth in Christ, and Christ in him, and by Christ he hath eternal life.

What need we any other witness? when Christ himself doth testify the matter so plainly, that whosoever eateth his flesh and drinketh his blood, hath everlasting life; and that to eat his flesh and to drink his blood, is to believe in him; and whosoever believeth in him, hath everlasting life. Whereof it followeth necessarily, that ungodly persons, being limbs of the Devil, do not eat Christ's flesh nor drink his blood: except the papists would say, that such have everlasting life.

But as the Devil is the food of the wicked, which he nourisheth in all iniquity, and bringeth up unto everlasting damnation : so is Christ the very food of all them that be the lively members of his body, and them he nourisheth, feedeth, bringeth up, and cherisheth unto everlasting life.[a]

---

[a] Aug. *In Joan. Hom.* 26. super hunc locum : *Patres vestri manducaverunt manna in deserto, et mortui sunt.* " Quantum, " inquit, pertinet ad mortem istam visibilem et corporalem, " numquid nos non morimur, qui manducamus panem de cœlo " descendentem ? " Et mox, " Quantum autem pertinet ad illam " mortem de qua terret Dominus, quia mortui sunt patres isto- " rum, manducavit manna et Moses, manducavit et Aaron, man- " ducavit manna et Phinees, manducaverunt ibi multi, qui " Domino placuerunt, et mortui non sunt. Quare ? Quia " visibilem cibum spiritualiter intellexerunt, spiritualiter esuri- " erunt, spiritualiter gustaverunt, ut spiritualiter satiarentur. " Nam et nos hodie accepimus visibilem cibum, sed aliud est sac- " ramentum, aliud virtus sacramenti. Quam multi de altari ac- " cipiunt et moriuntur, et accipiendo moriuntur ? Unde dicit " Apostolus : (1 Cor. xi.) *Judicium sibi manducat et bibit.* "Nonne buccella dominica venenum fuit Judæ ? (John xiii.) Et " tamen accepit, et cum accepit, in eum inimicus intravit, non " quia malum accepit, sed quia bonum malus male accepit. " Vide te ergo, fratres, panem cœlestem spiritualiter manducate." Et mox : " *Patres vestri manna manducaverunt, et mortui* " *sunt;* non quia malum erat manna, sed quia male manduca- "verunt. *Hic est panis qui de cœlo descendit,* hunc panem " significavit manna, hunc panem significavit altare Dei. Sac- " ramenta illa fuerunt, in signis diversa sunt, sed in re quæ " significatur, paria sunt," &c. Et mox : " Ut *si quis mandu-* " *caverit ex ipso non moriatur in æternum.* Sed quod pertinet " ad virtutem sacramenti, non quod pertinet ad visibile sacra- " mentum. Qui manducat intus, non foris, qui manducat in " corde, non qui premit dente." EMBD.

CHAP. II.
What is the eating of Christ's flesh, and drinking of his blood.

And every good and faithful Christian man feeleth in himself how he feedeth of Christ, eating his flesh and drinking of his blood. For he putteth the whole hope and trust of his redemption and salvation in that only sacrifice, which Christ made upon the cross, having his body there broken, and his blood there shed for the remission of his sins. And this great benefit of Christ the faithful man earnestly considereth in his mind, chaweth [cheweth] and digesteth it with the stomach of his heart, spiritually receiving Christ wholly into him, and giving again himself wholly unto Christ.

And this is the eating of Christ's flesh and drinking of his blood, the feeling whereof is to every man the feeling how he eateth and drinketh Christ, which none evil man nor member of the Devil can do.

CHAP. III.
Christ is not eaten with teeth, but with faith.

For as Christ is a spiritual meat, so is he spiritually eaten and digested with the spiritual part of us, and giveth us spiritual and eternal life, and is not eaten, swallowed, and digested with our teeth, tongues, throats, and bellies.

"Therefore," saith St. Cyprian[b], "*he that*

[b] Cyprianus, *De Cœna Domini*. [See note i, p. 49.]

THE EATING AND DRINKING. 203

"*drinketh of the holy cup, remembering this*
"*benefit of God, is more thirsty than he was*
"*before.* And lifting up his heart unto the living
" God, is taken with such a singular hunger and
" appetite, that *he abhoreth all gally and bitter*
" *drinks of sin;* and all savour of carnal pleasure
" is to him, as it were, sharp and sour vinegar. And
" the sinner being converted, receiving the holy
" mysteries of the Lord's Supper, giveth thanks
" unto God, and boweth down his head, knowing
" that his sins be forgiven, and that he is made
" clean and perfect; and his soul, which God hath
" sanctified, he rendereth to God again as a faithful
" pledge, and then he glorieth with Paul, and
" rejoiceth, saying, *Now it is not I that live, but it*
" *is Christ that liveth within me.* These things
" be practised and used among faithful people;
" and to pure minds the eating of his flesh is no
" horror but honour, and the spirit delighteth in
" the drinking of the holy and sanctifying blood.
" And doing this, *we whet not our teeth to bite, but*
" *with pure faith we break the holy bread.*"
These be the words of Cyprian.

And according unto the same, St. Austen
saith, "*Prepare not thy jaws, but thy heart*[c]."
And in another place[d], he saith, "*Why dost*
"*thou prepare thy belly and thy teeth? believe,*
"*and thou hast eaten.*" But of this matter is
sufficiently spoken before, where it is proved, that

[c] *In Joan. Tract.* 25.
[d] August. *De Verbis Domini, Serm.* 33.

BOOK IV.
"to eat Christ's flesh" and "drink his blood" be figurative speeches[e].

CHAP. IV.
The good only eat Christ.

And now to return to our purpose, that only the lively members of Christ do eat his flesh and drink his blood, I shall bring forth many other places of ancient authors before not mentioned.

First, Origen[f] writeth plainly after this manner: "The Word was made flesh and very meat, "which whoso eateth shall surely live for ever; "*which no evil man can eat.* For if it could be "that he that continueth evil might eat the Word "made flesh, seeing that he is the Word and "bread of life, it should not have been written, "*Whosoever eateth this bread, shall live for ever.*"

[e] Aug. *In Joan. Tract.* 26. "Credere in eum, hoc est mandu-"care panem vivum. Qui credit in eum, manducat, invisibili-"ter saginatur, quia et invisibiliter renascitur. Infans intus "est, novus intus est, ubi novellatur, ibi satiatur." Idem, *Psal.* 21 *in Expositione Prima,* "Sacramenta corporis et sanguinis "mei reddam coram timentibus eum. *Edent pauperes et* "*saturabuntur,* edent humiles et contemptores seculi et imita-"buntur. Ita enim nec copiam hujus seculi concupiscent nec "timebunt inopiam. *Et laudabunt Dominum qui requirunt* "*eum:* nam laus Domini est eructatio saturitatis illius. *Vivent* "*corda eorum in seculum seculi;* nam cibus ille cordis est."
Clemens Alexandrinus in *Pædagogo,* lib. ii. cap. 2. "Hoc "est bibere Jesu sanguinem, esse participem incorruptionis "Domini."
De Consecrat. dist. 2. "Utrum:" "Quia Christum fas "vorari dentibus non est," &c. EMBD.

[f] Origenes, *In Matt.* cap. 15.

These words be so plain, that I need say nothing for the more clear declaration of them. Wherefore you shall hear how Cyprian agreeth with him.

Cyprian, in his Sermon ascribed unto him of the Lord's Supper[g], saith, "The author of this "tradition said, that except we eat his flesh and "drink his blood we should have no life in us; in-"structing us with a spiritual lesson, and opening "to us a way to understand so privy a thing, that "we should know that *the eating is our dwelling* "*in him, and our drinking is as it were an incor-*"*poration in him,* being subject unto him in "obedience, joined unto him in our wills, and "united in our affections. *The eating therefore of* "*this flesh, is a certain hunger and desire to* "*dwell in him.*"

Thus writeth Cyprian of the eating and drinking of Christ. And a little after he saith, that "none do eat of this Lamb, but such as be true "Israelites, that is to say, pure Christian men, "without colour or dissimulation."

And Athanasius[h], speaking of the eating of Christ's flesh and drinking of his blood, saith, that "for this cause he made mention of his ascension "into heaven, to pluck them from corporal phan-"tasy, that they might learn hereafter that his "flesh was called the celestial meat that came "from above, and *a spiritual food* which he would "give. For those things that I speak to you,

[g] Cyprianus in *Sermo. de Cœna Domini.* [See note i, p. 49.]
[h] Athanasius, *De Peccato in Spiritum Sanctum.*

"saith he, *be spirit and life*. Which is as much "to say, as that thing which you see, shall be "slain and given for the nourishment of the world, "that it may be distributed to every body *spiri-* "*tually*, and be to all men a conservation unto "the resurrection of eternal life."

In these words Athanasius declareth the cause why Christ made mention of his ascension into heaven, when he spake of the eating and drinking of his flesh and blood. The cause after Athanasius's mind was this, that his hearers should not think of any carnal eating of his body with their mouths; for as concerning the presence of his body, he should be taken from them, and ascend into heaven; but that they should understand him to be a spiritual meat, and spiritually to be eaten, and by that refreshing to give eternal life, which he doth to none but to such as be his lively members.

And of this eating speaketh also Basilius[1], that "we eat Christ's flesh and drink his blood, being "made, by his incarnation and sensible life, par- "takers of his word and wisdom. For his *flesh* "*and blood he called all his mystical conversation* "*here in his flesh and his doctrine*, consisting of "his whole life, pertaining both to his humanity "and Divinity, whereby the soul is nourished and "brought to the contemplation of things eternal."

Thus teacheth Basilius how we eat Christ's

[1] Basilius, *Epistola* 141.

THE EATING AND DRINKING.

flesh and drink his blood, which pertaineth only to the true and faithful members of Christ.

St. Hierome also saith[k], "*All that love pleasure "more than God, eat not the flesh of Jesu, nor "drink his blood;* of the which himself saith, *He "that eateth my flesh and drinketh my blood, hath "everlasting life.*"

And in another place[l], St. Hierome saith, that "*heretics do not eat and drink the body and blood "of the Lord.*"

And moreover he saith[m], that "*heretics eat not "the flesh of Jesu,* whose flesh is the meat of "faithful men."

Thus agreeth St. Hierome with the other before rehearsed, that heretics and such as follow worldly pleasures, eat not Christ's flesh nor drink his blood, because that Christ said, *He that eateth my flesh, and drinketh my blood, hath everlasting life.*

And St. Ambrose saith[n], that "Jesus is the "bread which is the meat of saints; and that he "that taketh this bread, *dieth not a sinner's "death; for this bread is the remission of sins.*"

And in another book to him entitled[o], he writeth thus: "This bread of life which came from "heaven doth minister everlasting life, and *who- "soever eateth this bread shall not die for ever, "and is the body of Christ.*"

[k] Hieronymus *In Esaiam*, cap. 66.
[l] *In Hieremiam*, cap. 22.   [m] *In Oseam*, cap. 8.
[n] Ambrosius, *De Benedictione Patriarcharum*, cap. 9.
[o] *De iis qui Mysteriis initiantur.* [See note pp. 53 and 54.]

And yet in another book[p] set forth in his name, he saith on this wise: "He that did eat manna "died, but *he that eateth this body shall have* "*remission of his sins, and shall not die for ever.*" And again he saith[q], "*As often as thou drinkest,* "*thou hast remission of thy sins.*"

These sentences of St. Ambrose be so plain in this matter, that there needeth no more but only the rehearsal of them.

But St. Augustine in many places plainly discussing this matter, saith[r]: "*He that agreeth* "*not with Christ, doth neither eat his body nor* "*drink his blood*, although to the condemnation "of his presumption he receive every day the "sacrament of so high a matter."

And moreover St. Augustine most plainly resolveth this matter in his book *De Civitate Dei*[s], disputing against two kinds of heretics: Whereof the one said, that as many as were christened and received the sacrament of Christ's body and blood should be saved, howsoever they lived or believed; because that Christ said, *This is the bread that came from heaven; that whosoever shall eat thereof shall not die. I am the bread of life, which came from heaven; whosoever shall eat of this bread, shall live for ever.* Therefore, said these heretics, all such men must needs be delivered from eternal death and at length be

---

[p] *De Sacramentis*, lib. iv. cap. 5.   [q] Lib. v. cap. 3.
[r] *Lib. Sentent. Prosperi ex Augustino*, cap. 339.
[s] *De Civitate Dei*, lib. xxi. cap. 25.

brought to eternal life. The other said, that heretics and schismatics might eat the sacrament of Christ's body, but not his very body; because they be no members of his body. And therefore they promised not everlasting life to all that received Christ's baptism and the sacrament of his body, but to all such as professed a true faith, although they lived never so ungodly. For such, said they, do eat the body of Christ, not only in a sacrament but also in deed, because they be members of Christ's body.

But St. Augustine, answering to both these heresies, saith, that neither heretics, nor such as profess a true faith in their mouths and in their living show the contrary, have either a true faith which worketh by charity and doth none evil, or are to be counted among the members of Christ. For they cannot be both members of Christ and members of the Devil[t]. "Therefore," saith he, "*it may not be said, that any of them eat the body "of Christ.*" "For when Christ saith, *He that*

[t] "Qui ergo est," inquit [Augustinus], "in corporis Christi "unitate, id est, in Christianorum compage membrorum (cujus "corporis sacramentum fideles communicantes de altari sumere "consueverunt) ipse vere dicendus est manducare corpus "Christi et bibere sanguinem Christi. Ac per hoc hæretici et "schismatici, ab hujus unitate corporis separati, possunt idem "percipere sacramentum, sed non sibi utile, immo vero etiam "noxium." Et mox: "Recte intelligunt non dicendum eum "manducare corpus Christi, qui in corpore non est Christi." Et mox: "Nec isti, ergo, dicendi sunt manducare corpus Christi, "quoniam nec in membris computandi sunt Christi. Ut enim "alia taceam, non possunt simul esse et membra Christi, et "membra meretricis. Denique ipse dicens: *Qui manducat*," &c. EMBD.

"eateth my flesh and drinketh my blood, dwelleth "in me and I in him; he showeth what it is, not "sacramentally, but *in deed*, to eat his body and "drink his blood: which is, when a man dwelleth "so in Christ, that Christ dwelleth in him. For "Christ spake those words, as if he should say, "*He that dwelleth not in me, and in whom I* "*dwell not, let him not say or think, that he eateth* "*my body or drinketh my blood.*"

These be the plain words of St. Augustine, that such as live ungodly, although they may seem to eat Christ's body, because they eat the sacrament of his body, yet in deed they neither be members of his body, nor do eat his body.

Also upon the Gospel of St. John[u] he saith, that "he that doth not eat his flesh and drink his "blood, hath not in him everlasting life. And he "that eateth his flesh and drinketh his blood, hath "everlasting life. But it is not so in those meats "which we take to sustain our bodies; for "although without them we cannot live, yet it is "not necessary that whosoever receiveth them "shall live, for they may die by age, sickness, or "other chances.

"But in this meat and drink of the body and "blood of our Lord, it is otherwise; for both they "that eat and drink them not have not everlasting "life: *and contrariwise, whosoever eat and drink* "*them have everlasting life*[x]."

[u] *In Joan. Tract.* 26.

[x] Et mox: "Hunc itaque cibum et potum societatem vult "intelligi corporis et membrorum suorum, quod est sancta

THE EATING AND DRINKING. 211

Note and ponder well these words of St. Augustine, that the bread and wine and other meats and drinks which nourish the body, a man may eat, and nevertheless die; but the very body and blood of Christ no man eateth but that hath everlasting life. So that wicked men cannot eat nor drink them, for then they must needs have by them everlasting life.

And in the same place St. Augustine saith further: " The sacrament òf the unity of Christ's " body and blood is taken in the Lord's table of " some men to life, and of some men to death; " but *the thing itself*, whereof it is a sacrament, *is* " *taken of all men to life, and of no man to* " *death.*" And moreover he saith, " This is to " eat that meat and drink that drink, to dwell in " Christ and to have Christ dwelling in him. " And for that cause, *he that dwelleth not in* " *Christ, and in whom Christ dwelleth not, without* " *doubt he eateth not spiritually his flesh, nor* " *drinketh his blood,* although carnally and visibly " with his teeth he bite the sacrament of his body " and blood[y]."

Thus writeth St. Augustine in the twenty-sixth Homily of St. John. And in the next Homily

CHAP.
IV.

"Ecclesia in prædestinatis et vocatis et justificatis et glorifi-
"catis sanctis et fidelibus ejus." Et mox: "Hujus rei sacra-
"mentum, id est, unitatis corporis et sanguinis Christi, alicubi
"quotidie, alicubi certis intervallis dierum, in Dominica mensa
"præparatur, et de mensa Dominica sumitur quibusdam ad
"vitam, quibusdam ad exitium," &c. EMBD.

[y] "Sed magis tantæ rei sacramentum ad judicium sibi man-
"ducat." EMBD.

following[z] he writeth thus: "This day our sermon "is of the body of the Lord, which he said he "would give to eat for eternal life. And he de- "clared the manner of his gift and distribution, "how he would give his flesh to eat, saying, *He* "*that eateth my flesh, and drinketh my blood,* "*dwelleth in me, and I in him.* This therefore "*is a token or knowledge, that a man hath eaten* "*and drunken, that is to say, if he dwell in Christ* "*and have Christ dwelling in him;* if he cleave so "to Christ, that he is not severed from him. "This therefore Christ taught and admonished by "these *mystical or figurative words*, that we "should be in his body under him our head "among his members, eating his flesh, not "forsaking his unity"

And in his book *De Doctrina Christiana*[a], St. Augustine saith, (as before is at length declared,) that "to *eat Christ's flesh and to drink his blood,* "*is a figurative speech*, signifying the participa- "tion of his passion, and the delectable remem- "brance to our benefit and profit, that his flesh "was crucified and wounded for us."

And in another Sermon also, *De Verbis Apostoli*[c], he expounded what is the eating of Christ's body, and the drinking of his blood, saying, "*The eating* "*is to be refreshed, and the drinking, what is it* "*but to live?* Eat life, drink life. And that "shall be, when that which is taken visibly in the

[z] *In Joan. Tract.* 27.
[a] *De Doctrina Christiana*, lib. iii. cap. 14.
[c] *De Verbis Apostoli*, Serm. 2.

"sacrament, is in very deed eaten spiritually and "drunken spiritually."

By all these sentences of St. Augustine, it is evident and manifest, that all men, good and evil, may with their mouths visibly and sensibly eat the sacrament of Christ's body and blood ; but the very body and blood themselves be not eaten but spiritually, and that of the spiritual members of Christ, which dwell in Christ, and have Christ dwelling in them, by whom they be refreshed, and have everlasting life.

And therefore, saith St Augustine[d], that when the other Apostles did eat bread that was the Lord, yet *Judas did eat but the bread of the Lord, and not the bread that was the Lord.* So that the other Apostles, with the sacramental bread, did eat also Christ himself, whom Judas did not eat. And a great number of places mo hath St. Augustine[e] for this purpose, which for eschewing of tediousness I let pass for this time, and will speak something of St. Cyril.

[d] *In Joan. Tract.* 59.
[e] August. *In Psal.* 21, *in Expositione* 2[da.] "*Vota mea* "*reddam coram timentibus eum.* Quæ sunt vota sua? Sac-"rificium quod obtulit Deo. Nostis quale sacrificium? Norunt "fideles vota quæ reddit coram timentibus eum. Nam sequitur: "*Edent pauperes, et saturabuntur.* Beati pauperes, quia ideo "edunt, ut saturentur. Edunt enim pauperes, qui autem "divites sunt, non satiantur, quia non esuriunt. Comedent "pauperes, inde erat piscator ille Petrus, inde erat alius pisca-"tor Joannes, et Jacobus frater ipsius, inde erat etiam publi-"canus Matthæus de pauperibus. Ipsi erant, qui comederunt "et saturati sunt, talia passi, qualia manducaverunt. Cœnam "suam dedit, passionem suam dedit. Ille saturatur qui imita-

Cyril, upon St. John in his Gospel[f], saith, that " those which eat manna died, because they " received thereby no strength to live ever, (for it " gave no life, but only put away bodily hunger;) " but *they that receive the bread of life shall be* " *made immortal, and shall eschew all the evils* " *that pertain to death, living with Christ for* " *ever.*" And in another place[g] he saith: " *For-* " *asmuch as the flesh of Christ doth naturally* " *give life, therefore it maketh them to live that be* " *partakers of it. For it putteth death away from* " *them,* and utterly driveth destruction out of " *them.*"

And he concludeth the matter shortly in another place[h] in few words, saying, that " *when we eat* " *the flesh of our Saviour, then have we life in us.* " For if things that were corrupt were restored

"tur. Imitati sunt pauperes, ipsi enim sic passi sunt, ut "Christi vestigia sequerentur." &c. Et mox: "Sacrificium "pacis, sacrificium charitatis, sacrificium corporis sui norunt "fideles, disputari inde modo non potest. *Vota mea reddam* "*coram timentibus eum.* Edant publicani, edant piscatores, "manducent, imitentur Dominum, patiantur, saturentur."
Idem. *De Verbis Domini, Sermon.* 53. "Quicunque in cor- "pore ejus et membrorum ejus esse voluerit, non miretur quia "odit eum mundus. Corporis autem ejus sacramentum multi "accipiunt, sed non omnes qui accipiunt sacramentum, habi- "turi sunt apud eum etiam locum promissum membris ejus. "Pene quidem sacramentum omnes corpus ejus dicunt, quia "omnes in pascuis ejus simul pascunt, sed venturus est, qui "dividat, et alios ponat ad dexteram, alios ad sinistram."
Beda, in *Homilia quadam Paschali.* "Aderit nobis Christus "in fractione panis, cum sacramenta corporis ejus, videlicet, "panis et vini, casta et simplici conscientia sumimus." EMBD.

[f] Cyrillus, *In Joan.* lib. iv. cap. 10.   [g] Cap. 12.
[h] Cap. 14.

THE EATING AND DRINKING.

"by only touching of his clothes, *how can it be* "*that we shall not live that eat his flesh?*" And further[1] he saith, that "as two waxes that be "molten together do run every part into other, "so *he that receiveth Christ's flesh and blood must* "*needs be joined so with him, that Christ must be* "*in him, and he in Christ.*"

Here St. Cyril declareth the dignity of Christ's flesh, being inseparably annexed unto his Divinity, saying, that it is of such force and power, that it giveth everlasting life. And whatsoever occasion of death it findeth, or let of eternal life, it putteth out and driveth clean away all the same from them that eat that meat and receive that medicine. Other medicines or plasters sometimes heal, and sometimes heal not; but this medicine is of that effect and strength, that it eateth away all rotten and dead flesh, and perfectly healeth all wounds and sores that it is laid unto.

This is the dignity and excellency of Christ's flesh and blood joined to his Divinity; of the which dignity Christ's adversaries, the papists, deprive and rob him, when they affirm that such men do eat his flesh and receive this plaster, as remained still sick and sore, and be not holpen thereby.

---

[1] Cap 17.

And now for corroboration of Cyril's saying, I would thus reason with the papists, and demand of them: When an unrepentant sinner receiveth the sacrament, whether he have Christ's body within him or no?

If they say no, then have I my purpose, that evil men, although they receive the sacrament of Christ's body, yet receive they not his very body. If they say yea, then I would ask them further: Whether they have Christ's Spirit within them or no?

If they say nay, then do they separate Christ's body from his Spirit, and his humanity from his Divinity, and be condemned by the Scripture as very Antichrists that divide Christ.

And if they say yea, that a wicked man hath Christ's Spirit in him, then the Scripture also condemneth them, saying, that as he which hath no Spirit of Christ's is none of his; so he that hath Christ in him, liveth, because he is justified. And, *If his Spirit that raised Jesus from death dwell in you, he that raised Christ from death shall give life to your mortal bodies for his Spirit's sake which dwelleth in you.*

Thus on every side the Scripture condemneth the adversaries of God's word.

And this wickedness of the papists is to be wondered at, that they affirm Christ's flesh, blood, soul, holy Spirit, and his Deity to be in a man that is subject to sin and a limb of the Devil. They be wonderful jugglers and conjurers, that

THE EATING AND DRINKING. 217

with certain words can make God and the Devil to dwell together in one man, and make him both the temple of God and the temple of the Devil. It appeareth that they be so blind, that they cannot see the light from darkness, Belial from Christ, nor the table of the Lord from the table of devils.

Thus is confuted this third intolerable error and heresy of the papists, that they which be the limbs of the Devil do eat the very body of Christ and drink his blood, manifestly and directly contrary to the words of Christ himself, who saith, *Whosoever eateth my flesh, and drinketh my blood, hath everlasting life.*

CHAP. V.

But lest they should seem to have nothing to say for themselves, they allege St. Paul, in the eleventh to the Corinthians, where he saith, *He that eateth and drinketh unworthily, eateth and drinketh his own damnation, not discerning the Lord's body.*

CHAP. VI.
The answer to the papists.
1 Cor. xi.

But St. Paul in that place speaketh of the eating of the bread and drinking of the wine, and not of the corporal eating of Christ's flesh and blood, as it is manifest to every man that will read the text: for these be the words of St. Paul: *Let a man examine himself, and so eat of the bread, and drink of the cup; for he that eateth* and *drinketh unworthily eateth and drinketh his own damnation, not discerning the Lord's body.*

In these words St. Paul's mind is, that forasmuch as the bread and wine in the Lord's Supper do represent unto us the very body and blood of our Saviour Christ, by his own institution and ordinance ; therefore, although he sit in heaven at his Father's right hand, yet should we come to this mystical bread and wine with faith, reverence, purity, and fear, as we would do, if we should come to see and receive Christ himself sensibly present. For unto the faithful, Christ is at his own holy table present with his mighty Spirit and grace, and is of them more fruitfully received, than if corporally they should receive him bodily present. And therefore they that shall worthily come to this God's board, must after due trial of themselves consider, first who ordained this table, also what meat and drink they shall have that come thereto, and how they ought to behave themselves thereat. He that prepared the table is Christ himself. The meat and drink wherewith he feedeth them that come thereto as they ought to do, is his own body, flesh, and blood. They that come thereto must occupy their minds in considering, how his body was broken for them, and his blood shed for their redemption. And so ought they to approach to this heavenly table with all humbleness of heart, and godliness of mind, as to the table wherein Christ himself is given. And they that come otherwise to this

THE EATING AND DRINKING. 219

holy table, they come unworthily, and do not eat and drink Christ's flesh and blood, but eat and drink their own damnation; because they do not duly consider Christ's very flesh and blood, which be offered there spiritually to be eaten and drunken, but despising Christ's most holy Supper, do come thereto as it were to other common meats and drinks, without regard of the Lord's body, which is the spiritual meat of that table.

But here may not be passed over the answer unto certain places of ancient authors, which at the first show seem to make for the papists' purpose, that evil men do eat and drink the very flesh and blood of Christ. But if those places be truly and thoroughly weighed, it shall appear that not one of them maketh for their error, that evil men do eat Christ's very body.

The first place is of St. Augustine, *Contra Cresconium Grammaticum*[k], where he saith, that "although Christ himself say, *He that eateth not my flesh and drinketh not my blood, shall not have life in him:* yet doth not his Apostles teach "that the same is pernicious to them which use it "not well?* for he saith, *Whosoever eateth the "bread and drinketh the cup of the Lord un-*

[k] Augustinus, *Contra Cresconium*, lib. i. cap. 25.

"*worthily, shall be guilty of the body and blood of the Lord.*"

In which words St. Augustine seemeth to conclude, that as well the evil as the good do eat the body and blood of Christ, although the evil have no benefit, but hurt thereby.

But consider the place of St. Augustine diligently, and then it shall evidently appear, that he meant not of the eating of Christ's body, but of the sacrament thereof. For the intent of St. Augustine there is to prove, that good things avail not to such persons as do evil use them; and that many things which of themselves be good, and be good to some, yet to other some they be not good. As the light is good for whole eyes, and hurteth sore eyes; that meat which is good for some, is ill for other some; one medicine healeth some, and maketh other sick; one harness doth arm one, and cumbreth another; one coat is meet for one, and too strait for another. And after other examples, at the last St. Augustine showeth the same to be true in the sacraments both of baptism and of the Lord's body, which, he saith, do profit only them that receive the same worthily.

And the words of St. Paul, which St. Augustine citeth, do speak of the sacramental bread and cup, and not of the body and blood. And yet St. Augustine calleth the bread and the cup, the flesh and blood; not that they be so indeed, but that they so signify: as he saith in another place,

THE EATING AND DRINKING. 221

Contra Maximinum[1]. "In sacraments," saith he, CHAP. VII.
"is to be considered, not what they be, but what
"they show; for they be signs of other things,
"being one thing, and signifying another."
Therefore, as in baptism, those that come
feignedly and those that come unfeignedly, both
be washed with the sacramental water, but both
be not washed with the Holy Ghost, and clothed
with Christ; so, in the Lord's Supper, both eat
and drink the sacramental bread and wine, but
both eat not Christ himself, and be fed with his
flesh and blood, but those only which worthily
receive the sacrament.

And this answer will serve to another place[m]
of St. Augustine against the Donatists, where he
saith, that "*Judas received the body and blood of*
"*the Lord.*" For as St. Augustine in that place
speaketh of the sacrament of baptism, so doth he
speak of the sacrament of the body and blood,
which nevertheless he called the body and blood,
because they signify and represent unto us the
very body, flesh, and blood.

And, as before is at length declared, a figure CHAP. VIII.
hath the name of the thing that is signified
thereby. As a man's image is called a man, a Figures be called by the names
lion's image a lion, a bird's image a bird, and an of the

[1] *Contra Maximinum*, lib. iii. cap. 22.
[m] *De Baptism. contra Donat.* lib. v. cap. 8.

image of a tree and herb is called a tree or herb. So were we wont to say, our lady of Walsingham, our lady of Ipswich, our lady of Grace, our lady of Pity, St. Peter of Milan, St. John of Amyas, and such like, not meaning the things themselves, but calling their images by the name of the things by them represented. And likewise we were wont to say, Great St. Christopher of York or Lincoln; our lady smileth, or rocketh her child; let us go in pilgrimage to St. Peter at Rome, and St. James in Compostella; and a thousand like speeches, which were not understand of the very things, but only of the images of them.

So doth St. John Chrysostome say, that we see Christ with our eyes, touch him, feel him, and grope him with our hands, fix our teeth in his flesh, taste it, break it, eat it, and digest it, make red our tongues and dye them with his blood, and swallow it, and drink it.

And in a Catechism by me translated, and set forth, I used like manner of speech, saying that with our bodily mouths we receive the body and blood of Christ. Which my saying, divers[o] ignorant persons (not used to read old ancient authors, nor acquainted with their phrase and manner of speech) did carp and reprehend, for lack of good understanding.

[o] [Smythe probably was the person pointed at, (see Cranmer's *Answer to his Preface;*) but the remark may also be applied to Gardyner, who in his *Explication* repeatedly urged the inconsistency between the doctrines of the *Catechism* and of the *Defence;* and to Martyn, who brought forward a similar charge

THE EATING AND DRINKING. 223

For this speech and other before rehearsed of Chrysostome, and all other like, be not understand of the very flesh and blood of our Saviour Christ, which in very deed we neither feel nor see, but that which we do to the bread and wine, by a figurative speech is spoken to be done to the flesh and blood, because they be the very signs, figures, and tokens instituted of Christ, to represent unto us his very flesh and blood.

And yet as with our corporal eyes, corporal hands, and mouths, we do corporally see, feel, taste, and eat the bread and drink the wine, being the signs and sacraments of Christ's body, even so with our spiritual eyes, hands, and mouths, we do spiritually see, feel, taste, and eat his very flesh and drink his very blood.

As Eusebius Emissenus saith[p], "When thou "comest to the reverend altar to be filled with "spiritual meats, with thy faith look upon the "body and blood of him that is thy God, honour "him, touch him with thy mind, take him with "the hand of thy heart, and drink him with the "draught of thine inward man." And these spiritual things require no corporal presence of Christ himself, who sitteth continually in heaven, at the right hand of his Father.

upon his Examination of Cranmer at Oxford in 1555. See the Archbishop's justification in his *Answers to Gardyner*, and *Smythe*, and in his *Examination before Brokes*. This whole clause is omitted in the translation printed at Embden, in 1557: probably because it was thought unnecessary to weary continental readers with English disputes.—*Jenkyns.*]

[p] Eusebius Emissenus, in *Serm. de Eucharistia*.

BOOK IV.

And as this is most true, so it is full and sufficient to answer all things that the papists can bring in this matter, that hath any appearance for their party.

CHAP. IX.

The adoration in the sacrament.

Now it is requisite to speak something of the manner and form of worshipping of Christ, by them that receive this sacrament; lest that in the stead of Christ himself be worshipped the sacrament. For as his humanity, joined to his Divinity, and exalted to the right hand of his Father, is to be worshipped of all creatures in heaven, earth, and under the earth: even so, if in the stead thereof we worship the signs and sacraments, we commit as great idolatry as ever was, or shall be to the world's end[q].

The simple people be deceived.

And yet have the very Antichrists, the subtlest enemies that Christ hath, by their fine inventions and crafty scholastical divinity, deluded many simple souls, and brought them to this horrible idolatry, to worship things visible and made with their own hands, persuading them that creatures were their Creator, their God, and their Maker.

For else what made the people to run from their seats to the altar, and from altar to altar, and from sacring, as they called it, to sacring,

[q] De adoratione lege Roffen, et Œcolamp. lib. iii. cap. 4, and 5. [1580.]

THE EATING AND DRINKING. 225

peeping, tooting, and gazing at that thing which the priest held up in his hands, if they thought not to honour that thing which they saw? What moved the priests to lift up the sacrament so high over their heads? or the people to cry to the priest, 'Hold up, hold up;' and one man to say to another, 'Stoop down before;' or to say, 'This day have I seen my Maker;' and, 'I cannot be quiet except I see my Maker once a day?' What was the cause of all these, and that as well the priest as the people so devoutly did knock and kneel at every sight of the sacrament, but that they worshipped that visible thing which they saw with their eyes, and took it for very God? For if they worshipped in spirit only Christ, sitting in heaven with his Father, what needed they to remove out of their seats to toot and gaze, as the Apostles did after Christ when he was gone up into heaven? If they worshipped nothing that they saw, why did they rise up to see? Doubtless many of the simple people worshipped that thing which they saw with their eyes.

And although the subtle papists do colour and cloak the matter never so finely, saying, that they worship not the sacraments which they see with their eyes, but that thing which they believe with their faith to be really and corporally in the sacraments, yet why do they then run from place to place to gaze at the things which they see, if they worship them not, giving thereby occasion to them that be ignorant, to worship that which they see? Why do they not rather quietly sit still in their seats, and move the people to do the like, worshipping God in heart and in spirit, than to gad about from place to place, to see that thing which they confess themselves is not to be worshipped?

And yet to eschew one inconvenience, that is to say, the worshipping of the sacrament, they fall into another as evil, and worship nothing there at all. For they worship that thing, as they say, which is really and corporally and yet invisibly present under the kinds of bread and wine, which, as before is expressed and proved, is utterly nothing. And so they give unto the ignorant occasion to worship bread and wine, and they themselves worship nothing there at all.

But the papists, for their own commodity, to keep the people still in idolatry, do often allege a certain place[r] of St. Augustine upon the Psalms, where he saith, that "*no man doth eat the flesh of* "*Christ, except he first worship it,*" and that "*we do not offend in worshipping thereof, but we* "*should offend if we should not worship it.*"

That is true which St. Augustine saith in this place. For who is he that professeth Christ, and is spiritually fed and nourished with his flesh and blood, but he will honour and worship him, sitting at the right hand of his Father, and render unto him, from the bottom of his heart, all laud, praise, and thanks, for his merciful redemption?

[r] August. *In Psal. xcviii.*

THE EATING AND DRINKING. 227

And as this is most true which St. Augustine saith, so is that most false which the papists would persuade upon St. Augustine's words, that the sacramental bread and wine, or any visible thing, is to be worshipped in the sacrament. For St. Augustine's mind was so far from any such thought, that he forbiddeth utterly to worship Christ's own flesh and blood alone, but in consideration, and as they be annexed and joined to his Divinity. How much less then could he think or allow that we should worship the sacramental bread and wine, or any outward or visible sacrament, which be shadows, figures, and representations of Christ's very flesh and blood!

And St. Augustine was afraid, lest in worshipping of Christ's very body we should offend; and therefore he biddeth us, when we worship Christ, that we should not tarry and fix our minds upon his flesh, which of itself availeth nothing, but that we should lift up our minds from the flesh to the Spirit which giveth life: and yet the papists be not afraid, by crafty means, to induce us to worship those things which be signs and sacraments of Christ's body.

But what will not the shameless papists allege for their purpose, when they be not ashamed to maintain the adoration of the sacrament by these words of St. Augustine, wherein he speaketh not one word of the adoration of the sacrament, but only of Christ himself?

And although he say, that Christ gave his

flesh to be eaten of us, yet he meant not that his flesh is here corporally present and corporally eaten, but only spiritually. As his words declare plainly which follow in the same place, where St. Augustine, as it were in the person of Christ, speaketh these words: "It is the Spirit that "giveth life, but *the flesh profiteth nothing. The* "*words which I have spoken unto you, be spirit* "*and life. That which I have spoken, understand* "*you spiritually.* You shall not eat this body "*which you see,* and drink that blood which they "shall shed that shall crucify me. I have com- "mended unto you a sacrament, *understand it* "*spiritually*, and it shall give you life. And "although it must be visibly ministered, yet it "must be invisibly understand."

These words of St. Augustine, with the other before recited, do express his mind plainly, that Christ is not otherwise to be eaten than spiritually, which spiritual eating requireth no corporal presence; and that he intended not to teach here any adoration either of the visible sacraments, or of any thing that is corporally in them. For indeed there is nothing really and corporally in the bread to be worshipped, although the papists say, that Christ is in every consecrated bread.

But our Saviour Christ himself hath given us warning beforehand, that such false Christians and false teachers should come, and hath bid us to beware of them, saying, If any man tell you that Christ is here, or Christ is there, believe him not; *for there shall arise false Christs and false prophets, and shall show many signs and wonders, so that if it were possible the very elect should be brought into error. Take heed, I have told you beforehand.*

CHAP. IX.

Thus our Saviour Christ, like a most loving Pastor and Saviour of our souls, hath given us warning beforehand of the perils and dangers that were to come, and to be wise and ware, that we should not give credit unto such teachers as would persuade us to worship a piece of bread, to kneel to it, to knock to it, to creep to it, to follow it in procession, to lift up our hands to it, to offer to it, to light candles to it, to shut it up in a chest or box, to do all other honour unto it, more than we do unto God; having alway this pretence or excuse for our idolatry, 'Behold here is Christ.' But our Saviour Christ calleth them false prophets, and saith, *Take heed, I tell you before, believe them not: if they say to you, Behold, Christ is abroad, or in the wilderness, go not out; and if they say that he is kept in close places, believe them not.*

Matt. xxiv.

And if you will ask me the question, who be those false prophets and seducers of the people, the answer is soon made: the Romish Antichrists and their adherents, the authors of all error,

CHAP. X.

They be the papists that have deceived the people.

ignorance, blindness, superstition, hypocrisy, and idolatry.

Innocentius Tertius. For Innocentius the Third, one of the most wicked men that ever was in the see of Rome, did ordain and decree that the host should be diligently kept under lock and key.

Honorius Tertius And Honorius the Third not only confirmed the same, but commanded also that the priests should diligently teach the people from time to time, that when they lifted up the bread called the *Host*, the people should then reverently bow down, and that likewise they should do, when the priest carrieth the Host unto sick folks. These be the statutes and ordinances of Rome, under pretence of holiness, to lead the people unto all error and idolatry; not bringing them by bread unto Christ, but from Christ unto bread.

CHAP. XI.

An exhortation to the true honouring of Christ in the sacrament.

But all that love and believe Christ himself, let them not think that Christ is corporally in the bread, but let them lift up their hearts unto heaven, and worship him sitting there at the right hand of his Father. Let them worship him in themselves, whose temples they be, in whom he dwelleth and liveth spiritually: but in no wise let them worship him as being corporally in the bread; for he is not in it, neither spiritually, as he is in man; nor corporally, as he is in heaven;

but only sacramentally, as a thing may be said to be in the figure, whereby it is signified.

Thus is sufficiently reproved the third principal error of the papists, concerning the Lord's Supper, which is, that wicked members of the Devil do eat Christ's very body, and drink his blood.

THUS ENDETH THE FOURTH BOOK.

The Fifth Book is of the Oblation and Sacrifice of our Saviour Christ.

CHAP. I.

The sacrifice of the mass.

The greatest blasphemy and injury that can be against Christ, and yet universally used through the popish kingdom, is this, that the priests make their mass a sacrifice propitiatory, to remit the sins as well of themselves as of other, both quick and dead, to whom they list to apply the same. Thus, under pretence of holiness, the papistical priests have taken upon them to be Christ's successors, and to make such an oblation and sacrifice as never creature made but Christ alone, neither he made the same any more times than once, and that was by his death upon the cross.

CHAP. II.

The difference between the sacrifice of Christ, and of the priests of the old law.

For as St. Paul in his Epistle to the Hebrews witnesseth, *Although the high priests of the old law offered many times, at the least every year once, yet Christ offereth not himself many times, for then he should many times have died: but now he offereth himself but once, to take away sin by that offering of himself. And as men must die once, so was Christ offered once, to take away the sins of many.*

Heb. ix.

And furthermore St. Paul saith, that *the*

sacrifices of the old law, although they were continually offered from year to year, yet could they not take away sin, nor make men perfect. For if they could once have quieted men's consciences by taking away sin, they should have ceased, and no more have been offered. But Christ, with once offering, hath made perfect for ever them that be sanctified; putting their sins clean out of God's remembrance. And where remission of sins is, there is no more offering for sin.

CHAP. II.
Heb. x.

And yet further he saith, concerning the old testament, that *it was disannulled and taken away, because of the feebleness and unprofitableness thereof; for it brought nothing to perfection. And the priests of that law were many, because they lived not long, and so the priesthood went from one to another; but Christ liveth ever, and hath an everlasting priesthood, that passeth not from him to any man else. Wherefore he is able perfectly to save them that come to God by him, forasmuch as he liveth ever to make intercession for us. For it was meet for us to have such an High Priest that is holy, innocent, without spot, separated from sinners, and exalted up above heaven; who needeth not daily to offer up sacrifice, as Aaron's priests did, first for his own sins, and then for the people. For that he did once, when he offered up himself.*

Heb. vii.

Here, in his Epistle to the Hebrews, St. Paul hath plainly and fully described unto us the difference between the priesthood and sacrifices of the old testament, and the most high and worthy priesthood of Christ, his most perfect and necessary sacrifice, and the benefit that cometh to us thereby.

For Christ offered not the blood of calves, sheep, and goats, as the priests of the old law used to do; but he offered his own blood upon the cross. And he went not into an holy place made by man's hand, as Aaron did, but he ascended up into heaven, where his eternal Father dwelleth; and before him he maketh continual supplication for the sins of the whole world, presenting his own body, which was torn for us, and his precious blood, which of his most gracious and liberal charity he shed for us upon the cross.

And that sacrifice was of such force, that it was no need to renew it every year, as the bishops did of the old testament; whose sacrifices were many times offered, and yet were of no great effect or profit, because they were sinners themselves that offered them, and offered not their own blood, but the blood of brute beasts; but Christ's sacrifice, once offered, was sufficient for evermore.

CHAP. III.

Two kinds of sacrifices.

And that all men may the better understand this sacrifice of Christ, which he made for the great benefit of all men, it is necessary to know the distinction and diversity of sacrifices.

One kind of sacrifice there is, which is called a propitiatory or merciful sacrifice, that is to say, such a sacrifice as pacifieth God's wrath and indignation, and obtaineth mercy and forgiveness for all our sins, and is the ransom for our redemption from everlasting damnation.

And although in the old testament there were certain sacrifices called by that name, yet in very deed there is but one such sacrifice whereby our sins be pardoned and God's mercy and favour obtained, which is the death of the Son of God our Lord Jesu Christ; nor never was any other sacrifice propitiatory at any time, nor never shall be.

The sacrifice of Christ.

This is the honour and glory of this our High Priest, wherein he admitteth neither partner nor successor. For by his one oblation he satisfied his Father for all men's sins, and reconciled mankind unto his grace and favour. And whosoever deprive him of this honour, and go about to take it to themselves, they be very Antichrists, and most arrogant blasphemers against God and against his Son Jesus Christ whom he hath sent.

Another kind of sacrifice there is, which doth not reconcile us to God, but is made of them that be reconciled by Christ, to testify our duties unto God, and to show ourselves thankful unto him; and therefore they be called sacrifices of laud, praise, and thanksgiving.

The sacrifices of the Church.

The first kind of sacrifice Christ offered to God for us; the second kind we ourselves offer to God by Christ.

BOOK V.

And by the first kind of sacrifice Christ offered also us unto his Father; and by the second we offer ourselves and all that we have, unto him and his Father.

And this sacrifice generally is our whole obedience unto God, in keeping his laws and commandments. Of which manner of sacrifice speaketh the prophet David, saying, *A sacrifice to God is a contrite heart.* And St. Peter saith of all Christian people, that *they be an holy priesthood, to offer spiritual sacrifices, acceptable to God by Jesu Christ.* And St. Paul saith, that *alway we offer unto God a sacrifice of laud and praise by Jesus Christ.*

Psal. l.

1 Pet. ii.

Heb. xiii.

CHAP. IV.

A more plain declaration of the sacrifice of Christ.

But now to speak somewhat more largely of the priesthood and sacrifice of Christ: he was such an high Bishop, that he once offering himself, was sufficient by one effusion of his blood to abolish sin unto the world's end. He was so perfect a Priest, that by one oblation he purged an infinite heap of sins, leaving an easy and a ready remedy for all sinners, that his one sacrifice should suffice for many years unto all men that would not show themselves unworthy. And he took unto himself not only their sins that many years before were dead and put their trust in him, but also the sins of those that until his coming

Heb. vii.

1 John ii.

again should truly believe in his Gospel. So that now we may look for none other priest, nor sacrifice, to take away our sins, but only him and his sacrifice. And as he, dying once, was offered for all, so, as much as pertained to him, he took all men's sins unto himself. So that now there remaineth no more sacrifices for sin, but extreme judgment at the last day, when he shall appear to us again, not as a man to be punished again, and to be made a sacrifice for our sins, as he was before; but he shall come in his glory, without sin, to the great joy and comfort of them which be purified and made clean by his death, and continue in godly and innocent living; and to the great terror and dread of them that be wicked and ungodly.

CHAP. IV.
Heb. ix. and x.

Matt xxiv.

Heb. ix.

Thus the Scripture teacheth, that if Christ had made any oblation for sin more than once, he should have died more than once; forasmuch as there is none oblation and sacrifice for sin, but only his death. And now there is no more oblation for sin, seeing that by him our sins be remitted, and our consciences quieted.

Heb. ix.

And although in the old testament there were certain sacrifices, called sacrifices for sin, yet they were no such sacrifices that could take away our sins in the sight of God; but they were ceremonies

CHAP. V.
The sacrifices of the old law.

ordained to this intent, that they should be, as it were, shadows and figures, to signify beforehand the excellent sacrifice of Christ that was to come, which should be the very true and perfect sacrifice for the sins of the whole world.

And for this signification they had the name of a sacrifice propitiatory, and were called sacrifices for sins, not because they indeed took away our sins, but because they were images, shadows, and figures, whereby godly men were admonished of the true sacrifice of Christ then to come, which should truly abolish sin and everlasting death.

And that those sacrifices which were made by the priests in the old law could not be able to purchase our pardon and deserve the remission of our sins, St. Paul doth clearly affirm in his said Epistle to the Hebrews, where he saith, *It is impossible that our sins should be taken away by the blood of oxen and goats.*

Wherefore all godly men, although they did use those sacrifices ordained of God, yet they did not take them as things of that value and estimation, that thereby they should be able to obtain remission of their sins before God.

But they took them partly for figures and tokens ordained of God, by the which he declared, that he would send that seed which he promised, to be the very true sacrifice for sin, and that he would receive them that trusted in that promise, and remit their sins for the sacrifice after to come.

And partly they used them as certain ceremonies, whereby such persons as had offended against the law of Moses, and were cast out of the congregation, were received again among the people, and declared to be absolved.

As for like purposes we use, in the church of Christ, sacraments by him instituted. And this outward casting out from the people of God, and receiving in again, was according to the law and knowledge of man; but the true reconciliation and forgiveness of sin before God, neither the fathers of the old law had, nor we yet have, but only by the sacrifice of Christ, made in the mount of Calvary. And the sacrifices of the old law were prognostications and figures of the same then to come, as our sacraments be figures and demonstrations of the same now passed.

CHAP. VI.

The mass is not a sacrifice propitiatory.

Now by these aforesaid things may every man easily perceive, that the offering of the priest in the mass, or the appointing of his ministration at his pleasure to them that be quick or dead, cannot merit and deserve, neither to himself, nor to them for whom he singeth or sayeth, the remission of their sins: but that such popish doctrine is contrary to the doctrine of the Gospel, and injurious to the sacrifice of Christ.

For if only the death of Christ be the oblation, sacrifice, and price, wherefore our sins be pardoned, then the act or ministration of the priest cannot have the same office. Wherefore it is an abominable blasphemy to give that office or dignity to a priest which pertaineth only to Christ; or to affirm that the Church hath need of any such sacrifice; as who should say, that Christ's sacrifice were not sufficient for the remission of our sins; or else that his sacrifice should hang upon the sacrifice of a priest.

But all such priests as pretend to be Christ's successors in making a sacrifice of him, they be his most heinous and horrible adversaries. For never no person made a sacrifice of Christ, but he himself only. And therefore St. Paul saith, that *Christ's priesthood cannot pass from him to another.* For what needeth any mo [more] sacrifices, if Christ's sacrifice be perfect and sufficient? And as St. Paul saith, that if the sacrifices and ministration of Aaron and other priests of that time had lacked nothing, but had been perfect and sufficient, then should not the sacrifice of Christ have been required, (for it had been but in vain to add any thing to that which of itself was perfect;) so likewise, if Christ's sacrifice which he had made himself be sufficient, what need we every day to have mo [more] and mo [more] sacrifices? Wherefore all popish priests that presume to make every day a sacrifice of Christ, either must they needs make Christ's sacrifice vain, unperfect, and unsufficient, or else is their sacrifice in vain, which is added to the sacrifice which is already of itself sufficient and perfect.

But it is a wondrous thing to see what shifts and cautels the popish Antichrists devise to colour and cloke their wicked errors. And as a chain is so joined together, that one link draweth another after it; so be vices and errors knit together, that every one draweth his fellow with him. And so doth it here in this matter.

CHAP. VI.

For the papists to excuse themselves do say, that they make no new sacrifice, nor none other sacrifice than Christ made; for they be not so blind, but they see that then they should add another sacrifice to Christ's sacrifice, and so make his sacrifice unperfect; but they say, that they make the selfsame sacrifice for sin that Christ himself made.

CHAP. VII.

A confutation of the papists' cavillation

And here they run headlong into the foulest and most heinous error that ever was imagined. For if they make every day the same oblation and sacrifice for sin that Christ himself made, and the oblation that he made was his death and the effusion of his most precious blood upon the cross for our redemption and price of our sin; then followeth it of necessity, that they every day slay Christ and shed his blood: and so be they worse than the wicked Jews and Pharisees, which slew him and shed his blood but once.

Heb. ix.

BOOK V.
CHAP. VIII.
The true sacrifice of all Christian people

Almighty God, the Father of light and truth, banish all such darkness and error out of his Church, with the authors and teachers thereof; or else convert their hearts unto him, and give this light of faith to every man, that he may trust to have remission of his sins, and be delivered from eternal death and hell, by the merit only of the death and blood of Christ: and that by his own faith every man may apply the same unto himself, and not take it at the appointment of popish priests, by the merit of their sacrifices and oblations.

If we be indeed, as we profess, Christian men, we may ascribe this honour and glory to no man, but to Christ alone. Wherefore let us give the whole laud and praise hereof unto him; let us fly only to him for succour; let us hold him fast, and hang upon him, and give ourselves wholly to him. And forasmuch as he hath given himself to death for us, to be an oblation and sacrifice to his Father for our sins, let us give ourselves again unto him, making unto him an oblation, not of goats, sheep, kine, and other beasts that have no reason, as was accustomed before Christ's coming; but of a creature that hath reason, that is to say, of ourselves, not killing our own bodies, but mortifying the beastly and unreasonable affections that would gladly rule and reign in us.

So long as the law did reign, God suffered dumb beasts to be offered unto him; but now that we be spiritual, we must offer spiritual oblations, in the place of calves, sheep, goats, and doves   We must kill devilish pride, furious anger, insatiable covetousness, filthy lucre, stinking lechery, deadly hatred and malice, foxy wiliness, wolvish ravening and devouring, and all other unreasonable lusts and desires of the flesh. And as many as belong to Christ must crucify and kill these for Christ's sake, as Christ crucified himself for their sakes.

CHAP. VIII.

Gal. v.

These be the sacrifices of Christian men ; these hosts and oblations be acceptable to Christ. And as Christ offered himself for us, so is it our duties after this sort to offer ourselves to him again. And so shall we not have the name of Christian men in vain ; but as we pretend to belong to Christ in word and profession, so shall we indeed be his in life and inward affection. So that within and without we shall be altogether his, clean from all hypocrisy or dissimulation. And if we refuse to offer ourselves after this wise unto him, by crucifying our own wills, and committing us wholly to the will of God, we be most unkind people, superstitious hypocrites, or rather unreasonable beasts, worthy to be excluded utterly from all the benefits of Christ's oblation.

And if we put the oblation of the priest in the stead of the oblation of Christ, refusing to receive

CHAP. IX.

the sacrament of his body and blood ourselves, as he ordained, and trusting to have remission of our sins by the sacrifice of the priest in the mass, and thereby also to obtain release of the pains in purgatory, we do not only injury to Christ, but also commit most detestable idolatry. For these be but false doctrines, without shame devised and feigned by wicked popish priests, idolaters, monks, and friars, which for lucre have altered and corrupted the most holy Supper of the Lord, and turned it into manifest idolatry. Wherefore all godly men ought with all their heart to refuse and abhor all such blasphemy against the Son of God.

And forasmuch as in such masses is manifest wickedness and idolatry, wherein the priest alone maketh oblation satisfactory, and applieth the same for the quick and the dead at his will and pleasure; all such popish masses are to be clearly taken away out of Christian Churches, and the true use of the Lord's Supper is to be restored again, wherein godly people assembled together may receive the sacrament every man for himself, to declare that he remembereth what benefit he hath received by the death of Christ, and to testify that he is a member of Christ's body, fed with his flesh, and drinking his blood spiritually.

CHAP. X.

Christ did not ordain his sacraments to this

use, that one should receive them for another, and the priest for all the lay people; but he ordained them for this intent, that every man should receive them for himself, to ratify, confirm, and stablish his own faith and everlasting salvation. Therefore as one man may not be baptized for another, (and if he be, it availeth nothing,) so ought not one to receive the holy Communion for another. For if a man be dry or hungry, he is never a whit eased, if another man drink or eat for him; or if a man be all defiled, it helpeth him nothing another man to be washed for him: so availeth it nothing to a man, if another man be baptized for him, or be refreshed for him with the meat and drink at the Lord's table. And therefore, saith St. Peter, *Let every man be baptized in the name of Jesu Christ.* And our Saviour Christ said to the multitude, *Take, and eat.* And further he said, *Drink you all of this.* Whosoever therefore will be spiritually regenerated in Christ, he must be baptized himself. And he that will live himself by Christ, must by himself eat Christ's flesh and drink his blood.

And briefly to conclude: he that thinketh to come to the kingdom of Christ himself, must also come to his sacraments himself, and keep his commandments himself, and do all things that pertain to a Christian man and to his vocation himself; lest if he refer these things to another man to do them for him, the other may with as good right claim the kingdom of heaven for him.

CHAP. X.

Every man ought to receive the sacrament himself, and not one for another.

Acts ii

Matt xxvi

BOOK V.
CHAP. XI.

The difference between the priest and the layman.

Therefore Christ made no such difference between the priest and the layman, that the priest should make oblation and sacrifice of Christ for the layman, and eat the Lord's Supper from him all alone, and distribute and apply it as him liketh. Christ made no such difference; but the difference that is between the priest and the layman in this matter is only in the ministration; that the priest, as a common minister of the Church, doth minister and distribute the Lord's Supper unto other, and other receive it at his hands. But the very Supper itself was by Christ instituted and given to the whole Church, not to be offered and eaten of the priest for other men, but by him to be delivered to all that would duly ask it.

As in a prince's house the officers and ministers prepare the table, and yet other, as well as they, eat the meat and drink the drink; so do the priests and ministers prepare the Lord's Supper, read the Gospel, and rehearse Christ's words; but all the people say thereto, Amen; all remember Christ's death, all give thanks to God, all repent and offer themselves an oblation to Christ, all take him for their Lord and Saviour, and spiritually feed upon him; and in token thereof, they eat the bread and drink the wine in his mystical Supper.

THE SACRIFICE OF CHRIST. 247

And this nothing diminisheth the estimation and dignity of priesthood and other ministers of the Church, but advanceth and highly commandeth their ministration. For if they are much to be loved, honoured and esteemed, that be the king's chancellors, judges, officers, and ministers in temporal matters; how much then are they to be esteemed that be ministers of Christ's words and sacraments, and have to them committed the keys of heaven, to let in and shut out, by the ministration of his word and gospel!

CHAP. XI.
The dignity of priests.

Now, forasmuch as I trust that I have plainly enough set forth the propitiatory sacrifice of our Saviour Jesu Christ, to the capacity and comfort of all men that have any understanding of Christ; and have declared also the heinous abomination and idolatry of the popish mass, wherein the priests have taken upon them the office of Christ, to make a propitiatory sacrifice for the sins of the people, and I have also told what manner of sacrifice Christian people ought to make; it is now necessary to make answer to the subtle persuasions and sophistical cavillations of the papists, whereby they have deceived many a simple man, both learned and unlearned.

CHAP. XII.
The answer to the papists

The place of St. Paul unto the Hebrews, which they do cite for their purpose, maketh quite and

Heb. v.

clean against them. For where St. Paul saith, that *every high priest is ordained to offer gifts and sacrifices for sins,* he spake not that of the priests of the new testament, but of the old; which, as he saith, offered calves and goats. And yet they were not such priests, that by their offerings and sacrifices they could take away the people's sins, but they were shadows and figures of Christ our everlasting Priest, which only by one oblation of himself taketh away the sins of the world. Wherefore the popish priests that apply this text unto themselves, do directly contrary to the meaning of St. Paul, to the great injury and prejudice of Christ, by whom only, St. Paul saith, that the sacrifice and oblation for the sin of the whole world was accomplished and fulfilled.

And as little serveth for the papists' purpose the text of the Prophet Malachi, that *every where should be offered unto God a pure sacrifice and oblation.* For the Prophet in that place spake no word of the mass, nor of any oblation propitiatory to be made by the Priests; but he spake of the oblation of all faithful people, in what place soever they be, which offer unto God, with pure hearts and minds, sacrifices of laud and praise; prophesying of the vocation of the Gentiles, that God would extend his mercy unto them, and not be the God only of the Jews, but of all nations from east to west, that with pure faith call upon him and glorify his name.

But the adversaries of Christ gather together a great heap of authors, which, as they say, call the mass, or holy communion, a sacrifice. But all those authors be answered unto in this one sentence, that they call it not a sacrifice for sin, because that it taketh away our sin, which is taken away only by the death of Christ, but because it was ordained of Christ to put us in remembrance of the sacrifice made by him upon the cross. And for that cause it beareth the name of that sacrifice, as St. Augustine declareth plainly in his Epistle *Ad Bonifacium*[b], before rehearsed in this book, p. 140 and foll.; and in his book *De fide ad Petrum Diaconum*[c], before rehearsed also. And in his book *De Civitate Die*[d], he saith, "*That which men call a sacrifice, is a* "*sign or representation of the true sacrifice*[e]."

CHAP. XIII.
An answer to the authors.

[b] Augustinus *Ad Bonifacium*.
[c] [This has been proved to be the work of Fulgentius instead of Augustine. See Ed. Bened. tom. vi. App. p. 18.—*Jenkyns.*]
[d] *De Civitat.* lib. x. cap. 5. ad fin.
[e] Idem, *In Psal.* 21. *in Præfatione Expositionis secundæ.*
"Passio Domini, (sicut scimus,) semel facta est, semel enim "Christus mortuus est, justus pro injustis. Et scimus et cer- "tum habemus, et fide immobili retinemus, quia *Christus resur-* "*gens a mortuis jam non moritur, et mors ei ultra non* "*dominabitur.* Verba ista Apostoli sunt, tamen ne oblivisca- "mur quod factum est semel, in memoria nostra omni anno "fit. Quoties Pascha celebratur, numquid toties Christus "moritur? Sed tum anniversaria recordatio quasi repræsentat, "quod olim factum est, et sic nos facit moneri, tanquam "videamus in cruce pendentem Dominum." EMBD.

And the Master of Sentences, of whom all the school authors take their occasion to write, judged truly in this point, saying, "That which is offered " and consecrated of the priest, *is called a sacrifice* " *and oblation, because it is a memory and repre-* " *sentation of the true sacrifice and holy oblation,* " *made in the altar of the cross*[g]."

And St. John Chrysostome[h], after he hath said that Christ is our Bishop which offered that sacrifice that made us clean, and that we offer the same now, lest any man might be deceived by his manner of speaking, he openeth his meaning more plainly, saying, " *That which we do, is done* " *for a remembrance of that which was done by* " *Christ.* For Christ saith, *Do this in remem-* " *brance of me.*" Also Chrysostome declaring at length, that the priests of the old law offered ever new sacrifices, and changed them from time to time, and that Christian people do not so, but offer ever one sacrifice of Christ; yet by and by, lest some men might be offended with this speech, he maketh as it were a correction of his words, saying, " *But rather we make a remembrance of* " *Christ's sacrifice.*" As though he should say; Although in a certain kind of speech we may say,

[f] [The Embden translator, as if dissatisfied with the plainness of Cranmer's language, has added a simile. "Lombardus autem "(e cujus scriptis, tanquam ex equo Trojano, omnis scholasti-"corum turba profluxit) vere hac in causa judicasse videtur." Ed. Embd. fol. 149.]
[g] Lombardus, lib. iv. dist. 12.
[h] Chrysost. *In Epist. ad Heb. Hom.* 17. [See Gardyner, *Detection, &c.* fol. 87.]

that every day we make a sacrifice of Christ; yet in very deed, to speak properly, we make no sacrifice of him, but only a commemoration and remembrance of that sacrifice, which he alone made, and never none but he. Nor Christ never gave this honour to any creature, that he should make a sacrifice of him, nor did not ordain the sacrament of his holy Supper, to the intent that either the people should sacrifice Christ again, or that the priests should make a sacrifice of him for the people : but his holy Supper was ordained for this purpose, that every man eating and drinking thereof should remember that Christ died for him, and so should exercise his faith, and comfort himself by the remembrance of Christ's benefits ; and so give unto Christ most hearty thanks, and give himself also clearly unto him.

Wherefore the ordinance of Christ ought to be followed ; the priest to minister the sacrament to the people, and they to use it to their consolation. And in this eating, drinking, and using of the Lord's Supper, we make not of Christ a new sacrifice propitiatory for remission of sin.

But the humble confession of all penitent hearts, their knowledging of Christ's benefits, their thanksgiving for the same, their faith and consolation in Christ, their humble submission

CHAP. XIII.

CHAP. XIV. The lay persons make a sacrifice as

and obedience to God's will and commandments, is a sacrifice of laud and praise, accepted and allowed of God no less than the sacrifice of the priest. For Almighty God, without respect of person, accepteth the oblation and sacrifice of priest and lay person, of king and subject, of master and servant, of man and woman, of young and old, yea of English, French, Scot, Greek, Latin, Jew, and Gentile; of every man according to his faithful and obedient heart unto him; and that through the sacrifice propitiatory of Jesu Christ.

CHAP. XV.

The papistical mass is neither a sacrifice propitiatory, nor of thanksgiving. Luke xvi.

And as for the saying or singing of mass by the priest, as it was in time passed used, it is neither a sacrifice propitiatory, nor yet a sacrifice of laud and praise, nor in any wise allowed before God, but abominable and detestable; and thereof may well be verified the saying of Christ, *That thing which seemeth an high thing before men, is an abomination before God.*

They therefore which gather of the doctors, that the mass is a sacrifice for remission of sin, and that it is applied by the priest to them for whom he saith or singeth; they which so gather of the doctors, do to them most grievous injury and wrong, most falsely belying them.

THE SACRIFICE OF CHRIST. 253

For these monstrous things were never seen nor known of the old and primitive Church, nor there was not then in one church many masses every day, but upon certain days there was a common table of the Lord's Supper, where a number of people did together receive the body and blood of the Lord: but there were then no daily private masses, where every priest received alone, like as until this day there is none in the Greek churches but one common mass in a day. Nor the holy fathers of the old Church would not have suffered such ungodly and wicked abuses of the Lord's Supper.

But these private masses sprang up of late years, partly through the ignorance and superstition of unlearned monks and friars, which knew not what a sacrifice was, but made of the mass a sacrifice propitiatory, to remit both sin and the pain due for the same; but chiefly they sprang of lucre and gain, when priests found the means to sell masses to the people; which caused masses so much to increase, that every day was said an infinite number, and that no priest would receive the communion at another priest's hand, but every one would receive it alone; neither regarding the godly decree of the Council of Nice[i], which appointeth in what order priests should be placed above deacons at the communion; nor yet the Canons of the Apostles[k], which command

CHAP. XVI.

There were no papistical masses in the primitive Church.

---

[i] *Concilium Nicenum*, cap. 14.
[k] *Canones Apostolorum*, cap. 8.

that when any communion is ministered, all the priests together should receive the same, or else be excommunicate. So much the old fathers misliked, that any priest should receive the sacrament alone.

Therefore when the old fathers called the mass, or Supper of the Lord, a sacrifice, they meant that it was a sacrifice of lauds and thanksgiving, and so as well the people as the priest do sacrifice; or else that it was a remembrance of the very true sacrifice propitiatory of Christ: but they meant in no wise that it is a very true sacrifice for sin, and applicable by the priest to the quick and dead.

For the priest may well minister Christ's words and sacraments to all men both good and bad, but he can apply the benefit of Christ's passion to no man being of age and discretion, but only to such as by their own faith do apply the same unto themselves. So that every man of age and discretion taketh to himself the benefits of Christ's passion, or refuseth them himself, by his own faith, quick or dead; that is to say, by his true and lively faith, that worketh by charity, he receiveth them, or else by his ungodliness or feigned faith rejecteth them.

And this doctrine of the Scripture clearly condemneth the wicked inventions of the papists in these latter days, which have devised a purgatory to torment souls after this life, and oblations of masses said by the priests to deliver them from the said torments; and a great number of other commodities do they promise to the simple ignorant people by their masses.

CHAP. XVI.

Now the nature of man being ever prone to idolatry from the beginning of the world, and the papists being ready by all means and policy to defend and extol the mass for their estimation and profit; and the people being superstitiously enamoured and doted upon the mass, because they take it for a present remedy against all manner of evils; and part of the princes being blinded by papistical doctrine, part loving quietness, and loth to offend their clergy and subjects, and all being captive and subject to the Antichrist of Rome; the state of the world remaining in this case, it is no wonder that abuses grew and increased in the Church, that superstition with idolatry was taken for godliness and true religion, and that many things were brought in without the authority of Christ:

CHAP. XVII.
The causes and means how papistical masses entered into the Church

As purgatory, the oblation and sacrificing of Christ by the priest alone, the application and appointing of the same to such persons as the priest would sing or say mass for, and to such abuses as they could devise, to deliver some from purgatory, and some from hell, if they were not there finally by God determined to abide, as they

The abuses of the papistical masses.

termed the matter; to make rain or fair weather, to put away the plague and other sicknesses both from man and beast, to hallow and preserve them that went to Jerusalem, to Rome, to St. James in Compostella, and to other places in pilgrimage; for a preservative against tempest and thunder, against perils and dangers of the sea; for a remedy against murrain of cattle, against pensiveness of the heart, and against all manner afflictions and tribulation.

And, finally, they extol their masses far above Christ's passion; promising many things thereby, which were never promised us by Christ's passion: as that if a man hear mass, he shall lack no bodily sustenance that day, nor nothing necessary for him, nor shall be letted in his journey; he shall not lose his sight that day, nor die no sudden death; he shall not wax old in that time that he heareth mass, nor no wicked spirits shall have power of him, be he never so wicked a man, so long as he looketh upon the sacrament. All these foolish and devilish superstitions the papists of their own idle brain have devised of late years, which devices were never known in the old Church.

CHAP. XVIII.
Which Church is to be followed.

And yet they cry out against them that profess the Gospel, and say that they dissent from the Church, and would have them to follow the example of their Church. And so would they

THE SACRIFICE OF CHRIST. 257

gladly do, if the papists would follow the first Church of the Apostles, which was most pure and incorrupt; but the papists have clearly varied from the usage and example of that Church, and have invented new devices of their own brains, and will in no wise consent to follow the primitive Church; and yet they would have other to follow their Church, utterly varying and dissenting from the first most godly Church.

CHAP. XVIII.

But thanks be to the eternal God, the manner of the holy communion, which is now set forth within this realm, is agreeable with the institution of Christ, with St. Paul and the old primitive and apostolic Church, with the right faith of the sacrifice of Christ upon the cross for our redemption, and with the true doctrine of our salvation, justification, and remission of all our sins by that only sacrifice.

Now resteth nothing but that all faithful subjects will gladly receive and embrace the same, being sorry for their former ignorance; and every man repenting himself of his offences against God, and amending the same, may yield himself wholly to God, to serve and obey him all the days of his life, and often to come to the holy Supper, which our Lord and Saviour Christ hath prepared; and as he there corporally eateth the very bread, and drinketh the very wine; so spiritually he may feed of the very flesh and blood of Jesu Christ his Saviour and Redeemer, remembering his death, thanking him for his benefits, and

A short instruction to the holy communion.

looking for none other sacrifice at no priest's hands for remission of his sins, but only trusting to his sacrifice, which being both the High Priest, and also the Lamb of God prepared from the beginning to take away the sins of the world, offered up himself once for ever in a sacrifice of sweet smell unto his Father, and by the same paid the ransom for the sins of the whole world; who is before us entered into heaven, and sitteth at the right hand of his Father, as a Patron, Mediator, and Intercessor for us; and there hath prepared places for all them that be lively members of his body, to reign over him for ever, in the glory of his Father; to whom with him, and the Holy Ghost, be glory, honour, and praise, for ever and ever. Amen.

END.

(259)

SUPPLEMENTARY NOTES BY THE EDITOR.

No. 1. Page 6.

Archbishop Cranmer, writing against Bishop Gardiner on the misinterpretation which the latter Bishop had put on John vi., points out that Christ did not speak there of corporal or bodily, eating of his flesh. Cranmer speaks on this point as follows (Parker Society edition, p. 25):—

"Cyril, I grant, agreed to Nestorius in the substance "of the thing that was eaten (which is Christ's very "flesh), but in the manner of eating they varied. For "Nestorius imagined a carnal eating (as the Papists do) "with mouth, and tearing with teeth. But Cyril, in "the same place, saith (Cyril Anathemastismo, 11), "that Christ is eaten only by a pure faith, and not that "he is eaten corporally with our mouths, as other meats "be, nor that he is eaten in the sacrament only. . . ."

But your understanding of the sixth of John is such as never was uttered of any man before your time, and as declareth you to be utterly ignorant of God's mysteries. For who ever said or taught before this time that the sacrament was the cause why Christ said: "If we eat "not the flesh of the Son of man, we have not life in us?"

The spiritual eating of his flesh, and drinking of his blood by faith, by digesting his death in our minds, as our only price, ransom, and redemption from eternal damnation is the cause wherefore Christ said: "That if "we eat not his flesh, and drink his blood, we have not "life in us; and if we eat his flesh, and drink his blood we "have everlasting life." And if Christ had never ordained the sacrament, yet should we have eaten his flesh and drunken his blood, and have had thereby everlasting life; as all the faithful did before the sacrament was ordained, and do daily when they receive not the sacrament. And so did the holy men that wandered in the wilderness, and in all their life-time very seldom received the sacrament; and many holy martyrs, either exiled or kept in prison, did daily feed of the food of Christ's body, and drank daily the blood that sprang out of his side, or else they could not have had everlasting life, as Christ himself said in the Gospel of St. John, and yet they were not suffered with other Christian people to have the use of the sacrament. . . . And that in the sixth of John, Christ spake neither of corporal nor sacramental eating of his flesh, the time manifestly sheweth. For Christ spoke of the same present time that was then, saying, "The bread which I will give is my flesh," and, "He that eateth my flesh and drinketh my blood, " dwelleth in me, and I in him, and hath everlasting life;" at which time the sacramental bread was not yet Christ's flesh. For the sacrament was not then ordained; and yet at that time all that believed in Christ did eat his flesh, and drink his blood, or else they could not have dwelled in Christ, nor Christ in them.

No. 2. P. 21; end of first paragraph in ch. xiii

Cyprian, in a letter to Cæcilius *(Epist.* lxii.), severely condemned those who in his day used water in place of wine in the Lord's Supper. Cyprian strongly urged the necessity of employing a mixture of water and wine in the cup used in the celebration of the Lord's Supper. His argument is of special interest: "For because Christ " loves us all in that he also bore our sins, we see that in " the water is understood the people, but in the wine is "showed the blood of Christ. But when the water is "mingled in the cup with wine, the people are made one " with Christ, and the assembly of believers is associated "and conjoined with him in whom it believes; which "association and conjunction of water and wine is so "mingled in the Lord's cup that that mixture cannot any "more be separated. .... Thus, therefore in conse-"crating the cup of the Lord, water alone cannot be "offered, even as wine alone cannot be offered. For if "any offer wine only, the blood of Christ is dissociated from "us; but if the water be alone, the people are dissociated "from Christ. .... On the other hand, the body of "the Lord cannot be flour alone, or water alone, unless "both be united and joined together and compacted in "the mass of one bread; in which very sacrament our "people are shown to be made one, so that in like manner "as many grains, collected, and ground, and mixed to-"gether into one mass, make one bread, so in Christ, who "is the Heavenly Bread, we may know that there is one "body, with which our number is joined and united."— See *Writings of Cyprian*, vol. i., Epist. lxii., § 13, pp. 216-17. Translated by Dr. Wallis in the *Ante-Nicene Library*. Edinburgh: T. & J. Clark.

The same idea substantially is contained in the "Thanksgiving," which is directed to be used after the bread has been broken, as given in the recently discovered *Didaché*, or *Teaching of the Apostles*. For that book, which may probably be as early as A.D. 80 or 100, gives the prayer of thanksgiving then used over the bread as follows: "We thank thee, O our Father, for the life and "knowledge which thou hast made known to us by thy "Servant ($\pi\alpha\hat{\imath}\varsigma$) Jesus—thine be the glory for ever. As "this broken bread was once scattered [in grains] upon "the mountain, and being gathered together became one; "so let thy Church be gathered together from the ends "of the earth unto thy kingdom. For thine is the glory "and the power, through Jesus Christ for ever."

See also Dr. C. H. H. Wright: *Service of the Mass in*

the Greek and Roman Churches. London: Religious Tract Society; pp. 73-75.

No. 3.

After the death of Archbishop Cranmer (who suffered at the stake in Oxford, March 21, 1556), an edition of his *Defence* was published by English exiles on the Continent at Embden in 1557. The Embden edition has a few corrections of quotations from the Fathers, which appear in Cranmer's own work, and some other passages from the same source were added in defence of the views advocated by Cranmer in his book.

These additions are in Mr. Jenkyns' edition marked "EMBD." The explanation of the contraction is given in his Preface. The object of the present edition has been in general to give Jenkyns' text and notes without any minute critical examination of the Patristic passages, which would have demanded an immense amount of extra work and have largely increased the cost of production.

No. 4.

It may be well to notice the peculiarity that in Cranmer's Book on the Lord's Supper, in the Parker Society's edition, the confutation of the Second Book comes after the third and fourth books. This was designedly done by the Reformer, because he desired his refutation to adhere strictly to the order which Gardiner followed in his work against him. Thus the arguments adduced against Transubstantiation close the work in place of following the first book which treats of the Sacrament in general. Mr. Jenkyns has some noteworthy remarks on this subject on p. xciii. of his Preface.

THE END.